OAKWOOD LIBRARY OF RAILWAY HISTC

The MANCHESTER SOUTH JUNCTION & ALTRINCHAM RAILWAY

by

Frank Dixon

THE OAKWOOD PRESS

ISBN 0 85361 454 7

First published April 1973
Second Enlarged Edition: 1994

Typeset by Gem Publishing Company, Brightwell, Wallingford, Oxfordshire.

Printed by Alpha Print (Oxon) Ltd, Witney, Oxfordshire.

David and Janet Blewett, and David Salmond
In Memoriam

Sale station approach and entrance *c.*1900. *Courtesy Sale Library*

Published by
The OAKWOOD PRESS
P.O.Box 122, Headington, Oxford.

Contents

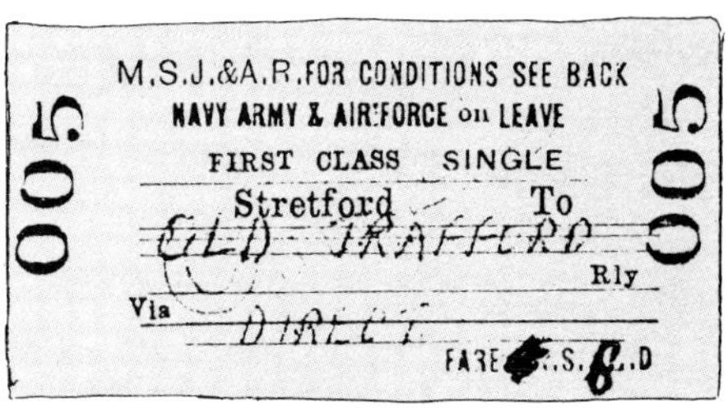

M.S.J.&A.R. FOR CONDITIONS SEE BACK
NAVY ARMY & AIR FORCE on LEAVE
FIRST CLASS SINGLE
Stretford To
OLD TRAFFORD
Rly
Via DIRECT
FARE
005
005

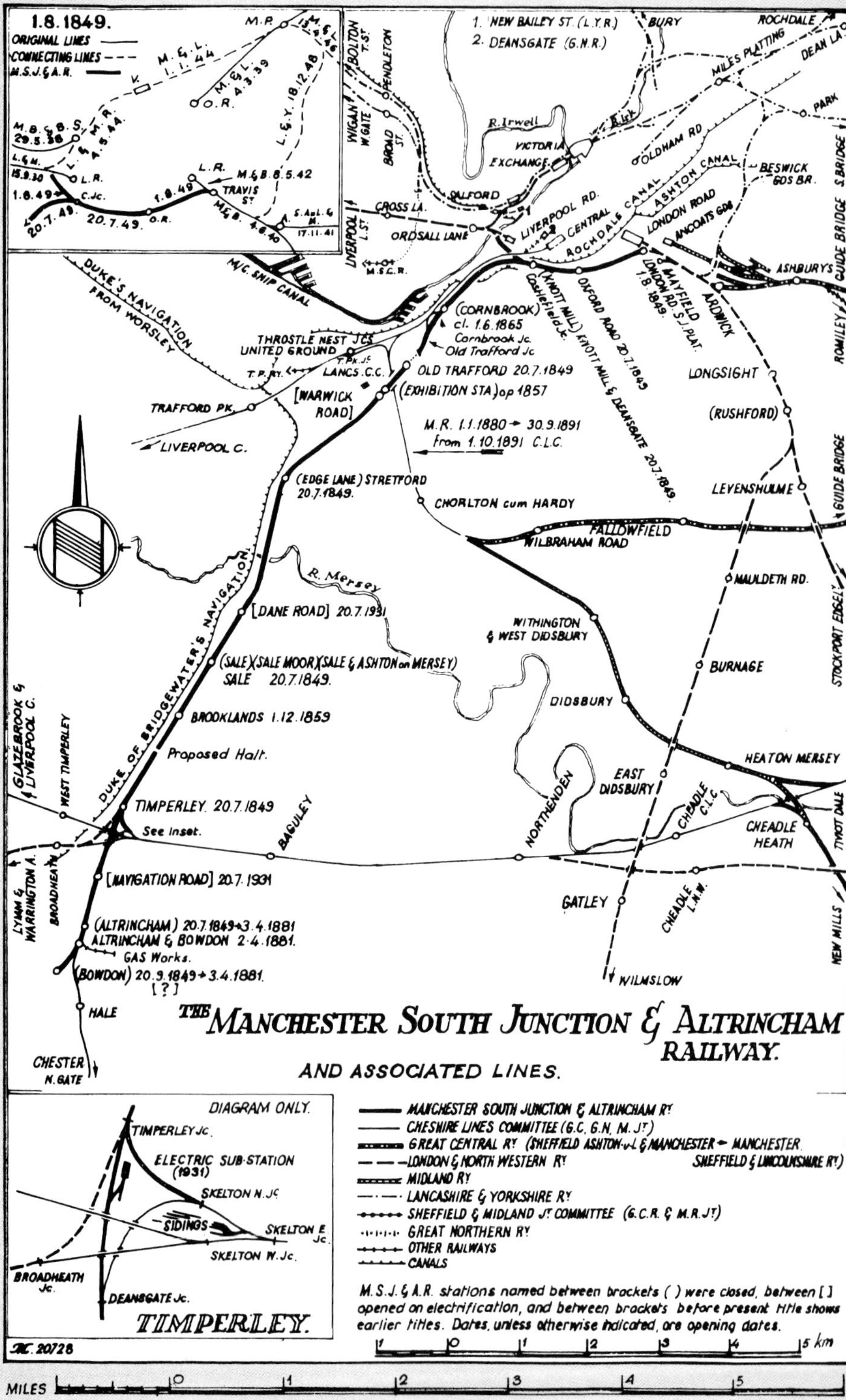
1.8.1849.
ORIGINAL LINES
CONNECTING LINES
M.S.J.& A.R.
1. NEW BAILEY ST. (L.Y.R.)
2. DEANSGATE (G.N.R.)
BURY
ROCHDALE
MILES PLATTING
DEAN LA.
PARK
BOLTON T.ST.
PENDLETON
WIGAN W.GATE
BROAD ST.
R. Irwell
VICTORIA
EXCHANGE
SALFORD
OLDHAM RD
ASHTON CANAL
BESWICK GDS BR.
CROSS LA.
LIVERPOOL L.ST.
ORDSALL LANE
LIVERPOOL RD.
CENTRAL
ROCHDALE CANAL
LONDON ROAD
ANCOATS GDS
ASHBURYS
GUIDE BRIDGE
M.S.C.R.
M/C. SHIP CANAL
MAYFIELD
LONDON RD. S.J. PLAT. 1.8.1849
ARDWICK
(KNOTT MILL) Castlefield Jc.
OXFORD ROAD 20.7.1849
KNOTT MILL & DEANSGATE 20.7.1849
DUKE'S NAVIGATION FROM WORSLEY
(CORNBROOK) cl. 1.6.1865
Cornbrook Jc.
Old Trafford Jc
THROSTLE NEST JCS
UNITED GROUND
LANCS. C.C.
OLD TRAFFORD 20.7.1849
(EXHIBITION STA) op 1857
[WARWICK ROAD]
TRAFFORD PK.
LIVERPOOL C.
M.R. 1.1.1880 → 30.9.1891 from 1.10.1891 C.L.C.
LONGSIGHT
(RUSHFORD)
ROMILEY
(EDGE LANE) STRETFORD 20.7.1849.
CHORLTON cum HARDY
LEVENSHULME
FALLOWFIELD
WILBRAHAM ROAD
R. Mersey
MAULDETH RD.
[DANE ROAD] 20.7.1931
WITHINGTON & WEST DIDSBURY
DUKE OF BRIDGEWATER'S NAVIGATION
(SALE)(SALE MOOR)(SALE & ASHTON on MERSEY) SALE 20.7.1849.
BURNAGE
STOCKPORT EDGELY
BROOKLANDS 1.12.1859
DIDSBURY
Proposed Halt.
HEATON MERSEY
GLAZEBROOK & LIVERPOOL C.
WEST TIMPERLEY
EAST DIDSBURY
TIMPERLEY 20.7.1849
See inset.
BAGULEY
NORTHENDEN
CHEADLE C.L.C.
CHEADLE HEATH
TIVIOT DALE
[NAVIGATION ROAD] 20.7.1931
LYMM & WARRINGTON A.
BROADHEATH
GATLEY
CHEADLE L.N.W.
NEW MILLS
(ALTRINCHAM) 20.7.1849→3.4.1881
ALTRINCHAM & BOWDON 2.4.1881.
GAS Works.
(BOWDON) 20.9.1849→3.4.1881.
[?]
WILMSLOW
HALE
CHESTER N.GATE
THE MANCHESTER SOUTH JUNCTION & ALTRINCHAM RAILWAY.
AND ASSOCIATED LINES.
DIAGRAM ONLY.
TIMPERLEY Jc.
ELECTRIC SUB-STATION (1931)
SKELTON N.Jc.
SIDINGS
SKELTON E. Jc.
SKELTON W. Jc.
BROADHEATH Jc.
DEANSGATE Jc.
TIMPERLEY.
MANCHESTER SOUTH JUNCTION & ALTRINCHAM RY
CHESHIRE LINES COMMITTEE (G.C., G.N., M. JT)
GREAT CENTRAL RY (SHEFFIELD ASHTON-U-L & MANCHESTER → MANCHESTER SHEFFIELD & LINCOLNSHIRE RY)
LONDON & NORTH WESTERN RY
MIDLAND RY
LANCASHIRE & YORKSHIRE RY
SHEFFIELD & MIDLAND JT COMMITTEE (G.C.R. & M.R.JT)
GREAT NORTHERN RY
OTHER RAILWAYS
CANALS
M.S.J. & A.R. stations named between brackets ( ) were closed, between [ ] opened on electrification, and between brackets before present title shows earlier titles. Dates, unless otherwise indicated, are opening dates.
km
MILES
JC. 20728

Introduction to the First Edition

The Manchester South Junction and Altrincham Railway was a small line of less than 10 miles route-length, and a joint line right from the start; promoted, constructed, operated, owned by two large railway companies and, for a short while, a peer. For a while it had its own management, until just after the turn of the century, when the owners decided to take turns to be 'responsible' for it. In steam days, its motive power (mere tanks) was provided by the owners and only a quarter of the trains running over its lines were its own; the rest, passenger and goods, were using running-powers to Warrington, Liverpool, Northwich, Chester etc.

But it was not so small that it could be ignored. It created the suburbs along its route and served them well; at its peak it was booking 8,000,000 passengers per year (plus season tickets) and carrying 1 in 8 of Manchester's rail-borne commuters. Its services were frequent and punctual, so much so that its initials were said to stand for 'Many Short Journeys And Absolute Reliability' and no-one using the line dare make as an excuse for being late for work that 'the train was late'.

In 1931 the line became the first passenger-carrying line in the UK to be electrified at 1500v dc overhead – the system that was meant to become the standard for British electrifications. The rolling-stock introduced then lasted until 1971, when BR re-electrified the line at 25,000v ac and banished the last vestiges of its individuality. Hence this history.

I like to think that this history is correct; I like to daydream. I would be delighted to hear from any reader with corrections or amendments or additional information. Any reader interested in the Altrincham Electric Railway Preservation Society, which has preserved two 'old electric' coaches, could get in touch with them through the author.

Hale, Cheshire *Frank Dixon*
15th May, 1972

Introduction to the Second Edition

There have been considerable changes on the MSJA in recent years, and it has regained the individuality that was lost in 1971: trams now run from Altrincham, over most of the MSJA and onto the streets of central Manchester. Most of the Altrincham branch was converted, in 1992, to form part of Metrolink, the first modern light-rail system in the UK with on-street running. And the South Junction line is now used by a great variety of through services, with the construction of the Windsor Link (in Salford) enabling services to run between Oxford Road and Bolton and beyond.

For this Second Edition, therefore, extra chapters have been added to cover the developments since 1971. While Metrolink features prominently, I should stress that this book does *not* provide a full history of Metrolink, nor a detailed description of the system. (Those wanting to know all about Metrolink should read one of the books mentioned in the bibliography.)

Altrincham station from the south, in 1910, with the photographer standing with his back to Moss Lane bridge. The tracks to the left led to the old Bowdon station and carriage sheds whilst the single track to the right led into the goods yards and, after reversal, into the gasworks.

N. Dodson Collection

Instead, I have provided only a summary of the Metrolink story, concentrating principally on matters affecting the Altrincham branch and the services to Piccadilly and Victoria, with little or no mention of the Victoria to Bury section. This book is a history of the MSJA, not of Metrolink.

I have also taken the opportunity to make a number of changes to the sections dealing with the story up to 1971. Many of these are of minor importance; there are a few places where an extra half-page (or so) of text has been inserted. Similarly, some additional old photographs have been added, along with some extra statistics, some examples of tickets, and so forth. (Unfortunately, it has not been possible to reproduce for this edition some of the photographs which were included in the first edition.)

At the time of writing, the future of the MSJA looks bright. The Metrolink services are well-patronised, and large operating profits have been forecast. The South Junction line is heavily-used, and a crucial link in the provision of many of Manchester's rail services. It will be interesting to see what further changes have occurred if a Third Edition of this book is produced, perhaps 20 years from now.

Edinburgh *Frank Dixon*
15th May, 1993

An MSJA coach axle box showing the company's initials in the casting. *H.C. Casserley*

A cast-iron notice, photographed in October 1952. *J.D. Darby*

Notes

Note on station names and abbreviations

Since the Manchester South Junction & Altrincham Railway (MSJA) was opened, certain of the stations have had their names changed at various times; to avoid confusion today's names are used with the following exceptions: London Road has been called Piccadilly since 12th September, 1960; Knott Mill has been known as Deansgate since 3rd May, 1971; and the former 'Old Trafford' station was renamed as 'Trafford Bar' on 15th June, 1992, on which date the former 'Warwick Road' station became the new 'Old Trafford' station.

It should also be mentioned that pre-1881 'Altrincham station' refers to a station at Stockport Road; post-1881 'Altrincham station' refers to today's station. Bowdon station was situated at Lloyd Street in Altrincham, and both 'Altrincham' and 'Bowdon' stations were closed in 1881 when a new 'Altrincham & Bowdon' station was built between them to replace them. For the first 100-or-so years of its existence, the new station was officially called 'Altrincham & Bowdon', but its name is now simply 'Altrincham'.

Abbreviations are standard; e.g.: LNW = London & North Western, and all are introduced thus when first used *viz.:* . . . the London & North Western (LNW) . . .

It should be noted that while the Manchester, Sheffield & Lincolnshire (MSL) was building its branch to London it changed its name to the Great Central (GC) on and from 1st August, 1897.

Note on the accidents mentioned in the text

The only ones mentioned are the serious collisions, derailments etc. that have occurred on the line. No mention has been made of the numerous cases of people walking under or falling out of trains; lest it be thought that the MSJA was free of them, I regret to say it wasn't. There were also many occasions when staff were injured, especially during shunting operations. However, to the best of my knowledge only two drivers and one passenger have died as a result of accidents to trains (collisions, derailments) – not a bad record for a line as busy as the MSJA.

Acknowledgements

Most of the research for the First Edition was done in the Manchester Central Reference Library, and the bulk of the remainder in the British Transport Archives and the National Library of Scotland, and I would like to thank the staffs concerned for their help. Material consulted included the MSJA minute-books, contemporary newspapers, periodicals and railway publications, the Acts of Parliament and Plans, and the various books mentioned in the Bibliography.

On a more personal level I would thank Mrs E.J. Mather and Messrs A. Bowden, G.G. Cooper, A. Lewis, R. Hill, G.S. Johnson, J.W. Pickup, N.K. Wardleworth and D. Walton for advice, assistance and aid; and Mark Coyne for assistance with researches in London; Messrs J.A. Dean, W.H. Tate, A. Tyson, J.D. Darby and R.E. Gee for checking the draft and supplying photographs; Messrs D. Getgood, G.D. Whitworth and G. Platt who made a valuable contribution by placing their specialist knowledge of signalling, locomotives, coaching-stock and electrical matters at my disposal; Messrs J.I.C. Boyd, N. Dodson, R.M. Dunne and D. Rendell who also supplied photographs; and Mr J.M. Lloyd who drew the maps, diagrams, graph and crest. On behalf of Mr Lloyd the help given by the staffs of Altrincham, Sale and Stretford Libraries and the Manchester Local History Library, the Sale Borough Engineer's Department and BR staff 'all along the line' is gratefully acknowledged.

To the many above, my thanks are no less due to Olga Neubert for typing, my family for checking and correcting my abysmal spelling, and Vincent Rutland who provided much information and, as co-founder of the Altrincham Electric Railway Preservation Society with Chris Davies, unwittingly precipitated the whole thing.

☆ ☆ ☆ ☆ ☆

I would like to thank several people for their help with the preparation of the Second Edition of this book. Nick Dodson, Andrew Macfarlane, Jonathan Rowse and David Walton of the Altrincham Electric R.P.S. read the early draft versions of the additional sections, commented upon them and provided some material for use in the book: their help was much appreciated. I am also grateful to other people, who kindly provided information or extra photographs: Messrs B. Avery, C.E. Box, W.A. Camwell, H.C. and R.M. Casserley, R. Chapman, G. Ellis, F.R.M. Fysh, R.S.B. Hamilton, R.L. Harris, P.G. Heath, T. Heavyside, L.M. Hobdey, Lens of Sutton, P. Mallaband, N.D. Mundy, J.D. Royle, E.K. Skelhorn, N.B.W. Thompson and E.R. Whitworth, and M. Warburton and Jonathan Rowse for the use of tickets from their collections. Thanks are also due to my brother and his family, and Mark Coyne and his family, for putting up with me on my visits to the area, and to my wife for her help with the proof-reading.

I am also grateful to the staff of the Altrincham, Sale and Manchester Central Reference libraries, and to the staff of the Reading Room at the National Railway Museum. My greatest debt is, probably, to all those who have, over the years, edited or otherwise contributed to *Live Wires*, the Altrincham Electric R.P.S. journal that has chronicled developments on the line since 1971.

If anyone has been unintentionally omitted, my sincere apologies.

'Princess Coronation' class 4–6–2 No. 46229, *Duchess of Hamilton* running through Navigation Road on 2nd September, 1991. The train is heading north on what used to be the south-bound (down) track and is now the single 'heavy rail' track, following the changes made prior to the introduction of Metrolink. *B. Avery*

A six-car train seen here in 1952, standing in the 'new carriage siding' south of Sale. *British Rail*

Chapter One

Construction

In the late 1830s and early 1840s, the five railway companies serving Manchester, the Manchester & Leeds (M&L), Manchester, Bolton & Bury (MB&B), Liverpool & Manchester (L&M), Manchester & Birmingham (M&B), and the Sheffield, Ashton-under-Lyne & Manchester (SA&M), ran from four separate Manchester terminals. These were Oldham Road (M&L), New Bailey Street (MB&B), Liverpool Road (L&M) and London Road (shared by the M&B and the SA&M). This separation was an inconvenience and a hindrance to through traffic, and steps were soon taken to link up the various stations. In the autumn of 1839 the M&L proposed connecting itself, the MB&B and the L&M with a line from Miles Platting on the M&L to Ordsall Lane on the L&M via the environs of New Bailey Street. A little later an alternative proposal was made: the construction of a multi-company central station at London Road and connecting lines from the L&M and M&L.

For a while the merits of these schemes were argued over, and pressures applied, until, in the spring of 1842, the L&M and M&L agreed to build the northern line, which was opened between Miles Platting and Victoria station on 1st January, 1844 and between Victoria and Ordsall Lane on 4th May, 1844.

This left the M&B and the SA&M isolated at London Road. Both companies wanted access to the city and port of Liverpool, and so they decided to build the line from London Road to the L&M themselves. Their original intention was to build only this South Junction line, but it was later decided to incorporate a branch to Altrincham, then a small market-town of around 4,000 people. As the branch would take traffic from the nearby Bridgewater Canal, Lord Francis Egerton, Chief Trustee of the Bridgewater Canal, was invited to participate, thus securing his support and avoiding his opposition. In July 1846 Lord Egerton became Earl of Ellesmere, and will be henceforth referred to as such.

On 29th January, 1845 agreement was made between the railways and the Earl for the construction of the MSJA line. The Earl would guide through Parliament the Bill authorising construction of the line, provide some of the land required for the line (especially a 3¼ mile stretch between Stretford and Timperley where it runs alongside the canal, which was then 'black and filthy, winding like some huge snake through the meadows, emitting an exceedingly offensive and noisome stench'), and, once the line was opened, withdraw the competing 'swift packets' (passenger-carrying flyboats) that plied the canal between Timperley and Castle Quay in Manchester, terminating boats from the west at Timperley where the passengers would have to change to a train to complete their journey. In return, he would receive £50,000 worth of shares and effectively be guaranteed an 8 per cent per annum return on his 'investment'. The railways would each take up £175,000 worth of shares. No shares would be offered to the public.

The MSJA crest, which decorated the coaching stock up to nationalisation, symbolised this tripartite ownership. Incorporated into the design, amidst all the frills and trills, are the arms of Altrincham, Manchester, Birmingham, Sheffield and the Egerton family.

On 21st July, 1845 the Manchester South Junction and Altrincham Railway Company's Act of Incorporation received the Royal Assent. It confirmed the agreement of 29th January and set out how the MSJA was to be run. Full details appear in the appendices.

In 1845/6 several mergers took place. The L&M, M&B and some other lines became part of the London & North Western (LNW) and the SA&M formed the basis of the Manchester Sheffield & Lincolnshire (MSL).

On 2nd July, 1847 the LNW got an Act authorising the joint purchase by it and the MSL of the Earl of Ellesmere's shares in the MSJA. The Earl received £62,500 and withdrew his Directors from the MSJA Board, which now became half-MSL and half-LNW. The LNW act modified the MSJA constitution so that each owning company nominated the Chairman at alternate Board meetings. As the Chairman had a casting vote, this meant that contentious decisions could be reversed at subsequent Board meetings by the Chairman's casting vote – a sort of dynamic deadlock.

A survey of the proposed route was carried out and plans produced in 1844 by three engineers: Messrs Joseph Locke, George Watson Buck and William Baker. Their route, with minor modifications,is the one taken by the line today. For the purposes of construction, the line was split in two. On 23rd October, 1845 the tenders of David Bellhouse of Garrett Road (for the South Junction section) and of John Brogden of Sale (for the Altrincham branch) were accepted. William Baker was appointed Chief Engineer, and Henry Hemberow Resident Engineer.

Construction did not start at once. Before work could begin, land had to be bought. The South Junction line passed entirely through built-up areas, and, although the route was chosen to make the best possible use of large plots of land, especially land controlled by Ellesmere, it could not avoid having to take a large number of other plots. The railways, having compulsory purchase powers, were determined to pay as little as possible, the owners were determined to get all they could; much haggling ensued. Two solicitors were required to cope with the bargaining, one working west of Oxford Road and the other east, and such was the pressure that the health of the elder one broke down, and Baker and some assistants and officials had to be brought in to speed up the purchasing. The same sort of trouble occurred on the Altrincham branch, but to a lesser extent. Further delays were caused by a cartographer called Shorlands not completing some plans on schedule, and a dispute with Brogden over the exact terms of the contract. Work eventually got under way, and by 30th October, 1846 sufficient had been done for the first report on the state of the works to be presented.

Unfortunately, the costs of building the line had been underestimated and there was a general shortage of investment funds following the Railway Mania of 1845. By the summer of 1847, the MSJA was running out of money and had to start advertising for 5 year loans at 5 per cent interest. Many local people responded with small sums (£100 here, £500 there) and another £50,000 or so was raised in this way. However, this only delayed the inevitable. By the end of October work had to come to a halt on the Altrincham branch, and by November 1847 on the whole line, much to the distress of Bellhouse and Brogden.

In order that the line might be completed, it was necessary to obtain an Act of Parliament (22nd July, 1848) authorising a £250,000 increase in capital (to £650,000) and a £83,333 increase in borrowing powers (to £216,666). The two owning companies each provided half the increased capital. With more money available, work restarted immediately.

Only one serious mishap occurred during the construction of the line – the collapse on 20th January, 1849 of part of the viaduct near Oxford Road. The section of viaduct just west of Oxford Road station and east of Gloucester Street had been built just before Christmas 1848 and left to stand, supported by scaffolding, while the mortar set. Normal procedure was to leave the arches for two to three weeks, after which time the mortar would have set, the scaffolding could be removed, and the arches would stand on their own two feet.

At about 2 pm on Saturday 20th January, 1849, carpenters started to loosen the scaffolding under the arch next to the bridge over Gloucester Street. The arch settled about an inch, which was less than normal for an arch of its type, indicating all was well; and so the men proceeded to dismantle all the scaffolding.

Several men were involved, some working on the abutments, others on the ribs of the scaffolding. There were 12 of these ribs in all, and four had been removed. Work was in progress on removing a fifth when, without any warning, part of the arch fell.

Men on the ground under the arch escaped through the side-openings and through doors at the ends of the arch; one man on the ribs leapt down and escaped through a side-opening. Others were not so fortunate. James Oates and Thomas Davies, who had been standing on the abutments, were struck by falling materials and were buried. Ralph Beresford, on one of the ribs, fell to the ground and was buried by falling materials. When the dust had settled their workmates started digging them out. They were brought out dead. Other men were injured: Murphy broke his arm and Crosby his leg. The bodies were taken to the Atlas Inn for the inquest.

The inquest opened on the following Monday and was eventually adjourned until Thursday. As luck would have it, at about 5.30 am on the morning of Thursday, 25th, the arch next to the fallen one fell. No one was hurt: two watchmen heard it creaking a while before it fell. At 10 am the next arch towards Oxford Road fell, despite much propping up. Again, no one was hurt.

Examination of the mortar in the rubble of the fallen arches showed that it had not completely set. The stuff was of the highest quality, as the suppliers testified, and it was agreed that the reason the mortar had not set was that the recent wet weather had kept it wet. The two subsequent falls were attributed to the non-setting mortar (the arches were built at the same time) and to the fact that the fall of the first arch had weakened the others.

As this was the first fatal accident on Bellhouse's section, and as it had been previously believed that any arch that had been standing for almost a month would certainly have set, no blame was attached to anyone; although it was hoped that in future more setting-time would be allowed for wet weather.

A 'rural' scene, *c*.1910: Timperley station photographed from Park Road bridge looking north. The barges on the 'Duke of Bridgewater's Navigation' are a bygone transport system. Note the well tended platform gardens. *Courtesy Altrincham Library*

The South Junction Line (1¾ miles)

This formed a junction with the LNW by Ordsall Lane station and was carried eastwards on the viaduct, crossing the Irwell with two 65-foot span brick arches supported by a pillar in the middle of the river. (Following an 1882 Act of Parliament, the short stretch of the South Junction line to the west of the Irwell was transferred to the LNW, and so the west end of the bridge became the new end of the MSJA.) At Castlefield a canal branch is crossed by an 80-foot span brick arch – at the time this was the largest brick arch in the country. Near here the viaduct runs on top of a culvert containing the River Medlock (which was diverted when the nearby canal's 'Giant's Basin' weir overflow was made), roughly from arch 113 to arch 118. At Castlefield Junction it connects with the Altrincham branch and proceeds eastwards through Knott Mill station (now called Deansgate station) and Oxford Road station to London Road station (now called Piccadilly station) where it passes through the MSJA platforms and makes a junction with the line from the main part of London Road station.

The South Junction line is entirely elevated, and, including the stretch of viaduct at the north end of the Altrincham branch, there are over 2 miles of continuous viaduct, requiring 224 arches, on the MSJA. The viaduct averages 30 feet in height and 28 feet in width, with foundations 30–35 feet below ground. The average arch spans 30 feet. The line's course crossed, in addition to the two already mentioned, 26 streets and canals which were spanned with cast-iron bridges. It had been intended to use flat-girder bridges; however, while work was in progress on these, a flat-girder bridge over the Dee at Chester collapsed under a train (24th May, 1847) and doubts were cast on the safety of such bridges. The half-built ones were scrapped and replaced by arched bridges 'of very superior workmanship' obtained by David Bellhouse from the foundries of E.T. Bellhouse, Hunt Street, off Garrett Road. Twenty-eight of these were required (three at Knott Mill) all with spans of 70 feet except the one over the Rochdale Canal which spanned 105 feet.

The construction of the MSJA viaduct required 50,000,000 bricks, 300,000 cu. ft of stone and 3,000 tons of cast iron.

Near Castlefield the line passes the remains of an old Roman castle, and, during the excavations, part of a Roman wall was discovered. The Earl of Ellesmere 'watched the safety of the fragment of Roman Wall during excavation and caused it to be supported by brick-work. He legally secured it from further molestation' and subsequently an arch was built over it and rented by a timber-merchant. This was one way of preserving it for posterity, as the merchant would not allow the curious (who are liable to pull it to pieces for souvenirs) to wander around his yard. Posterity was grateful: apparently, A.J.P. Taylor described it as 'the least interesting Roman remain in England'.

The Altrincham Branch (7½ miles)

This starts from a junction with the South Junction line at Castlefield Junction and runs generally south-westwards. A description of the line as it was when it was opened (from the 1899 souvenir booklet) follows:

> The line, after its divergence from South Junction at Castlefield and crossing the 'Duke's' Canal, passes the site of the Old Hulme Hall close to the river, the Pomona Gardens, and under the Chester Road at Old Trafford by means of a short tunnel (the only one on the line) to [what used to be called] Old Trafford Station [and is now called Trafford Bar Station], which is just two miles distant from Oxford Road. Immediately after quitting this station the Blind Asylum, the Deaf and Dumb School, and the joint Chapel were [in 1849] the most prominent objects passed on the right side of the line, and following them the leafy groves of the Botanical Gardens, and the neat Pavilion and lawn-like ground of the Manchester Cricket Club came into view. Next was seen the front of Mr T. Bazley's residence, whilst on the left, from amidst the well-wooded landscape, could at that early period be descried the turrets of the Lancashire Independent College and the taper spire of St Margaret's Church, Whalley Range. The line then lay along a straight and nearly level course, through meadows and fields, with here and there a cottage and its garden, or a road or footpath carried by a light bridge over the line, till the Edge Lane (or Stretford) Station was reached, three-and-a-half miles from Oxford Road. This station was built to accommodate the, even then, populous village of Stretford, which lay a short distance to the right, its brick-towered church a landmark for the neighbourhood. Hence the line was taken along an embankment over the level vale of the Mersey, and side by side with the Bridgewater Canal. The Mersey was crossed by an iron bridge, supported on tubular girders on Mr Fairbairn's principle, and beyond the river, Sale Priory was to be seen on the left of the railway, and also two houses built by Mr Samuel Brooks. Reaching Sale, at a distance of five-and-a-quarter miles from Oxford Road, another station was provided. The only portion of [the area that was *then* called] Sale Moor at that period remaining in an uncultivated state was a small strip of land between the railway and the canal, and another small piece on the east side of the line. The house of Mr Roebuck was visible to the right, and further on were various other residences on the Manchester and Altrincham turnpike road.
>
> The line proceeded in an open country, and the works were of a very light nature, with the exception of the bridges, the approaches to which, owing to the line being level, were necessarily heavy. There was no Brooklands station when the line was opened, but to the right of where it now stands were the floral and horticultural gardens of Mr Yates. At Timperley, seven miles from Oxford Road, there was another station, and a landing place from the canal, which runs parallel with the line, and but a few yards away, between Stretford and that point. At a little distance to the right were seen Timperley Lodge, the residence of Mr Clegg; Washway (on the high road), the abode of Mr Samuel Bury; and a little further off lay the hamlet of Broadheath, the canal station for Altrincham. To the left or east of the line and close to it stood the residence of Mr John Woollam, and at a little distance the buildings of Timperley Hall (Mr Pilling) were visible. Passing the Well House and other houses on the right, the then terminus of the line was reached at Altrincham, just eight miles from Oxford Road. The line was subsequently extended to the foot of the Downs, where its southern terminus was placed and known as Bowdon Station.

After passing Timperley, where the canal bears off to the right, several modifications were made to the 1844 plans. The original intention was that Deansgate Row, Navigation Lane and the Stockport turnpike should all bridge the line; but, for economy, level-crossings were installed. The line was also to bridge *over* Moss Lane in Altrincham, but now Moss Lane bridges it. The line ran to its terminus at Bowdon station on Altrincham's

Lloyd Street, keeping to the east of the built-up part of Altrincham.

Apart from the viaduct at the north end of the branch, there were few major works: Old Trafford tunnel (Bridge No. 59: 142 yards), and the embankment and bridge over the Mersey. Incidentally the five cast-iron bridges used by Brogden came from the foundries of Garforths of Dukinfield – not Bellhouses!

Illustrations from the souvenir booklet issued in 1899 to mark the line's jubilee. The booklet was printed by George Falkner & Sons, subsequently part of McCorquodale Printers Limited, who kindly provided permission for its reproduction.
George Falkner & Sons, per N. Dodson

Sale station, from the south photographed around 1870. *Courtesy Sale Public Library.*

Sale station buildings *c.*1904 as seen from the junction of Broad Road and Northenden Road, looking down School Road. These buildings were built across the running lines, as can be seen in the top view. *Lens of Sutton*

Chapter Two

Completion and Opening

By the end of May 1849 the line was sufficiently complete to allow the first proper train to run over the Altrincham branch. Brogden borrowed two first-class coaches and an engine from the LNW and invited railway officials, local dignitaries, and friends and relations to take a trip.

The special train left Manchester at noon on Whit Monday, 28th May, 1849, which was fortunately a fine day. The coaches carried Messrs Brogden, Kirkman (appointed on 5th May, 1849 as MSJA Secretary/Manager), Hemberow, etc. Another carriage carried the Stretford Temperance Band, clad in blue uniforms and with several blue silk banners. At Cornbrook it was greeted by cheering crowds; at Stretford (population then around 3,000) it stopped, the band played, and the excursionists amused themselves by inspecting the works and the neighbourhood. The train then went onward, past throngs of lineside onlookers, to Sale (population then about 1,500), where it was greeted with cannon salutes and cheers from the massed ranks of Brogden's workmen. They stopped at Sale and Timperley before arriving at Altrincham (population then 4,000 or so) where they alighted and the band, playing, led the way to the Unicorn Hotel where they ate and drank. Then they drove out to Rostherne before returning to the Unicorn at four o'clock for more eating, drinking and speechmaking. The train eventually returned to Oxford Road at about 10 pm.

Following this jaunt, an engine was used to help with the works up and down the line. The rest of the South Junction line was ready to take its first proper train on Monday 2nd July, when Bellhouse and guests travelled from London Road to Ordsall Lane, reversed there, returned to Castlefield and proceeded to visit Altrincham before returning to Manchester for celebrating in the Albion Hotel. This trip was unattended by festivities and lineside gogglers.

The MSJA was inspected by a Captain Wynne on Saturday 7th July, 1849; he passed it fit for use, apart from the uncompleted Bowdon extension, and for some points and a turntable at Ordsall Lane, also uncompleted.

On Friday 20th July, 1849, the MSJA was opened for traffic between Oxford Road and Altrincham. The opening was poorly publicised and the services poorly patronised. The competing horse-drawn omnibuses between Altrincham and Manchester ran 'as full as ever' and the horse-drawn flyboats continued to use the canal between Timperley and Manchester – they were not withdrawn from that section until the whole of the line was opened.

The first trains left each terminus at 8.00 am (Greenwich Time was in use at all stations) and called at all stations. The 8.00 am ex-Altrincham had an unfortunate maiden trip: it was delayed at Stretford and struggled into Oxford Road just before 9.00 am with the 8.40 am express from Altrincham hard on its heels. The 8.00 am carried 65 passengers into Manchester, the express 15 and the 9.00 am slow train 40. The initial service was 12 slow trains (booked time 30 minutes) each way and one express (20 minutes) each way per day.

Initial MSJA Service: July 1849 *Weekdays*

		1	2	3	4	5	6	7	8	9	10	11	12	13
Oxford Road	*dep.*	8.00	9.00	10.00	11.00	1.15	1.20	2.45	4.00	5.00	6.00	7.00	8.00	9.00
Knott Mill	,,	8.03	9.03	10.03	11.03	...	1.23	2.48	4.03	5.03	6.03	7.03	8.03	9.03
Old Trafford	,,	8.07	9.07	10.07	11.07	...	1.27	2.52	4.07	5.07	6.07	7.07	8.07	9.07
Edge Lane	,,	8.12	9.12	10.12	11.12	...	1.32	2.57	4.12	5.12	6.12	7.12	8.12	9.12
Sale Moor	,,	8.18	9.18	10.18	11.18	...	1.38	3.03	4.18	5.18	6.18	7.18	8.18	9.18
Timperley	,,	8.25	9.25	10.25	11.25	...	1.45	3.10	4.25	5.25	6.25	7.25	8.25	9.25
Altrincham	*arr.*	8.30	9.30	10.30	11.30	1.35	1.50	3.15	4.30	5.30	6.30	7.30	8.30	9.30

On Saturdays only train 13 departs Oxford Road at 10.00 pm.

Altrincham	*dep.*	8.00	8.40	9.00	10.00	11.00	1.00	2.45	4.00	5.00	6.00	7.00	8.00	9.00
Timperley	,,	8.04	...	9.04	10.04	11.04	1.04	2.49	4.04	5.04	6.04	7.04	8.04	9.04
Sale Moor	,,	8.11	...	9.11	10.11	11.11	1.11	2.56	4.11	5.11	6.11	7.11	8.11	9.11
Edge Lane	,,	8.18	...	9.18	10.18	11.18	1.18	3.03	4.18	5.18	6.18	7.18	8.18	9.18
Old Trafford	,,	8.23	...	9.23	10.23	11.23	1.23	3.08	4.23	5.23	6.23	7.23	8.23	9.23
Knott Mill	,,	8.27	...	9.27	10.27	11.27	1.27	3.12	4.27	5.27	6.27	7.27	8.27	9.27
Oxford Road	*arr.*	8.30	9.00	9.30	10.30	11.30	1.30	3.15	4.30	5.30	6.30	7.30	8.30	9.30

On Saturdays only train 13 departs Altrincham 9.30 pm.

Sunday Service:
All calling at all stations, and taking 30 minutes for the journey.
Trains from Oxford Road at 8.30 am, 9.30 am, 1.30 pm, 2.00 pm, 5.00 pm, 6.00 pm, 7.00 pm, 8.00 pm, 9.00 pm.

Trains from Altrincham at: 8.30 am, 9.30 am, 2.00 pm, 5.00 pm, 6.00 pm, 7.00 pm, 8.00 pm, 9.00 pm.

A copy of the opening timetable for July 1849. Note: Bowdon station did not open until September 1849.

Even then there were railway enthusiasts. Isaac Warburton, who lived at the Vale Farm, Langham Road, Bowdon, ran to Altrincham station, determined to buy the first ticket, which he obtained; it was handed on to his descendants and eventually given to Altrincham library where it can be seen today.

Oxford Road station, the terminus for Altrincham trains for the next 30 years, had at the time of opening one flagged platform on each side of the line, two sidings and precious little else of permanence. A temporary wooden booking-office was in use, and work was in progress on permanent buildings. At Knott Mill, too, there was only temporary accommodation; but all the stations on the Altrincham branch had permanent buildings. The stations at Old Trafford, Stretford, Sale and Timperley all had two platforms and two buildings: station master's house and booking-office/waiting room. At Altrincham station, just south of Stockport Road level crossing, the station building was in the form of a cottage with penthouse eaves, and the platforms were paved with square red and yellow tiles, laid diamondwise.

The rest of the line was soon opened. The London Road–Oxford Road and Castlefield Junction–Ordsall Lane sections of the South Junction line were opened for traffic on 1st August, 1849. At London Road the MSJA had its own platforms adjacent to the main body of the station; at Ordsall Lane trains to and from the MSJA would use the L&M station there. With the opening completing the South Junction line, goods traffic started flowing between Liverpool and Yorkshire via the LNW, MSJA and MSL, and a shuttle service ran between London Road and Ordsall Lane, connecting with Liverpool trains. However, the Altrincham trains continued to terminate at Oxford Road station.

The completion of the line – the extension to the 'Bowdon' terminus at Lloyd Street in Altrincham – was delayed by difficulties in making the Bowdon station. The site was on boggy ground – water kept filling up the excavations and a lot of work was needed to provide solid foundations. The extension was completed and opened in September 1849. The exact date of opening is uncertain. The date quoted by most authorities is Thursday 20th September, 1849. The *Guardian* of Wednesday, 26th, reports that the line was opened to Bowdon station on Sunday, 23rd, on which day the Bowdon Wakes commenced and a lot of extra traffic used the line. In the minute books, minute MSJ 1/2 No. 553 records that the Board meeting of 18th September resolved that 'the portion of line from Altrincham station to Goose Green bridge be opened on Saturday next the 22nd inst and that for the convenience of parties visiting Bowdon, Dunham Park etc. during the ensuing Wakes, extra trains be run between Manchester and the temporary station near Bowdon' – the 'temporary station' being, presumably, just north of Goose Green bridge. On 14th October, 1847, Baker had been requested by the Board to produce plans for a temporary Bowdon station and an estimate of the cost – but this may have been necessitated by the money shortage at the time. The author has been unable to find any minute or press report dealing with the opening of the Lloyd Street terminus and the miniscule section of line thence to Goose Green bridge.

The line was now complete and had cost about £575,000. Its effect on the area was immediate. The value of shops near Bowdon station rose, land prices increased, and villas and terraces blossomed on the Downs as people who could afford to move out 'into the country' succeeded in bringing the town out with them. Similar developments occurred at other stations along the line.

The seeds of the long tradition of vandalism that has plagued the MSJA had also been sown. On Wednesday evening, 19th September, 1849, a 'miscreant' placed a sleeper on the line near Sale station. A train hit it, and both engine and tender were derailed (no-one was hurt). The *Guardian* thundered: 'A more diabolical attempt to destroy life and property can scarcely be conceived and we trust that the perpetrator of it will ere long be discovered and speedily receive the extreme punishment the law will allow'. To assist in his apprehension, the MSJA offered a reward of £50.

By the end of 1849 the MSJA had attained its maximum route mileage. Double-track throughout, it would be quadrupled in parts and have its stations and sidings enlarged and new ones opened; but in terms of length it was complete. There were times when it might have been extended: in the 1850s the LNW and MSL worked the line to Warrington via Lymm as an extension of the MSJA; in the 1860s the MSL tried to get the LNW to agree to build the line to Northwich as an extension of the MSJA; in the 1930s, after the electrification had fired the imaginations of amateur planners, there was talk of extending the electrification through Hale, and of building new branches – but it all came to nothing.

One of the Sharp Brothers & Co. 2–2–2s, *Flora*, No. 78, built in 1849 at the Atlas Works in Manchester, for the Manchester South Junction and Altrincham Railway.

Chapter Three

The Warrington and Altrincham Railway

The Altrincham branch of the MSJA, practically an afterthought, was not intended to form a part of any through line; however, before the ink on the Act of Incorporation was dry, approaches were made to the MSJA by the Birkenhead, Lancashire & Cheshire Junction (BLCJ), a company formed in the Railway Mania to connect the Chester & Birkenhead at Hooton and Chester with Altrincham and Stockport. It was agreed that the BLCJ could use the MSJA to obtain access to Manchester. The BLCJ was incorporated in 1846, but fell foul of the money troubles following the Railway Mania and was only able to build the line from Chester to Walton Junction, just south of Warrington. In 1847 the BLCJ merged with the Chester & Birkenhead and kept the BLCJ name until it changed its name to Birkenhead Railway in 1859. Henceforth the BLCJ will be referred to as the Birkenhead Railway.

When better times came, it was not the Birkenhead that approached Altrincham from the west, but a new company, the Warrington & Altrincham Railway (W&A), incorporated on 3rd July, 1851 with powers to make a line from Timperley Junction on the MSJA to an end-on junction at Warrington with the St Helens Canal & Railway Co.'s line to Garston, together with a branch from Latchford to the LNW and Birkenhead lines at Walton Junction. The W&A was counting on using the MSJA to obtain access to Manchester and in the spring of 1853 approached the MSJA Board to discuss terms. Unfortunately for the W&A, the LNW stood to lose traffic between Warrington and Manchester if the W&A started running competing services between Warrington and Manchester, and therefore the LNW stood to gain by denying the W&A the use of the MSJA. At that time, the LNW and MSL were closely allied and consequently it came as no great surprise when the MSJA Board unanimously decided the W&A's proposals were unacceptable. (A Minute at that time suggests that meanness on the MSJA Board's part was not unusual: 'Resolved that the width of the seats in the new second-class compartments be a little reduced . . .' MSJ 1/3, 24.5.1853.)

The W&A desperately needed access to Manchester to make its line viable. If its trains had to terminate at Timperley Junction, and were restricted to running from Warrington to (in effect) nowhere, the Company's future would be bleak, as the local traffic was not expected to pay for the line. The W&A needed large population centres at each end of its route if it were to survive – and accordingly approached Parliament in the 1853 session for various powers, promoting two Bills to obtain them.

The first Bill was to give the W&A running powers over the MSJA into Manchester, and over other lines, and to allow it to construct its own terminus just off the MSJA at Granby Row. The W&A also applied for authority to abandon the Latchford–Walton link (on which construction had not yet started) and to replace it with a shorter Arpley–Walton link. The second Bill was to empower the construction of an extension of the W&A to Stockport, together with a change in the Company's name to Warrington & Stockport.

The MSJA Board unanimously decided to affix the MSJA's seal against the W&A application for running powers over the MSJA and a Granby Row station. In due course the Bills came before Parliament. The Stockport Extension Bill was passed on 4th August, 1853 and the Company's name duly changed to Warrington & Stockport (W&S). The first Bill, being controversial, met much opposition but was eventually passed, albeit severely mauled. The end result, while not what the W&S had hoped for, was still unacceptable to the LNW – as a result Kirkman was dispatched post haste to London to affix the MSJA seal to a Petition against the Bill.

The second Bill gave the W&S running-powers between Timperley and a point 100 yards short of Castlefield Junction (nowhere near Granby Row: Granby Row station would have been between Oxford Road and London Road stations) at all times for passenger traffic, and between the hours of 10.00 pm and 6.00 am for goods traffic. The MSJA was compelled to haul W&S passenger stock between Timperley and Oxford Road as the W&S required. Due to poor draftmanship, the Bill did *not* give the W&S running powers between Timperley Junction and Timperley station and a special resolution had to be passed at the MSJA Board allowing the W&S to run into Timperley station for the purposes of delivering and collecting its stock to and from the MSJA for and after haulage (MSJ 1/3 21.11.54). The W&S was allowed to use all the MSJA stations from Timperley to Oxford Road, at which the MSJA had to provide reasonable facilities for passenger traffic. The modification of the Walton branch was approved, and also the exchange of running powers with various other railways. The section about the Granby Row station was, however, deleted.

Most of the W&S was opened for traffic on 1st November, 1853. Unfortunately, as neither the bridge over the Mersey at Warrington nor the bridge over the canal at Broadheath had been completed, the line ran from nowhere to nowhere and was, all in all, rather useless. With the bridges completed, the line was opened from Warrington to Timperley Junction on 1st May, 1854 – but as the W&S and MSJA could not come to agreement over the tolls to be charged for the W&S's use of the MSJA, the W&S trains terminated at Broadheath. The matter of tolls was eventually sent to John Hawkshaw for arbitration and he decided, on 31st October, 1854, that the W&S should pay to the MSJA, for every passenger conveyed between Timperley and Oxford Road, a mileage rate with a small premium, the minimum payments being 1*s*. 2*d*. (1st class), 10½*d*. (2nd) and 8¾*d*. (3rd). The MSJA fares between Timperley and Oxford Road were 9*d*., 6¾*d*. and 5*d*. respectively.

The W&S had to accept these charges, at the same time complaining bitterly that the tolls were too high and that they would inhibit the growth of their traffic; however they had no alternative but to pay up and look pleasant. They had foolishly built a line that would compete with the LNW's L&M line for Warrington traffic and relied on using the MSJA – of which the LNW was half-owner – for access to Manchester on terms that would make their line pay, terms they should never have expected to get. Their financial situation was pretty poor and as a result they were unable to raise the money for the Stockport extension – consequently the powers for making the line lapsed and £20,000 worth of deposit, expenses etc. were lost.

The W&S was worked by the LNW from its opening (no-one else had any incentive to work it) at a small loss until the MSL was persuaded to agree that the line should be worked, from 1st October, 1856, as an extension of the MSJA to reduce working expenses and increase traffic.

Many companies obtained running-powers over the W&S, among them being the Great Western Railway (GWR). In the spring of 1855, the Arpley–Walton Junction link was opened, enabling the GWR, which had running powers over the Birkenhead to Walton, to reach Timperley. At this time, the LNW and GWR were at daggers drawn, and there was no chance of the GWR running into Manchester over the ex-L&M or the MSJA. Timperley was thus the nearest to Manchester that the GWR could get, and in August 1855 the GWR Directors reported that they were 'taking steps to procure accommodation' there for its Manchester traffic.

In 1857 the MSL-LNW alliance was broken and a Railway War developed. No longer bound to the LNW, the MSL was willing to co-operate with the GWR and in the spring of 1858 got two of its Directors appointed to negotiate with the GWR on the MSJA's behalf, with a view to agreeing terms for GWR use of the MSJA. However the LNW also started talking to the GWR, and the two agreed in November 1858 that the GWR should work into Manchester over the ex-L&M. And so the W&S-MSJA route from Walton, although shorter than the ex-L&M, was never used by the GWR for its Manchester traffic.

Timperley Junction: Altrincham line on the left, Lymm line to the right, Skelton Junction–Glazebrook line in the background. The 6.20 Warrington to London Road with Stanier class '3MT' 2–6–2T No. 40107 in charge, seen coming onto the MSJA in April 1952. *R.E. Gee*

A contemporary print of the Art Treasures Exhibition 1857, with what was then called Old Trafford station (and is now called Trafford Bar station) in the foreground. Note the signal at the end of the platform.
Courtesy J.M. Lloyd

Chapter Four

The Railway War

In the summer of 1857 the Manchester Art Treasures Exhibition was held on a site near Old Trafford station (before the introduction of Metrolink it was called Warwick Road station). The Exhibition was intended to bring together the country's art treasures, to amass (if only fleetingly) a collection the like of which the world had never seen – and to this end owners loaned irreplaceable works, to make it the exhibition to end all exhibitions. They succeeded. If there had been a fire the loss would have been incalculable.

To cater for the traffic to the Exhibition the MSJA installed a siding to the Exhibition buildings, a roofed Exhibition station slightly north of today's station, and extra sidings and platforms at Oxford Road and London Road. At London Road the extra platform and siding were installed on land owned by the LNW, land which had previously been used for goods exchange sidings.

To handle the extra traffic over the MSJA, three extra engines were required; and a fourth was deemed necessary to deal with the increase in W&S traffic. The MSL provided these for 11½*d.* per mile.

The Exhibition was opened by the Prince Consort on 5th May, and visited by the Queen on 30th June. Over 1 million people paid to get in and over 250,000 season tickets were sold. Special excursion trains were organised from all over the country, even from Ireland. Manchester was invaded by visitors, many of whom used the Exhibition station, and there was a pleasing increase in the MSJA's passenger receipts as a result.

As has been already mentioned, the LNW and the MSL were at that time closely allied. They were, in fact, involved in a LNW-MSL-Midland alliance that was based on an illegal 'common-purse' agreement. The alliance had been constructed by the LNW to maximise profits by minimising competition – for example the MSL connected with the Great Northern (GN) at Retford thus making possible a second (though longer) route to London (MSL London Road–Sheffield–Retford, GN Retford–Peterborough–London) which could compete with the LNW's route via Crewe. To make sure it did not, the MSL was required to ensure that none of its trains connected with any GN trains at Retford, so that no sane passenger would want to travel to London via Retford (with a long, long wait between trains). Not only did the alliance attempt to prevent the introduction of services competing with those already offered by one or more of the allied companies (e.g. Warrington & Altrincham from Manchester to Warrington), but it also attacked existing services offered by hostile (unallied) companies. The basic aim was to send as much traffic as they could over each other's systems, regardless of whether other routes were shorter and regardless of public convenience (or inconvenience).

Unfortunately for the allied companies, during a skirmish between the LNW and the GN over the 'little' North Western Railway, details of the existence of the illegal agreement were made known to the world at large, and the agreement had to be swiftly terminated or the Law would step in.

This photograph of the Art Treasures Exhibition building of 1857, shows details of early MSJA slotted-post signals (plus the roof of the signal box).
Courtesy Manchester Public Libraries

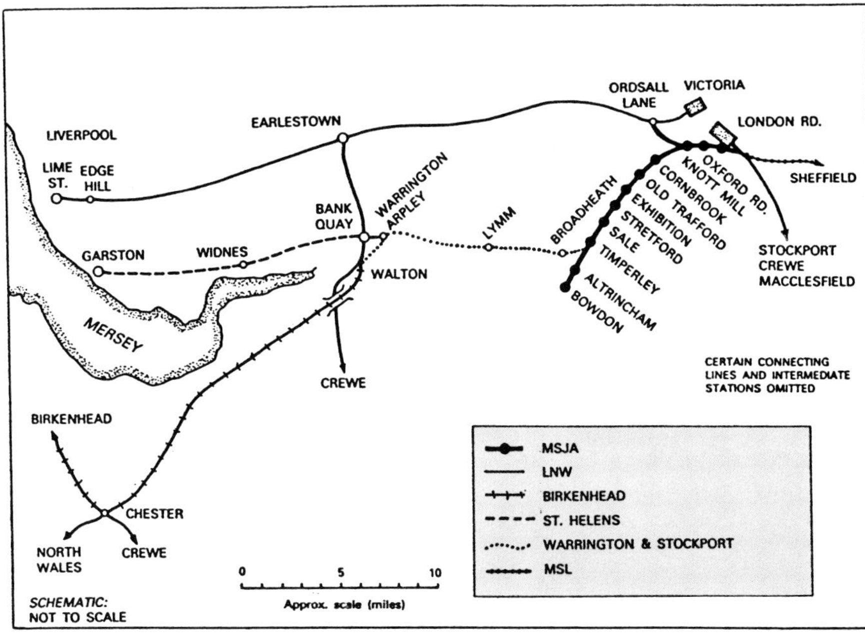

Map showing how the MSJA and Lymm lines were used to provide services to Liverpool and Chester, 1857–58.

The east end of South Junction line at London Road, which the LNW 'obstructed' during the railway war, seen here in 1923 with LNW locomotive No. 8840 on a special '567'. Note the elevated No. 2 signal box and the turntable. *L.M. Hobdey*

The foundation-stone of the alliance had been removed – would the alliance stand? In some matters all had the same interests – but in other matters, such as the building of lines to Buxton, where MSL and LNW interests differed, there was disagreement. Huish of the LNW seems to have judged that without the 'common-purse' the alliance would collapse and decided it would be in the best interests of his company to do a deal with someone else. Accordingly, he approached the GN and offered a division of traffic that would have left the MSL and Midland out in the cold.

The GN did not trust Huish at all, and much preferred to join hands with the MSL and open the junction at Retford. Accordingly, it informed the MSL of Huish's approach to it. The MSL, already suspicious of the LNW's intentions in the Buxton area and elsewhere, saw this as sufficient grounds for withdrawing from the alliance and signing a treaty with the GN on 8th July, 1857. The junction at Retford was opened, and plans put in hand for the introduction of a competitive service to London at the beginning of August. The LNW got to hear of this and arranged for its trains to be accelerated – and a railway war developed. Both sides cut their fares to attract traffic, and fares plummeted to uneconomic levels. There was keen competition for the Exhibition traffic and special trains were run from anywhere the two sides could physically compete, regardless of whether they made a profit, enabling many people who normally could not have afforded to visit the Exhibition to do so; and doubtless they thought favourably of the benevolent companies' efforts to bring culture to the masses, no matter what the cost to their shareholders.

On the MSJA, facilities for through booking via the MSL/GN route were introduced at the beginning of August and shortly afterwards Huish was complaining that the booking-clerks at the Exhibition station were persuading people to book by the MSL/GN rather than by the LNW, and also that the clerks were giving tickets by the MSL/GN route even when tickets for the shorter (LNW) route were requested. The MSJA management denied these charges.

As the railway war escalated, each side attacked more and more of the other's traffic. An example was the LNW's Liverpool traffic. The MSL had running powers over the MSJA, the W&S and the St Helens Co., so could run through trains over the MSJA to Timperley Junction, thence over the W&S to Warrington, and thence over the St Helens to Garston, 6 miles from Liverpool. The MSL decided to provide a competing Manchester–Liverpool service over this route to Garston, where connecting omnibuses took passengers into the centre of Liverpool. (At that time the LNW's Edgehill–Garston link had not been constructed: it was opened on 15th February, 1864 when the 'Lymm line' to Liverpool was completed.) Similarly, a competing service to Chester was provided using the W&S to Arpley and the W&S's running powers over the Birkenhead into Chester station.

Minor acts of violence were committed by the servants of the warring companies. At London Road, LNW men ejected MSL men from the MSL booking-office there and boarded it up. They also began 'frightening' people using MSL trains. The LNW also 'obstructed' the London Road end of the MSJA by blocking the junction there and using part of the South Junction line for making up goods trains.

On 17th October, 1857 the Exhibition closed, but the competition continued.

As the LNW and MSL had equal stakes in the MSJA and provided the casting-vote Chairman at alternate MSJA Board meetings, a remarkable situation developed in which controversial resolutions were passed by the casting vote of the Chairman at one meeting, rescinded at the next, re-affirmed at the third and so on. This sounds like a recipe for deadlock, but in fact is not necessarily so; some things got done, but in twice the time they normally took.

On 8th September, 1857 the first controversial resolutions were passed by the casting vote of a MSL Chairman: one to the effect that the chief officers of the LNW and MSL should be allowed to attend MSJA Board meetings in a non-voting capacity; the second that the MSJA should approach the Bridgewater Canal Trustees offering to make a branch to the Canal at Stretford at joint expense. At the next Board meeting, a fortnight later, a LNW man was in the chair and these two resolutions were rescinded. For the next year or so they would be reaffirmed and rescinded at alternate meetings – a harmless activity. The Stretford branch was never started. It is interesting to note, in connection with the first resolution, that after a MSL-chaired meeting reaffirming it, notice of the next MSJA Board meeting would be sent to Watkin of the MSL and Huish of the LNW. Huish couldn't be bothered about attending – but Watkin would often turn up for a LNW-chaired meeting and be requested to leave (unless he had something important to contribute)!

After the Exhibition closed, the LNW started to remove the extra platform and siding at London Road, as it needed the space for goods sidings. This annoyed the MSL, who wanted to extend the W&S trains to London Road. The MSL contended that, as the extra platform and siding had been put in at MSJA expense, the LNW could not arbitrarily remove it, and that the MSJA should sue the LNW for its replacement. Legal advice was that (a) the existing platforms at London Road could handle the traffic, (b) it had been understood when the extra platform was installed that it was only a temporary one to handle the Exhibition traffic and, most important, (c) the land on which it stood was the LNW's – there was no evidence to indicate that it had ever been transferred or rented to the MSJA, and therefore the LNW could dismantle the extra platform. The opinion was that the MSJA had a bad case, and should not get involved in protracted and practically hopeless litigation.

The MSL searched in vain for documents that would prove the land was MSJA-owned or rented but eventually gave up its search. The MSJA never sued. W&S trains did not start running from London Road until 1860, by which time the LNW was leasing the W&S.

In November 1857, a notice appeared in the papers giving details of a Bill which the MSJA was to apply for, in the coming Parliamentary session, to modify the MSJA's constitution to facilitate the solving of disputes. The promotion of a Bill had not been discussed at any Board meeting, nor had any authority been given for the placing of the notice. At the next Board meeting, which was MSL-chaired, the MSL Directors moved that retrospective approval be given for the placing of the notice. The LNW Board members protested, and at the next meeting passed a resolution rescinding this approval. At the following meeting, the MSL Directors proposed a resolution, carried by the casting vote, instructing the MSJA's solicitors to proceed with the proposed Bill. The MSJA Bill was drawn up and submitted, with the MSJA seal fixed sometimes in support of it and at other times against it, depending on whether the previous Board meeting had a MSL or LNW Chairman! It was eventually thrown out at the Committee stage. However, a MSL-promoted Bill modifying the MSJA's constitution was passed on 23rd July, 1858, allowing the appointment of a permanent arbitrator.

Another dispute concerned the charges that the MSJA was to levy on through traffic passing over its line. As the MSL was running services to Liverpool and Chester via the W&S and MSJA, it was to the LNW's advantage to make the tolls payable the maximum permitted, whereas it was in the MSL's interests for the tolls to be lower and based on a mileage rate. Every meeting reversed the decision of the previous one, until on 25th May, 1858 it was agreed that the Board of Trade should arbitrate. However the BOT declined to appoint an arbitrator, as there was nothing in the then MSJA constitution allowing one! The problem was resolved with the passage of the above-mentioned Bill.

When the MSL was running its services to Liverpool and Chester over the W&S, it seemed likely that the MSL and St Helens Co. would jointly lease the W&S, and in February 1858 the companies reached agreement on the terms – 3½ per cent in the first year rising to 5 per cent in the fourth and subsequent years. The LNW was offered a share in the lease, but declined. Parliamentary approval was sought in the 1858 session but the Bill, alternately supported by and opposed by the MSJA, was thrown out.

Shortly before the end of the railway war, the MSL Directors attempted to bring off a minor coup. The MSJA Act of Incorporation states that the MSJA Directors must be appointed under the seals of the company they represent. All the MSL Directors had sealed appointments, but the LNW appointed its Directors by letter alone. The MSL Directors contended that the LNW Directors were not validly appointed and therefore not entitled to take their seats on the MSJA Board. The Solicitor's opinion was that the LNW appointments were technically invalid, in which case all previous LNW appointments were invalid, and therefore it was possible that all the previous decisions taken by the Board were technically invalid. Therefore he recommended that the LNW appointments, made in good faith, be accepted.

The railway war came to an end in the autumn of 1858, after the warring companies had lost several hundred thousand pounds through the lowering of fares to unprofitable and even loss-making levels (in some cases the rates fell so low that they did not cover the terminal charges, leaving less than nothing to pay for the transport of the passenger or goods).

In November 1858 peace terms were agreed, including the withdrawal of the competing services to Liverpool and Chester provided by the MSL over the W&S.

Chapter Five

The Early Days

On 4th March, 1851 the MSJA accepted a tender from Mr Ashbury for the provision of three parcel vans with springs and covered tops at £8 each.

In the summer of 1852, the first advertisements appeared on MSJA stations. At first it handled the letting itself, but it was found to be more profitable for the MSJA to rent the advertising rights to a semi-national space-selling concern. Of the various tenders received, that of W.H. Smith for the advertising and bookstall rights was the most attractive and was accepted in 1856. Smith's were to provide the bookstalls and sell advertising space for the next 50 years, being replaced by Wymans on and from Lady Day 1906.

On Saturday 20th March, 1853, the 1.15 pm ex-Oxford Road was derailed at Castlefield because the pointsman had not set the points properly. No one was hurt and very little damage was done. The pointsman, who had a hut within one of the viaduct's turrets, was cautioned and requested to read carefully the company's rules. Just over a year later (Saturday 22nd March, 1854) two wagons and their contents, part of a LNW goods train, were derailed because of a similar mistake, this time by a pointsman at Oxford Road, who was dismissed from the service.

On 8th September, 1854 the Manchester & Liverpool Agricultural Society held a Show at Altrincham and the MSJA offered to carry all livestock and equipment to the show free, as well as carrying from the show any unsold goods free. This sort of offer was made many times in later years.

In the summer of 1855 the electric telegraph was installed on the MSJA at a cost of £5 per mile per year installation and maintenance.

In 1856 the MSJA had to pay up on two unusual claims for damages: to Francis Woods, who received £10 compensation and 3 guineas costs for 'false imprisonment'; and to Edward Worthington, whose horse took fright and bolted on seeing an engine on Oxford Road bridge, causing his carriage to be damaged. Worthington held the MSJA liable for the damage, claiming that the battlements on the bridge were lower than the minimum height specified by the Act of Parliament authorising its construction. The MSJA replied that the bridge had been built in accordance with plans approved by the Town Clerk – and discovered that the battlements of several bridges were indeed lower than Parliament said they should be. Worthington was threatening to sue; worriedly the MSJA instructed their law clerks to settle with him and started looking into the possibility of raising all the battlements.

Worthington's claim for damages was negotiated down from £25 18s. to £20 which he received. A while later he approached the MSJA with a petition requesting an aerial tunnel over Oxford Road instead of the existing open bridge; to which the Board replied that modifications to the bridge were under consideration.

On 1st June, 1856 a station was opened at Cornbrook, served by four trains each way per day, to handle local traffic and excursionists to the nearby Pomona Gardens. In the summer of 1856 mileposts were installed along the line.

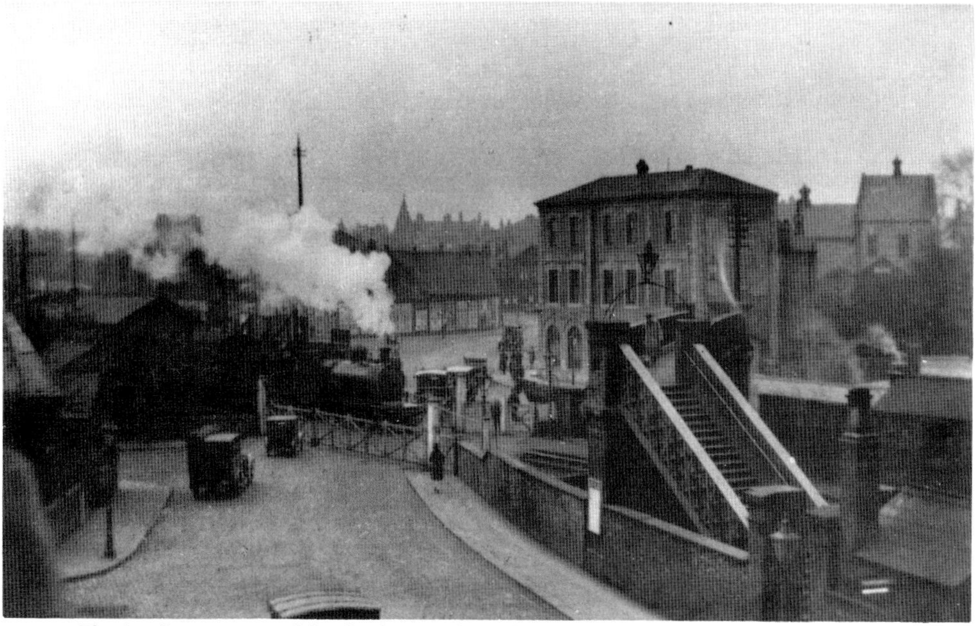

The level crossing and footbridge at Altrincham (*c*.1920). The footbridge has lights and the level crossing has wicket gates for pedestrians. *Courtesy Altrincham Library*

A view from the footbridge (*see above*) of the level crossing and signal box on 19th September, 1928; Altrincham Show Day. The two locomotives are Nos. 6919 and 8583. *E.R. Whitworth*

As previously mentioned, the W&S was in a pretty parlous financial state and, shortly after they started working it as an extension of the MSJA, it became necessary for the MSJA to inject £15,000 into it. The money was loaned at 5 per cent p.a. interest from 1st March, 1857, and as security the MSJA was issued with £15,000 worth (nominal value) of W&S shares, which were held by two MSJA nominee Directors.

Eighteen-fifty-seven was the year of the Art Treasures Exhibition and a peak year for revenue – it was also a peak year for accidents. On Whit Saturday, 6th June, an engine under the control of its fireman (the driver not being around) backed too fast into its train at the platform at Oxford Road and four passengers were hurt. On Wednesday, 5th August, at London Road, a LNW goods train ran into a train bound for the Exhibition. A first class carriage was damaged and some goods wagons derailed. Two days later the 3.15 pm to Bowdon pulled out of the bay at Oxford Road and hit a MSL Ordsall Lane–London Road train; several people were hurt. On Boxing Day the 1.10 pm ex-Oxford Road ran into a goods train at Sale; and on 9th January, 1858, Thomas Leigh was hit by the 4.10 pm express to Warrington while crossing the line at Old Trafford from the booking-office to the down platform. The jury at the inquest found that Old Trafford station was just not safe enough, and urged that both platforms be equipped with a footpath from the road and a booking office.

From 25th November to 31st December, 1857, a service of four trains a day each way between Oxford Road and London Road, connecting with Bowdon trains (which were still terminating at Oxford Road), was in operation and must rank as the most unsuccessful service the MSJA has ever operated. It was initiated when a MSL man was in the chair and lasted until these figures for a month's operation had been gathered: Passengers booked: 362. Receipts: £4 14*s*. 8*d*. Cost of service (wages and engines): £21 19*s*. 3*d*. The service was removed by the casting-vote of a LNW Chairman, the MSL Directors protesting that the service had no chance of becoming viable while LNW policemen accosted all the passengers using the service, demanding names and addresses. It was not, however, restored the next time the MSL provided the Chairman.

The Exhibition station and sidings were left standing after the Art Treasures Exhibition closed, pending a decision on whether the exhibition hall and buildings could be used as the venue for an industrial exhibition in 1858. Eventually those considering this decided against it; in the meantime high winds blew down the roof of the Exhibition station on the morning of 20th January, 1858; 28 of the 41 large columns and 5 of the 37 small ones were broken. James Lloyd paid £3 7*s*. 6*d*. per ton for the broken columns and the corrugated iron roof was also sold for scrap. Thirty tons of surplus rails were sold to the LNW for £5 per ton, lifted from the sidings put in to handle the exhibition traffic.

In September 1858 a turntable was installed at Bowdon station. Until then engines had to run in reverse from Bowdon to Altrincham to be turned round.

In March 1855, 45 residents signed a petition to the MSJA requesting the opening of a station at Marsland's Bridge (which was near Marsland's farm).

Brooklands station from the south on 8th June, 1927. Note the station buildings on the bridge. *Lens of Sutton*

An earlier view of Brooklands station, taken in the 1880s from the west bank of the Bridgewater Canal, and reproduced from the Birkenhead Series of postcards, printed in Belgium in the late 19th century. *Courtesy Sale Library*

The MSJA did not think that there would be enough traffic generated to justify the cost of building one and did nothing until it was approached by a local landowner called Brooks. Brooks was a Manchester banker who laid out an extensive speculative estate of large houses along a new road: Brooklands Road. Brooks and the MSJA negotiated until terms were agreed on 24th January, 1859 for the construction and opening of the station. Brooks would provide an acre of land for £200, the MSJA would build station and siding, and Brooks guaranteed that if the traffic receipts in the fifth year after opening were less than £100 he would pay the MSJA £300. The station was duly opened on 1st December, 1859, served by seven trains each way per day, and was taking over £100 per year within a couple of years. The station was christened Brooklands.

The MSL Act of 23rd July, 1858 authorised the appointment of a permanent MSJA arbitrator – the only qualification for the job being acceptability by both LNW and MSL. This proved an extremely difficult condition to satisfy – not until August 1859 was a suitable man found. Captain O'Brien of the North Eastern Railway was appointed on 31st October, 1859 and attended his first MSJA Board meeting on 15th November, 1859.

As previously mentioned, the peace terms at the end of the railway war included the withdrawal of MSL services over the Lymm line to Garston with bus connections to Liverpool, as these competed with the LNW's services over the L&M. This left the W&S of little use to the MSL, and no further attempts were made by the MSL to lease it.

The W&S therefore drifted into the clutches of the LNW. An Act of 13th August, 1859 empowered the LNW and St Helens Co. jointly to lease the W&S. Shortly thereafter the joint MSL/LNW working of the W&S ceased – from 1st November, 1859 all the trains of the W&S were LNW-worked. W&S services were extended to London Road at the beginning of 1860 (but the local MSJA services continued to terminate at Oxford Road). At this time there were only two tracks into the main part of London Road station, and frequently the engine of a W&S train arriving at the MSJA platforms at London Road was unable to venture onto the LNW tracks in order to get round its train because of all the traffic going to and from London Road station. Often W&S trains had to be pushed by their engines from London Road to Oxford Road where the engine was able to run round its train.

This blocking of the east end of the MSJA was relieved by the quadrupling of the approaches into London Road, plans for which were approved in March 1861. The work was completed in December 1866.

On 14th June, 1860 the LNW obtained an Act authorising it to lease the Warrington–Garston line of the St Helens Co. At the beginning of 1861 the LNW repaid to the MSJA the money owed by the W&S, and took possession of the W&S shares that the MSJA was holding as security. The final stage of the LNW takeover of the W&S and St Helens lines soon followed, in July 1864, when the LNW was empowered to swallow both companies. Following this, the Lymm line was used almost solely for local passenger traffic, and a fair amount of goods traffic.

Passengers alighting at the Cricket Ground station in July 1899, to watch a match at Old Trafford between England and Australia. *Railway Magazine*

The 8.40 am from Altrincham hurtling past Old Trafford! – card, posted in 1907, produced by the Cynicus Publishing Company of Tayport, Fife. 'Cynicus is the cognomen of Mr Anderson, that widely popular and clever Scottish caricaturist. So great has been the demand for the work of this artist that a commercial undertaking has been formed . . . who print and place on the market the works of this somewhat erratic genius'. *Courtesy Altrincham Library*

Chapter Six

Cheshire Lines Connections

Apart from a short curve put in by the MSL at Timperley, all the other lines connecting with the MSJA were part of the Cheshire Lines. The first of these to open was the line to Northwich. This was backed by the MSL, who suggested to the LNW that it be built as an extension of the MSJA; however the LNW would not join in. Incorporated as the Cheshire Midland (CM), the line was opened to Knutsford on 12th May, 1862 and to Northwich on 1st January, 1863. This was extended as far as Mouldsworth by the West Cheshire Railway, which opened to Helsby on 1st September, 1869, and from Mouldsworth to Chester Northgate by the Chester & West Cheshire Junction on 2nd November, 1874.

The line between Deansgate Junction and Stockport was promoted as the Stockport, Timperley & Altrincham Junction (STAJ) and was opened between Deansgate Junction and Stockport Tiviot Dale on 1st December, 1865. The link between the STAJ and the Lymm line, bridging the MSJA, was opened on 1st February, 1866. The MSL built a curve between Timperley station and the STAJ and opened it on 1st December, 1879.

The Cheshire Lines main line was opened from Skelton Junction to Garston via Glazebrook on 1st March, 1873, and from Cornbrook East Junction on the MSJA to Glazebrook on 1st September, 1873. The line from Cornbrook Junction West to the temporary Central station was brought into use on 9th July, 1877 and the connection from Old Trafford Junction on the MSJA to Cornbrook West was opened on 1st July, 1878, enabling Chester trains to use Central.

The Cheshire Lines Committee (CLC) was formed by an Act of 13th July, 1863 which authorised the formation of a committee to manage the Stockport & Woodley, CM, West Cheshire and STAJ: four MSL-backed Cheshire lines in which the GN was taking a half share. Just before the Midland gained access to the Manchester area with the completion of its line from Derby to New Mills (winter 1866/67) it obtained an Act on 5th July, 1865 allowing it to buy its way into the CLC, which became a joint line with three equal owners.

In 1862/63 the Cheshire Midland opened as detailed above, CM trains running from Oxford Road over the MSJA to the old Altrincham station, after which they branched off onto their own line. With increased traffic using Oxford Road, it was necessary to spend £12,500 enlarging it in 1864.

Following approaches from the Manchester Cricket Club, the old Art Treasures station near Warwick Road was adapted to serve Old Trafford Cricket Ground on match days only, at the beginning of the 1862 season. The Cricket Ground station was used on match days in many years, until Warwick Road station was opened for daily use in 1931. The Cricket Ground station was to the north of Warwick Road station, and for a long time traces of it could still be seen, in the form of banks of earth. For convenience, the Cricket Ground station will henceforth be referred to as 'Warwick Road'.

There was an unusual accident at Old Trafford station in 1864. In those days, certain trains were scheduled to stop at Old Trafford only if passengers were waiting to be picked up. The practice evolved of setting the signal

The previous signal box at Deansgate Junction, which was on the other side of the line from the present one, photographed on 16th May, 1956. In the background is the Skelton Junction–Lymm line. *R.E. Gee*

Deansgate Junction, 1932: the bridge in the foreground carried the Skelton Junction–Lymm line; and the one in the distance the Skelton Junction–Glazebrook line.
National Railway Musuem

north of Old Trafford tunnel to 'danger' if passengers were waiting at the station. The drivers of such trains would pass the signal, even though it was at 'danger', then start decelerating so as to stop at the station after emerging from the tunnel. On 6th August, shortly before 8.50 am, a joint GN/MSL passenger train to Liverpool (via Lymm) was derailed by faulty points at the west end of Old Trafford station. A few minutes later, a joint MSL/GN goods train to Liverpool halted behind it. The end of the goods train was protected by the signal north of the tunnel, which was set to 'danger'. Unfortunately, the next down train was the MSJA's 8.55 am service from Oxford Road to Altrincham, which was booked to stop at Old Trafford only if passengers were waiting. The driver saw the 'danger' signal, assumed that it meant 'passengers waiting' and passed it, and so was unable to avoid running into the goods train at about 10 mph, despite braking hard when he saw it: 28 passengers were injured. As well as an end to the unorthodox (and ambiguous) use of the 'danger' signal, and improvements to the points, better use of the telegraph was recommended. Apparently, 'commercial' messages had had priority over those relating to the controlling of the trains, so that although the Old Trafford station quickly telegraphed Oxford Road about the derailment, the message arrived too late to prevent the dispatch of the 8.55 am train.

Cornbrook station closed after the last trains had called on 31st May, 1865.

By now the MSJA was taking as much traffic as it could handle with a primitive time-interval system of signalling. From the west, traffic off the Lymm line, the L&M, the CM and from local MSJA stations; from the east, traffic from the MSL and its allied system, and the M&B and its branches; all this traffic converged on the South Junction viaduct. Delays of an hour on the viaduct were not unusual; relief was urgently needed and came with the opening of the Stockport–Timperley line in 1865/66 which took all the traffic from points east of Godley Junction to everywhere on the Lymm and Northwich lines off the South Junction viaduct. As can be seen from the graph (page 159), goods traffic over the MSJA fell dramatically at that time, whereas passenger traffic was pretty well unchanged, because the Stockport–Timperley line was little used for passenger traffic.

On 6th July, 1865 the MSL obtained an Act for the construction of the CLC Liverpool line, which authorised not only the construction of the CLC line but also the widening of the MSJA from just south of Old Trafford station, where the CLC was to branch off, into Manchester. This Act was passed despite having the MSJA seal fixed against it (O'Brien's decision as arbitrator) but the authorised widening was never carried out. The CLC line's route was later modified (MSL Act of 16th July, 1866) to commence with a junction with the MSJA at Cornbrook rather than Old Trafford.

With trains to Liverpool running from London Road via the Lymm line, and the probable opening of the CLC line to Liverpool, the need for and patronage of the Ordsall Lane service declined. Passenger receipts for traffic over the South Junction line fell from just under £1,000 in 1860 to £500 in the mid 1860s, and towards the end of that decade were down to double figures. The MSL stopped running trains between Ordsall Lane and London Road in the autumn of 1868, and the LNW (apart from through workings onto the L&M) in the summer of 1871.

In 1869 a Royal Agricultural Society Exhibition was held near Warwick Road and the station there went into service as 'Exhibition'. The MSJA handled the slightly increased traffic competently (apart from a collision between a LNW Lymm line train and a MSJA cattle train, on 16th July, near the Exhibition site). The Exhibition was visited by the Prince and Princess of Wales on 20th July.

In 1870 there were two accidents at Altrincham. The first was minor – an MSJA stock train was derailed at Altrincham Junction by faulty points; the second was a little more serious – and curious. On the evening of 27th December a CLC train was standing in Altrincham station delayed by a late connection from the Baguley line when an MSJA train ran into it from behind at about 4 mph. Fifteen passengers were hurt. The signalman in the box near Altrincham level crossing was in the habit of giving the 'all clear' to the Deansgate Junction signal box as soon as a train going south passed his box (instead of waiting until it left the Altrincham station). Thus, on the night of the accident, Deansgate Junction box got the 'all clear' although the train stayed in the station. The Altrincham distant and home signals should both have protected it, but unfortunately the distant signal was frozen at 'clear' and the driver of the MSJA train did not see the home signal reading 'danger' until it was too late. The signalman was severely reprimanded, but a previous good record kept him his job.

In the autumn of 1871, the MSJA decided to spend £400 installing a footbridge just north of Altrincham level crossing. It was also suggested that the Altrincham level crossing should be closed and replaced by a bridge – but the board baulked at having to spend £30,000 or more. (Nothing happened until a £500,000 flyover to take road traffic off Stockport Road level crossing was completed in autumn 1972.)

That summer, there had been a curious near accident. One Saturday afternoon, a carriage and pair stood in Holmfield, off Hope Road, Sale. A five-year-old boy jumped in and startled the horses, which charged out of the street, leapt over a hedge onto the line between Brooklands and Sale, and proceeded to gallop along the line towards Manchester, dragging the carriage after them. They passed through Sale station, startling passengers on the platforms, and disappeared northwards. Wardleworth, the station master at Sale, got on the telegraph and had all the trains stopped. Child and horses were rescued when they stopped just north of Mersey Bridge.

O'Brien died in September 1872 and was succeeded as Arbitrator by George Leeman (also of the North Eastern) who was appointed on 13th November, 1872.

By now, several of the stations needed improving. In 1871, plans to rebuild the old Altrincham station jointly with the CLC came to naught. At Timperley and Brooklands conditions were such that, a few years later, the passengers presented petitions for the improvement of the waiting-rooms. In 1874 Oxford Road was rebuilt – a task involving the demolition of a goods warehouse, a building yard and a few rooms, and replacing the lot by a new passenger station.

The cause of most of the complaints received by the MSJA was its viaduct. Shortly after the opening of the line the first complaint was received – about some offensive matter deposited under the arches in Little Ireland – and from then on they kept rolling in. The viaduct not only cut across north–south street-level communication, but was also untidy. Never averse to any extra income (£2,000 pa at the time) the MSJA let arches for smithies, marine stores, stables, mortar mills, the storage of old tubs, lumber, casks and other 'low-class trades' – and so one side of a street running alongside the viaduct would be cluttered up with horses and carts, haggling traders and miscellaneous junk. The unlet arches attracted tramps and general down-and-outs who needed a 'roof' for the night – and the rich complained.

On top of the viaduct the trains kept on running – in increasing numbers. Although the opening of the Baguley line had creamed off much east–west traffic, local traffic, together with that over the former L&M, was ever-growing. To handle it more competently the block system of signalling was introduced on the Altrincham branch in 1870 and on the South Junction line in 1874, and the Smith vacuum brake was fitted to all trains in 1875.

In 1872, 1874 and 1878 Acts were passed authorising increases in the MSJA's capital of £50,000, £50,000 and £60,000 respectively. Each owner provided half the total.

The mid-1870s were a peak period for accidents. On Sunday 30th March, 1873, a goods train from Ordsall Lane ignored some signals and ran into the back of the 2 pm from Bowdon which was standing in Knott Mill station; no-one was killed. On 6th August, 1873, while an engine was running round its train at London Road, some uncoupled wagons ran away to Oxford Road, where the signalman diverted them into a siding where they harmlessly derailed themselves. On 7th July, 1874 an MSL train of empty cattle wagons from Ordsall Lane ignored some signals and rammed a LNW passenger train at Oxford Road. No one was killed, but a few carriages were damaged; much the same happened 11 days later when a MSL light engine collided with a LNW excursion from Preston to Longsight (for Belle Vue). On Friday 14th July, 1876 the 4.25 pm from Bowdon was allowed onto a stretch of line at Cornbrook on which some platelayers were working; travelling at a fair speed it was derailed. The engine demolished a section of the viaduct wall, turned turtle and instantly killed the driver. The fireman had leapt out and survived, the passengers were shaken but unhurt. The MSJA board voted £250 compensation to the driver's widow – a sum increased to £325 after the vicar of Altrincham intervened. On 12th August, 1876 a CLC train from Knutsford ignored signals and collided with a MSJA train at Altrincham Junction. A few carriages were damaged and the passengers shaken but otherwise unharmed.

Until then, the CLC trains to Chester and Liverpool had started from Oxford Road. However, their traffic was increasing and they wanted their own terminal. In addition, there was overcrowding at London Road (into which the Midland now worked) and more accommodation was urgently required. A temporary Central station was opened on 9th July, 1877, when CLC Liverpool trains started using it as their terminus. Chester trains continued to run from Oxford Road until 1st July, 1878 when the Old Trafford Junction–Cornbrook West Junction link was brought into use, enabling them to use the temporary Central station. The permanent Central station was opened on 1st July, 1880.

An Act of Parliament passed on 16th April, 1878 authorised the construction by the MSL of a short curve between Timperley Junction and Skelton Junction which was duly brought into use on and from 1st December, 1879 when a circular service from Central to London Road via Stockport Tiviot Dale was introduced. The service, provided by the MSL, was very poorly patronised and was withdrawn as from 20th March, 1880. After this the curve was little used, and was broken in 1903. Houses now cover the ground where it ran.

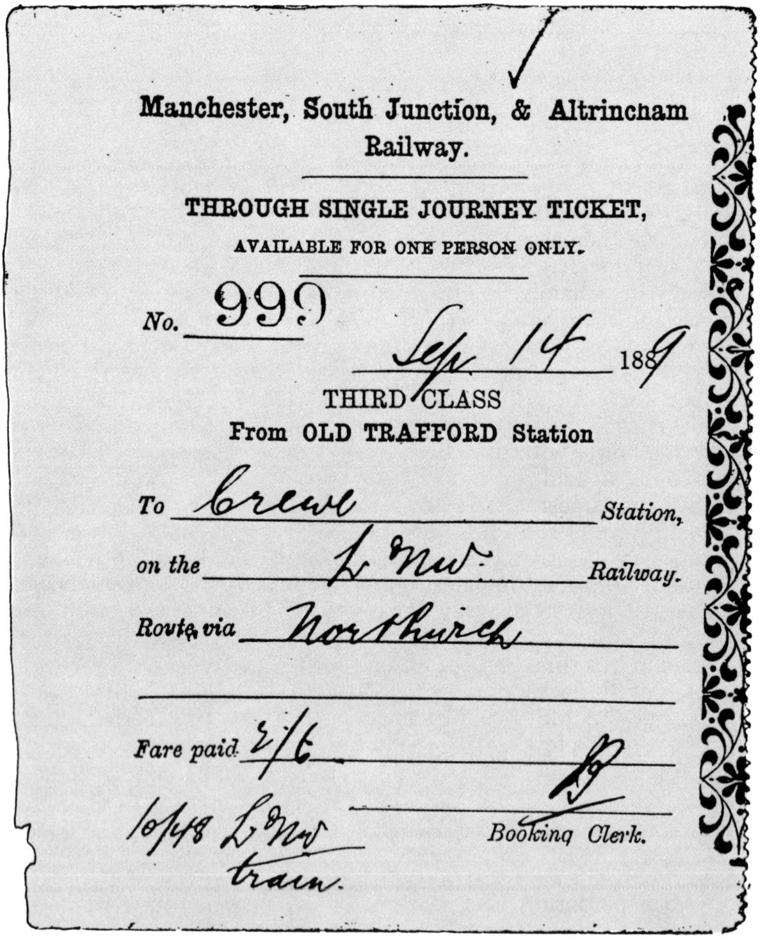
Manchester, South Junction, & Altrincham Railway.

THROUGH SINGLE JOURNEY TICKET,

AVAILABLE FOR ONE PERSON ONLY.

No. 999

Sep 14 1889

THIRD CLASS

From OLD TRAFFORD Station

To Crewe *Station,*

on the L & NW *Railway.*

Route, via Northwich

Fare paid 2/6

10/48 L&NW train

Booking Clerk.

Chapter Seven

New Termini

In 1880, the MSL and LNW came to agreement about the improvement of the stations at Altrincham and at Bowdon. It was decided to close both Altrincham station and Bowdon station and build a new station between them, to be called Altrincham & Bowdon.

Over 100 years later, it was described, in the newsletter of the Victorian Society's Manchester group, as:

> . . . a pleasant and spacious station. The main building is a long single-storey range in red-orange brick with stone dressings. A central block with a high hipped roof contains the booking hall, and this is linked by symmetrical wings to pavilions at either end. The building is given character by the use of coloured bricks in the voussoirs of the window and door arches. There is a good clock tower in the forecourt in the same style. The extensive platform awnings are glazed and are supported on cast iron columns and arched brackets. The effect is elegant and pleasing . . .
>
> The method of supporting the platform awnings and the use of coloured brick at Altrincham may also be seen in the brickwork and roof of the main shed at London Road (Piccadilly) station, and one may therefore conclude that the LNWR architect's office was responsible for the design of Altrincham.

The new Altrincham & Bowdon station had four platforms – two for the CLC and two for the MSJA. For the use of this improved accommodation the CLC's rent was increased from £250 p.a. (plus a share of working expenses) to £350 p.a. (plus etc.).

The new Altrincham & Bowdon station was brought into use on 3rd April, 1881 when the other two stations closed. Although the new station's official name for the next 100-or-so years was 'Altrincham & Bowdon', for simplicity (and in line with common practice) it will henceforth be referred to as Altrincham station.

About this time the whole of London Road station was enlarged, but we are concerned only with the MSJA's platforms. The existing platforms and bridge across Fairfield Street were demolished and two new girder bridges (at the time the largest in Europe) were installed to carry the MSJA. A new island platform 450 feet long was built, 20 feet wide with a 200-foot long glass awning covering it. The waiting-rooms were of blue and white bricks and 'furnished with all the latest improvements for the convenience of the passengers'. A covered stairway down to Fairfield Street was built: well-lit, ventilated and lined with white enamelled bricks. A new footbridge was constructed to link this island platform with the rest of London Road station.

The new platform was opened on 16th May, 1882, and became a new terminus. In 1878 MSJA local trains started running through to London Road, at first only a few, but in increasing numbers until by 1890 nearly all started at London Road. The southern face of the island platform, served by a bay line, was used for all the local trains except at rush hours, when the northern face of the island and the main station's platform serving the through lines were brought into use. At Oxford Road, the through trains used the through platform while the cricket trains and other specials ran from the bay platforms. At the time Oxford Road had only one through platform, which trains to and from London Road called at, involving the crossing and recrossing of tracks as trains entered and left; a complex

Mid. & Ches. Line sht.]   a Saturdays only.

Manchester, South Junction, and Altrincham Railway

b Saturdays excepted

Centrl. Station	..	650	..	d	..	..	..	..	..	d	d	d	..	1020	d	..	..	d
London Road	625	..	..	8 5	..	..	..	855	..	920	9 30	1010	1020	..	1110	..	12 0	1210
Oxford Road	628	..	715	810	815	830	845	9 0	915	925	9 45	1015	1023	..	1113	1115	12 5	1215
Knott Mill	630	..	717	..	817	..	847	..	917	..	9 47	1017	1025	..	..	1117	12 7	1217
Old Trafford	..	655	721	..	821	..	851	..	921	..	9 51	1021	1031	..	..	1121	1213	1221
Stretford	..	7 0	725	..	825	837	855	9 7	925	..	9 55	1025	..	1028	..	1125	1218	1225
Sale	..	7 5	730	..	830	842	9 0	912	930	..	10 0	1030	..	1033	..	1130	1224	1230
Brooklands	..	7 8	732	..	832	..	9 2	..	..	..	10 2	1032	..	..	..	1132	1227	1232
Timperley	640	713	735	828	835	..	9 5	..	..	936	10 5	1035	1048	..	1125	1135	1231	1235
Altrm. & Bwdn	..	717	740	..	840	847	910	917	935	.	1010	1040	..	1042	..	1140	..	1240

Centrl. Station	bd	ad	b	a	a		a	a	..	..	d	d	d	..	..	b	b	d
London Road	1240	1240	..	..	..	.	..	..	155	..	240	310	340	..	..	440	..	5 5
Oxford Road	1245	1245	1 5	1 5	113	1 15	135	155	2 0	215	245	315	343	345	415	445	5 5	515
Knott Mill	1247	1247	1 7	..	..	1 17	137	157	2 2	217	247	317	..	347	417	447	..	517
Old Trafford	...	1251	..	..	..	1 21	141	2 1	2 8	221	251	321	..	351	421	451	..	521
Stretford	1253	1255	113	..	..	1 25	145	2 5	214	225	255	325	..	355	425	455	..	525
Sale	1258	1 0	118	..	124	1 30	150	210	218	230	3 0	330	..	4 0	430	5 0	514	530
Brooklands	1 0	1 2	120	..	126	1 32	152	212	..	232	3 2	332	..	4 2	432	5 2	..	532
Timperley	...	1 5	..	..	130	1 35	155	215	226	235	3 5	335	357	4 5	435	5 5	..	535
Altrm. & Bwdn	1 5	1 10	125	120	..	1 40	2 0	220	..	240	310	340	..	410	440	510	520	540

Centrl. Station	d	b	..	b	d	..	d	..	..	d	..	d	845	..	..	..	..	..	..
London Road	520	..	..	..	6 0	6 5	625	..	..	740	750	827	..	..	..	..	1015	..	..
Oxford Road	525	530	545	6 0	6 5	615	628	645	715	745	755	830	..	9 0	930	10 0	1030	11 0	1130
Knott Mill	..	532	547	..	6 7	617	..	647	717	747	757	832	..	9 2	932	10 2	1032	11 2	1132
Old Trafford	..	536	551	..	..	621	..	651	721	751	8 2	836	..	9 6	936	10 6	1036	11 6	1136
Stretford	..	540	555	6 7	..	625	..	655	725	755	8 7	840	852	910	940	1010	1040	1110	1140
Sale	..	545	6 0	6 11	..	630	635	7 0	730	8 0	812	845	857	915	945	1015	1045	1115	1145
Brooklands	..	547	6 2	6 13	..	632	..	7 2	732	8 2	815	847	..	917	947	1017	1047	1117	1147
Timperley	540	..	6 5	..	620	..	640	7 5	735	8 5	820	850	..	920	950	1020	1050	1120	1150
Altrm. & Bwdn.	..	553	610	6 18	..	638	..	710	740	810	..	855	9 5	925	955	1025	1055	1125	1155

Sundays

Centrl. Station	..	850	..	..	..	..	..		..	..	..	..	..	..	..	..	..
London Road	740	..	9 35	1235	140	2 5	235	..	435	5 5	535	625	7 5	820	845	915	1015
Oxford Road	745	..	9 45	1245	145	215	245	3 0	445	515	545	630	715	830	855	930	1030
Knott Mill	747	..	9 47	1247	148	217	247	3 2	447	517	547	632	717	832	857	932	1032
Old Trafford	752	855	9 51	1251	153	221	251	3 6	451	521	551	640	721	836	9 1	936	1036
Stretford	757	9 0	9 55	1255	158	225	255	310	455	525	555	645	725	840	9 5	940	1040
Sale	8 2	9 5	10 0	1 0	2 3	230	3 0	315	5 0	530	6 0	650	730	845	910	945	1045
Brooklands	8 5	9 7	10 2	1 2	2 7	232	3 2	317	5 2	532	6 2	654	732	847	912	947	1047
Timperley	8 9	910	10 5	1 5	212	235	3 5	320	5 5	535	6 5	659	735	850	915	950	1050
Altrm. & Bwdn.	..	914	1010	1 10	..	240	310	325	510	540	610	..	740	855	920	955	1055

Altrm. & Bwdn.	640	..	726	740	8 0	..	810	8 25	..	..	835	845	9 0	9 15	930	9 45	10 0	..
Timperley	643	7 7	..	743	..	8 7	..	..	..	..	838	848	..	9 18	..	9 48	..	10 9
Brooklands	646	..	..	746	8 4	..	814	..	..	837	..	851	..	9 21	..	9 51	..	..
Sale	649	712	732	749	8 7	..	817	..	831	..	844	854	9 6	9 24	936	9 54	10 6	1014
Stretford	654	717	737	754	811	..	822	..	835	..	849	859	910	9 29	940	9 59	1010	..
Old Trafford	658	722	745	758	..	..	826	..	..	..	853	9 3	..	9 33	..	10 3	..	..
Knott Mill	7 4	727	..	8 4	819	820	832	8 38	843	848	859	9 9	918	9 39	948	10 9	1018	1023
Oxford Road	7 5	730	..	8 5	820	822	833	8 40	844	850	9 0	910	920	9 40	949	1010	1019	1025
London Road	..	735	..	..	..	825	..	8 45	..	855	9 5	915	925	9 45	..	1015	..	1030
Centrl. Station	e	..	750	..	e	..	e	..	..	..	e	..	..	e	..	..	e	..

Altrm. & Bwdn.	..	1030	1042	11 0	..	12 0	1217	1 0	..	130	135	2 0	230	3 0	..	330	345	4 0
Timperley	1023	1033	..	11 3	1155	12 3	..	1 3	113	133	138	2 3	233	3 3	310	333	..	4 3
Brooklands	..	1036	..	11 6	..	12 6	..	1 6	..	136	141	2 6	236	3 6	314	336	..	4 6
Sale	..	1039	..	11 9	..	12 9	1223	1 9	118	139	144	2 9	239	3 9	317	339	350	4 9
Stretford	..	1044	..	1114	..	1214	1227	114	123	144	149	214	244	314	322	344	355	414
Old Trafford	..	1048	1054	1118	..	1218	1232	118	..	148	153	218	248	318	327	348	4 3	418
Knott Mill	1036	1054	..	1124	12 4	1224	..	124	131	154	159	224	254	324	333	354	..	424
Oxford Road	1037	1055	..	1125	12 6	1225	..	125	133	155	2 0	225	255	325	335	355	..	425
London Road	1040	11 0	..	1130	1210	1230	..	..	138	..	..	230	3 0	334	340	..	..	430
Centrl. Station	..	e	11 0	e	..	e	1238	e	..	b	a	e	e	e	..	b	410	e

Altrm. & Bdn.	..	430	445	5 0	515	530	6 0	630	..	7 0	725	730	..	8 0	845	930	..	1015	1030	11 0
Timperley	425	433	..	5 3	518	533	6 3	633	638	7 3	..	733	745	8 3	848	933	9 50	1018	..	11 3
Brooklands	f	436	..	5 6	521	536	6 6	636	642	7 6	..	736	..	8 6	851	936	9 54	1021	..	11 6
Sale	433	439	..	5 9	524	539	6 9	639	645	7 9	730	739	750	8 9	854	939	9 58	1024	..	11 9
Stretford	438	444	455	514	529	544	614	644	650	714	735	744	755	814	859	944	10 4	1029	..	1114
Old Trafford	444	448	5 1	518	533	548	618	648	654	718	742	748	8 0	818	9 3	948	10 9	1033	1040	1118
Knott Mill	449	454	..	524	539	554	624	654	658	724	..	754	8 5	824	9 9	954	1016	1039	..	1124
Oxford Road	451	455	..	525	540	555	625	655	7 0	725	..	755	8 7	825	910	955	1020	1040	..	1125
London Road	455	..	..	..	..	6 0	..	..	7 8	730	..	..	810	..	..	100	1025	..	..	..
Centrl. Stn.	..	b	5 8	..	b e	..	..	e	..	e	750	e	..	..	..	..	..	..	1045	..

Sundays

Altrm. & Bdn.	754	845	..	9 45	1245	2 0	225	330	..	415	5 0	545	715	8 0	830	..	930
Timperley	..	848	928	9 48	1248	2 3	228	333	343	418	5 3	548	718	8 3	833	9 11	933
Brooklands	..	851	932	9 51	1251	2 6	231	336	347	421	5 6	551	721	8 6	836	9 14	936
Sale	8 0	854	937	9 54	1254	2 9	234	339	351	424	5 9	554	724	8 9	839	917	939
Stretford	8 5	859	942	9 59	1259	214	239	344	357	429	514	559	729	814	844	922	944
Old Trafford	810	9 3	947	10 3	1 3	218	243	348	4 2	433	518	6 3	733	818	848	927	948
Knott Mill	..	9 9	953	10 9	1 9	224	249	354	4 9	439	524	6 9	739	824	854	935	954
Oxford Road	..	910	955	1010	1 10	225	250	355	4 11	440	525	610	740	825	855	937	955
London Road	..	915	100	1015	1 15	230	..	4 0	415	445	530	615	745	830	9 0	942	100
Centrl. Stn.	818	..	..	..	..	..	..	..	..	..	..	..	..	..	..	..	..

d Passengers from London Road for South Junction Stations change at Oxford Road; **e** For London Road change at Oxford Road. **f** Stops at Brooklands, Sats.

From the 'Sale Guide', July 1885.

A montage from an 1899 souvenir booklet.
George Falkner & Sons, Courtesy N. Dodson

Altrincham station forecourt about 1920. *J.A. Dean*

(B 14)

Manchester, South Junction, and Altrincham Railway.

TICKET for Carriages, Luggage, &c., Horses, Cattle Asses, Mules, Dogs, and other Quadrupeds, and for Poultry and other Live Birds by Passenger Train.

No. 69
From .... To M'worth
Spl ....Train. Mch 7 1888.

No.	Description	Rate	Paid on £ s. d.	To Pay £ s. d.	Paid £ s. d.
	Carriage........Wheels......				
	Carriage Trucks.............				
	Covered Truck extra........				
	Luggage				
	Invalid Road Carriage				
1	Horses	8/8			8 8
	Bulls				
	Neat Cattle				
	Rams				
	Sheep......................				
	Pigs				
	Asses or Mules				
	Dogs......................				
	Other Quadrupeds, viz.:—				
	Poultry or other Birds, viz.:—				

Declared value, £...............
Insurance on £............at 5 per cent............
Total, £...

Name of Consignee..
Address..

NOTICE.—The Manchester, South Junction, and Altrincham Railway Company are not and will not be Common Carriers of Horses, Cattle, Sheep, Pigs, Asses, Mules, Dogs, or other Quadrupeds, or of Poultry, or other Live Birds, and receive, forward, and deliver the same solely on and subject to the following conditions:—

The Company will not be responsible for any loss of, or damage or delay to, any Horse, Cattle, or other Quadruped, or any Poultry or other Bird occasioned by any cause or means whatever, except upon proof of wilful misconduct or negligence on the part of the Company or their servants, nor will they be responsible in any case for a greater amount for loss, injury, or delay of or to any such Quadruped or Bird beyond the following sums, viz.:—Horses, £50 each, Neat Cattle, £15 each; Sheep or Pigs, £2 each; Asses or Mules, £5 each; Dogs, Deer, or Goats, £2 each; Rabbits or other small Quadrupeds, 5s. each; Poultry or other Birds, 5s. each, unless a higher value be declared at the time of delivery to the Company, and a percentage of 5 per cent. paid upon the excess value so declared. Neither will the Company be responsible for loss of market or any other special damages whatever.

In cases of consignments to shows or other places of a similar character, these conditions shall apply as well to the return as to the outward journey.

Please forward the above consignment on the terms contained in this note, which terms shall apply to the whole transit, and shall also apply as between the owner and any of the Companies whose lines are included in such transit, notwithstanding that the consignment may only be booked locally over the line upon which the transit commences.

....

Owner or on Owner's behalf.

operation but one whose successful execution emphasised the skill of the MSJA staff.

A short stretch of the South Junction line beyond the west end of the bridge over the Irwell was transferred to the LNW, following an 1882 Act that authorised various LNW modifications to it and at Ordsall Lane station.

In the early 1880s the Ordsall Lane service was revived (perhaps by the opening of the LNW Bolton line?) and was in use for a decade before being withdrawn. Since then, until the introduction of the Windsor Link services in 1988, the only passenger services over the South Junction line were occasional, irregular and sometimes short-lived services between, e.g. Liverpool and York, Liverpool and Buxton, Stockport and Blackpool, Stockport and Bolton, Bolton and London. For example, in 1958 the only passenger services using it were on summer Saturdays and occasional excursions.

In the late 1870s the CLC introduced the Altrincham–Stockport Tiviot Dale service, which was eventually withdrawn in April 1931. This was latterly worked by a Sentinel-Cammell railcar, known locally as the 'Baguley Bus'. In the early 1880s the LNW introduced a service from Oxford Road over the MSJA and CLC to Northwich, thence to Crewe and London. This service lasted until the autumn of 1933.

First and second class season tickets were available from just after the opening of the line; third class season tickets were not introduced until 1st January, 1883.

Shortly after the opening of the W&S, arrangements were made for season tickets from Broadheath, Altrincham or Bowdon to Manchester to be valid from any of the three; however although Peel Causeway (Hale) station was opened in 1862 it was not until 1881 that arrangements were made for season tickets from Altrincham or Hale to Central or Oxford Road to be valid from either station at each end – for an extra 10s. per year.

Mention of Peel Causeway leads to the following diversion: on 31st March, 1900 Hale became an Urban District, but its station was still called Peel Causeway, which was an affront to local pride. To quote from a contemporary handbook:

> The Cheshire Lines Committee have recently given courteous consideration to the application by the Parish Council for an alteration in the name, and it has now been changed to Peel Causeway for Hale; but this can hardly be deemed a satisfactory result as the station is within the parish boundary. Meanwhile the neighbourhood of the station has been recognised as Peel Causeway by the Postal Authorities and Ordnance Surveyors; but this is a barbarous innovation that should meet with every discouragement.

The desired renaming was made in 1902 and Hale became Hale.

On 16th July, 1885 an Act was passed authorising an increase in MSJA capital of £50,000 to £860,000.

In November 1884 Manchester Corporation approached the MSJA about the 'eyesore and nuisance' that was Knott Mill station and within the month a plan for its improvement was approved in principle, but not implemented as the MSL did not want to pay for the street reconstruction required. In 1889 a modified plan was produced; this time the LNW wanted

Further illustrations from the 1899 jubilee booklet.

George Falkner & Sons, Courtesy N. Dodson

nothing to do with it. Early in 1891 agreement was finally reached and an Act was obtained on 21st July, 1891 authorising reconstruction of the station, taking of land, etc. Work did not start at once, in fact an extension of time for the necessary powers had to be obtained in 1894. Eventually Robert Neill & Sons got a £20,000 contract in 1895 for the rebuilding of the station – over 10 years after the first approaches. Such are the benefits of joint lines.

The new station was described as follows in the Victorian Society's Manchester group's newsletter:

> [It] is awkwardly situated on a narrow angular site between Whitworth Street West and the stub end of Deansgate. It is in blue and red brick with stone dressings. The style is vaguely baronial and includes a sham (at least, I suppose it's a sham) portcullis in the main entrance, which is further protected by elaborate wrought iron gates. The original name – Knott Mill Station – appears on a carved stone scroll, and the date 1896 is carried on a shield motif. It is a pretty odd sort of building but one of undoubted character. The bridges carrying the line over Deansgate, the Bridgewater Viaduct and the canal are particularly good, especially the parapets and cast-iron spandrels.

Manchester South Junction and Altrincham Railway Company

TRAFFIC DEPARTMENT

EMPLOYEES'

Tontine Sick Society

CONTRIBUTION CARD

Name...

Chairman—
Mr. W. WILDE.

Secretary—
Mr J. BROWN,
155, Tatton Street, Salford.

Treasurer—
Mr. R. FENT,
1, The Grove, Brooklands.

Members are urgently requested to note that the rules do not permit Sick Money to be paid out unless **immediate** notice of illness be sent to the Secretary.

An early view of the entrance to Old Trafford station. *Lens of Sutton*

A derailment at Old Trafford station on 1st August, 1889. Note the 'birdcage' brake-end coach and the slotted-post signals. *Courtesy J.A. Dean*

Chapter Eight

The 1887 Exhibition

In 1887 the Royal Jubilee Exhibition was held at the old 1857 Exhibition site, and from May to October Warwick Road was used as 'Exhibition' station. New temporary platforms, made of old sleepers, were provided at the station, and a third track was laid from Old Trafford to stock sidings at Stretford; this, with branches, served the extra platforms. In all, only £5,610 was spent enlarging station accommodation and laying extra track.

In the next five months the Exhibition station handled over 2,500,000 passengers, with only one recorded accident – a woman's crutch got stuck in a knothole and, trying to free it, she broke the end off. She received 2*s*. 6*d*. compensation. (They were used to crowds at Warwick Road. At the close of play on matchdays they could dispatch 16 trains from siding-platforms, without disturbing the normal traffic, in the space of 45 minutes.)

The normal MSJA traffic of over 60 trains per day each way (including CLC and LNW) was augmented by 33 trains per day each way shuttling between Manchester and the Exhibition, plus a fair few untimetableable extra trains at the end of the day, to carry the people who stayed until they were thrown out, plus the various special excursions organised from all over the country. What was at times in reality a doubling of traffic was handled by what was effectively the normal staff – as few extra men as possible were taken on (a) to keep costs to a minimum and (b) because of the risks of inexperience causing accidents – as the following figures show. As a result of the extra pressure there were a few minor delays but the smoothness with which so much extra traffic was handled for so long was a tribute to the staff.

Half-year end	*Passenger traffic receipts*	*Wages bill*
30th June, 1886	£35,323 6*s*. 10*d*.	£1,739 7*s*. 2*d*.
31st December, 1886	£35,784 3*s*. 8*d*.	£1,581 7*s*. 4*d*.
30th June, 1887	£42,427 16*s*. 0*d*.	£2,023 12*s*. 0*d*.
31st December, 1887	£55,605 8*s*. 7*d*.	£1,778 1*s*. 5*d*.
30th June, 1888	£38,131 12*s*. 8*d*.	£1,668 2*s*. 11*d*.
31st December, 1888	£38,672 3*s*. 1*d*.	£1,616 11*s*. 4*d*.

The Exhibition was opened by the Prince and Princess of Wales (later Edward VII and Alexandra). After the opening ceremony, the royal party joined the royal train and were transported to Ashley, where they alighted and went to Tatton Hall to stay the night as the guests of the then Lord Egerton. The following day they visited Altrincham and joined the royal train there, the journey to the Exhibition station taking 10 minutes.

One of the items on display at the Exhibition was an experimental LNW Webb Compound tank engine. This was built in 1887 at Crewe and was in effect a 2–2–4–0T. The high-pressure cylinders drove the rear (four-coupled) wheels, and the low-pressure ones the leading driving wheels. It was numbered 777 by the LNW, renumbered 1977 in 1895, and scrapped in 1901.

On 1st August, 1889 the engine of a stock train fell on its side after passing over points at Old Trafford; no fault could be found with the track.

Another montage from the 1899 souvenir booklet.

George Falkner & Sons, Courtesy N. Dodson

On 21st July, 1891 an Act was passed authorising the quadrupling of the MSJA between Old Trafford and Timperley Junction, together with the construction of a connecting link to the CLC Chorlton line, via a second Old Trafford tunnel. To finance these works the authorised capital was increased by £200,000 to £1,060,000. The only widening done was between Old Trafford and Sale, and the link to the CLC was never commenced. Progress on the 3 miles of widening done was slow, and extensions to the time limit for its completion had to be obtained again and again. The first stage was the provision of a fourth set of rails between Old Trafford and Stretford, which was ordered by the MSJA in December 1896 and completed in 1897.

On the morning of 7th December, 1892 a driver backed his engine too fast into his coaches standing at Altrincham. The front brake van was damaged. On the evening of 1st December, 1893 a driver was brought to a halt by the gates of Altrincham level crossing being shut against him. He whistled, the signalman saw him and opened the gates for him. The driver tried to move off, but his brake got stuck. He climbed down to fiddle with it, and the signalman shut the crossing gates. The fault was only minor and swiftly mended, the driver hopped back into his cab, took off the brake (to check it was working?) and crashed through the level crossing gates, injuring a woman.

In 1897 the Royal Agricultural Society held another Exhibition at Old Trafford, and Warwick Road handled the marginal increase in traffic competently. In the same year, the MSL renamed itself the Great Central (GC).

In 1899 the line celebrated its 50th birthday, issuing a special souvenir booklet to mark the anniversary. By now it was booking over 5,000,000 passengers per year plus an 'immense number' of season ticket holders – whom it carried in its 81 daily passenger trains. Altogether 146 passenger trains used the MSJA per weekday: 81 MSJA trains, 34 CLC trains and 31 LNW trains, of which 6 (3 each way) ran via Ordsall Lane. In addition, each weekday saw 153 goods trains: 102 over the South Junction line, 7 between Altrincham and Central, and 44 between Altrincham and Deansgate Junction. By now £1,115,927 had been invested in the line and it was making a profit of some £75,000 per year.

Train from Altrincham approaching Sale *c.*1910 hauled by a LNWR 0–6–2T.
G.W. Smith Collection, per A. Tyson

'. . . a stern official, incapable of recognising anything but a ticket . . .' An MSJA ticket-collector at Sale (and Ashton-on-Mersey) station in the early 1900s.

M. S. J. & A. Rly. Coy.
Weekly Season Ticket 24 THIRD CLASS
No. 7503 AVAILABLE BETWEEN NOT TRANSFERABLE
Altrincham & Bowdon and Broadheath
AND
MANCHESTER (London Road)
UNTIL
8 [illegible] 4
(SEE OVER)

Chapter Nine

'Revolution on the South Junction line'

The following extract from the *Manchester City News*, 3rd September, 1904 indicates the relationship between the public and a railway that had become a part of Manchester's daily life.

ALL CONTRACTS READY!

REVOLUTION ON THE SOUTH JUNCTION LINE

For at least a quarter of a century passengers on the Manchester South Junction Railway have done pretty much as they pleased. Season ticket holders, when passing the barriers at the various stations, have been in the habit of either muttering 'Contract' or walking past the collector with an air of aloofness which suggested that for them such an official had absolutely no existence. But a rude awakening has come. The line is the joint possession of the London and North-Western and Great Central railways, and certain changes of management have now been made by which, for three years, the first-named company rules the roost. Excited passengers in every train are to be heard declaring that they have exchanged King Log for King Stork.

Why do the people so furiously rage together? Well, the fact is that everybody is being compelled to show his or her contract. For some weeks past, several trains each day have been singled out for this indignity, and the porter who knows you perfectly by sight has suddenly become a stern official, incapable of recognizing anything but a ticket. Of course a large proportion of contract holders had no ticket. They had left it at home, never dreaming that it would have to be produced. Names and addresses were taken, and then the astonished and indignant passengers were allowed to proceed. One of the weaknesses of the South Junction system is that, tickets being collected or shown on the outward journey at the station where you alight, the collector has no means of knowing which class of carriage you have travelled in. By way of a check, several of the late trains out of town at night were stopped at Knott Mill. Collectors boarded all the first and second class compartments and made quite a large haul in excess fares from people found in those carriages whose tickets or contracts only entitled them to third-class accommodation. Up to last Monday, however, most of the business trains, morning, noon, or teatime, escaped lightly. But this week, when the suburban resident reached his station in the morning, he found access to the platforms impossible until he showed a ticket. The excuse of 'contract left at home' was useless. No ticket, no journey was the order, and a number of contractors had to take an ordinary single or return ticket to town. Dreadful stories are current of how respectable contractors of many years' standing assaulted the ticket-collectors, or ran down to the opposite platform and stepped across the metals to gain the forbidden territory, and the air is full of impending cases in the law courts. It is certain that the general feeling of irritation is extremely strong, and were season tickets granted on the tramcars between Manchester and Stretford, that service would be exceedingly popular just at present.

VIEWS OF THE NORTH-WESTERN COMPANY

No doubt there are two sides to every question and a representative of the *City News* called this week upon Mr H. Linaker, the district superintendent of the North-Western, to see what the company thought about the complaints.

'I suppose you know,' he said, 'all the contract-holders signed an agreement, when they took their tickets, that they would show them when called upon or pay the ordinary fare. It seems to me that honest passengers ought to be glad we are

North Staffordshire Railway No. 2265 at South Junction platform, London Road in 1923. The footbridge in the background went over Fairfield Street to Mayfield station.
L.M. Hobdey

Altrincham locomotive shed and goods shed in 1929, from the footbridge at the then Stockport Road level crossing. *E.R. Whitworth*

finding out the tricksters.'

'But think of the annoyance of perpetually showing your ticket, Mr Linaker, some of the passengers declare they will wear them round their necks on a string.'

'We don't want to inconvenience the passengers, but merely to show them that contracts must be in readiness when required. It is done on most suburban lines, you know; one morning a week all contracts and tickets must be shown. That is what we shall do in the future, when things have settled down a bit.'

'How about the complaints that have been made of unpunctuality of the trains.'

'People have written to the papers a good deal, I know; but there has been very little unpunctuality. I've got a record of it all. Twice in August we stopped the trains in order to look at tickets, and the names of passengers who had no contracts had to be written down. Naturally that caused delay. Then the line is being altered between Stretford and Sale . . . and also at Oxford Road, and the trains have to slow down a little. From the same cause the use of the loopline between Stretford and Old Trafford has been temporarily lost to us. These things will soon be right again. We made some curious discoveries. Some of the people who had left their contracts at home gave names and addresses which could not be found; and in some cases other people's names were given. Other "contract-holders" when written to, sent on the fare, and a number of persons have been here to apologize and ask me not to prosecute. The amount of money paid has been quite a large item, so you see investigation was needed, as a result of the previous laxity. When the new lines are in use, and contract-holders realize that they should carry their tickets, we shall get on smoothly enough.'

'Do you think the staff on the South Junction stations is big enough to cope rapidly with all this extra supervision?'

'I have made inquiries,' said Mr Linaker, 'and I find that there is really a tremendous staff for so small a line, a staff far greater in proportion than any other line I know. Besides, additional men are sent down when required for the inspection of tickets. The fact is, folks have been making mountains out of molehills.'

The above article, although seemingly only concerned with season-tickets on the MSJA, also touches in passing upon many of the happenings on the MSJA at the turn of the century. First, it mentions changes in the MSJA management. As previously stated, the MSJA had its own Secretary/Manager and was run as an independent line, hiring its motive power and so on. At the turn of the century, the owning companies decided that it would be better if they were to dispense with the MSJA's separate management and take alternating responsibility for the line.

The then Secretary/Manager was R. H. Brown, who had been appointed to the position when Kirkman was dismissed in 1869. Brown retired on 31st December, 1903 and received a presentation gold casket. A. Ward was appointed as temporary MSJA Secretary/Manager from 1st January, 1904 until 1st July, 1904, when the LNW took over responsibility for the line for a three-year period. By an Act of 4th August, 1904 the MSJA was incorporated into the LNW and GC Joint Committee, of which body Ward became the Secretary.

The article refers to the widening of the line between Stretford and Sale, which cost some £30,000. Work started on this at the end of 1903 and was practically finished when the article appeared. By August 1904 the new track had been laid all the way, the old track slewed where necessary, the

Two views of the 'last MSJA steam train' to run from Altrincham in May 1931 with the LNER class 'F1' 2–4–2T being prepared (*above*) and with its crew and inspector (*below*). *Courtesy Altrincham Library*

Stanier class '3P' 2–6–2T No. 77 on the 4.55 pm London Road–Warrington, seen here passing Brooklands on 7th August, 1948. *J.D. Darby*

Before the introduction of the electric services: a six-coach MSJA train at Warwick Road on 4th May, 1931. The motor coach has the first type of pantograph. *British Rail*

Looking south from Warwick Road station 4th May, 1931. Note the variety of types of support for the overhead catenary, and several electric trains stabled in the sidings west of the slow running lines. *National Railway Museum*

Chapter Ten

The 1931 Electrification (1500 v DC)

The MSJA's main answer to road competition (e.g. the Manchester trams, which reached Sale in 1906 and Altrincham in 1907) was electrification. This was first considered and rejected in 1910–11. It was reconsidered in 1924; but the General Manager's report was against it. It was reconsidered in 1926; but again reported against. Finally, in 1928, the LMS/LNE Joint Committee recommended that the MSJA be electrified. The Ministry of Transport's Railway Electrification Committees (Pringle and Weir) had recommended that 1500v DC overhead be adopted as the standard railway electrification voltage. This recommendation was mainly based on other countries' experience (the only British use of the system until then had been on an LNE freight-only line in County Durham, between Shildon and Newport). As the MSJA was an important link between other lines, it was felt that the MSJA should use the new standard system which, it was thought, would be adopted for any 'main line' electrifications. Also it would provide valuable experience of the use of the system. And financial estimates showed a small balance in favour of using it (rather than a 'third rail' system) on the MSJA. So the MSJA became the first British passenger line to be electrified using the 1500v DC overhead system.

The electrification was designed by Lt-Col F.A. Cortez-Leigh, the LMS Chief Electrical Engineer, in conjunction with H.N. Gresley, the LNE's Chief Mechanical Engineer. The LMS was to be responsible for the work involved. The estimated cost, including new rolling-stock, was to be £500,000 (the out-turn was around £565,000); 28 track-miles were to be electrified, including the quadrupled section and certain sidings. The line between Castlefield Junction and Ordsall Lane was not electrified.

Work started in February 1929; and, with the aid of a special concrete-mixing train, the first overhead equipment went up in June 1929. Simultaneously work was going ahead on building the substations, the new stations and the new stock, and modifying the signals and platforms.

In the autumn of 1930 the first of the new electric trains was delivered – a three-coach set. There was no siding space available and so they were stored at Longsight and later (when more arrived) on the fast lines between Old Trafford and Warwick Road, and in sidings at the latter.

By now the substations were in working order, and sufficient of the overhead equipment completed to allow the first test run. On 25th November, 1930 a steam train pulled a three-car set from Longsight to Old Trafford, where the motor was tested and the train, watched by LMS, LNE and General Electric officials, made short trips up and down the line. This was the first multiple-unit 1500v DC overhead working in the UK.

Work proceeded, and on 14th April, 1931 the first electric train ran from London Road to Altrincham. It was driven by George Graver of Hale Barns, who had been a driver for 29 years. Thereafter test trains frequently ran over the line, while the steam service ran as normal.

In preparation for the electrification the drivers underwent 4 months' part-time training. This consisted of learning the theory of electric traction, various drills for various situations, and many practice drives. The practising generally took place on Sundays, and iron ballast was sometimes used to give the 'feel' of a loaded train. As the trains were more powerful

An Altrincham train at No. 1 platform Oxford Road, on the first day of electric services, 11th May, 1931. *Courtesy D. Rendell*

than those previously in use, much practice was needed before they were mastered.

On 6th May, 1931 an electrician working on the overhead equipment was electrocuted and died, and his mate was badly burned. They had accidentally touched the live wires.

On Sunday 10th May, 1931, a full dress rehearsal was held for the benefit of the staff. Two interleaved services were run: the normal Sunday steam passenger service; and the proposed Sunday electric service, with the trains carrying ballast instead of passengers. This was exceedingly successful (there was only one minor breakdown) and hopes were high for a successful first day of the electric service.

The line went all-electric overnight. On Monday 11th May, 1931, no MSJA steam trains ran. The company attempted to run a full electric service. In case of disasters, steam trains were kept at London Road, Warwick Road, Sale and Altrincham, to be brought into use if the electric services completely collapsed.

There were several mishaps, despite all the training and despite the dress rehearsal. At the stations, passengers were slow to get on and off (not realising the booked time for stopping had been reduced) and, in their haste to make up lost time, the drivers made mistakes and trains ground to a halt. The mishaps occurred in waves, after each new shift of drivers came on.

The first trains were at 5.30 am, which gave the drivers plenty of time to sort out their problems in time for the morning rush, which passed without incidents due to driver errors. However, the services were badly disrupted by a fault in a substation. A passenger at Sale, irate from a long wait, demanded 'What is this? Fred Karno's circus?' and received the reply 'No, madam, it is an electric railway'. Many passengers forsook the trains for the buses. Nor were they lucky with the evening rush-hour. At about 4.30 pm two trains (one up and one down) failed independently at Cornbrook and both lines were blocked for about half an hour. No sooner had that problem been sorted out than, at about 5.00 pm, a train entering London Road got into difficulties, and, due to poor communications, some trains were sent on from Oxford Road after it; there was a traffic jam on the viaducts while the stations filled up with cursing commuters. However, the reserve steam trains were not needed, for most of the mishaps were minor and easily sorted out in a few minutes.

For the first few days it proved difficult to operate the planned timetable, due to delays caused by slow passenger loading and the odd mishap; and the planned express service was never even attempted. However, once the drivers (and public) got used to the new working, they kept to the new timetable. The steam trains were no longer needed, and the stock was disposed of, mostly to the CLC. The engines kept at Altrincham shed were returned to their 'parent' sheds, and within a few weeks Altrincham shed was demolished.

As a result of the introduction of electric trains, the 'all stations' journey time between London Road and Altrincham was cut from 27 to 24 minutes and later to 22 minutes, despite there being three extra stops: a tremendous improvement in the service.

The station at Warwick Road was brought into daily use on 11th May, 1931; and the management must have been pleased to see 1,000 passengers booking from it on the first day, in addition to the cricket spectators (who saw Lancashire crumble from 84 for 1 to 153 all out; nothing ever changes). The two completely new stations, Dane Road and Navigation Road, were opened for traffic on 20th July, 1931. 'The whole of the stations on this line are illuminated by electricity', boasted the souvenir booklet issued to mark the electrification. The stations had also been spruced up and platforms adjusted, where necessary, for height and clearance.

In order to accommodate the 'Sale set' – an electric train stabled at Sale overnight and starting from there in the morning rush-hour – the up line was slewed out towards the canal south of Sale station and a siding put in between the up and down lines, with access from both.

Besides cutting the journey time, the new trains enabled an increased service to be provided. From 68 up and 67 down trains on weekdays the service was increased to 92 each way; starting and finishing earlier and later respectively.

To quote an advertisement in the *Guardian*, 9th May, 1931:

> Big, comfortable and roomy, the new coaches ride with a steadiness and a smoothness that makes the journey a pleasant break between the office and home. The new service is a great boon to those who live on the line and offers the prospect of fresh air and sunlight to those who still live in the city.

An interior of a third-class compartment of the 1931 electric stock. Note the typical lineside scenery! *British Rail*

The new rolling stock on the line was built by Metropolitan-Cammell Carriage Wagon and Finance Co. There were three different types of coach:

(a) *Motor coach* Weighing 57 tons and seating 72 third class passengers; this contained the motors and a guard's compartment (also for prams, mail, etc.). It had a pantograph on the roof, and a driving compartment.

(b) *Trailer* Weighing 30 tons when empty, this seated 40 first class and 48 third class (later modified to 24 first class and 72 third class).

(c) *Driving Trailer* Weighing 31 tons, seated 108 third class and had a driving compartment. Contained the 'ladies only' compartment.

The following measurements apply to all three types of coach:

Length over body 58 ft 1 in.; length over buffers 61 ft 8 in.; width over body 8 ft 11¼ in.; centre of bogies 38 ft 6 in.; height rail/roof 12 ft 4¾ in.; motor bogie wheel base 8 ft 9 in.; trailer bogie 9 ft 0 in.

The basic three-coach train unit was formed from one of each type of coach, with a driving compartment at each end. This had 268 seats (later 276). For peak times, a six-coach train was formed of two units marshalled normally with a motor coach at each end of the train (half the motor-coaches – the even-numbered ones – faced Manchester, and half – the odds – faced Altrincham. The same applied to the driving trailers). The total length was 370 ft and seating capacity 536 seats (later 552).

The coaches were basically of steel. The livery of the stock was initially: sides, green (very approximately that of GC locomotives) lined in yellow and black in the then-current LMS style, and decorated with the MSJA crest. Ends and underframes were black with red headstocks at the ends of the sets; roofs were dark grey.

Despite the contemporary trend to saloon-style carriages, the coaches were built compartment-style for swift loading and unloading at stations. The coaches were teak-framed with sheet-steel panels; the roofs were entirely angled steel sections covered with sheet-steel; the floors consisted of galvanised keystone corrugated steel covered with Induroleum, over which brown lino was laid.

The first-class compartments were finished in walnut, with blue cloth upholstery and seated eight passengers. The third-class were mahogany finished, upholstered in red and black moquette (latterly vandalised into patchwork) with seating for 12.

In both classes of compartments the luggage racks above the seats were of wooden frame and string netting (replaced by vandal-proof steel in 1969). Above the compartment doors were ventilators, there were bars across the door-windows and blinds were fitted to the seat-windows. Match-strikers were fixed to the door-frames. Set into position above the seats at eye-level were glass-covered pictures of beauty spots, a mirror, the MSJA route-map and (later) advertisements for British Transport Advertising Services Ltd. A few of these looking-glasses have been seen carrying paid advertisements (High Speed Gas – Just The Ticket).

Heating and lighting were controlled from the driving compartments. The

The longest MSJA train?: new coaching stock on the down fast line at Warwick Road on 16th April, 1931, prior to the introduction of the electric services

National Railway Museum

heating had three possible levels: full, half, none, and was provided by four 300-watt heaters in each compartment; wound for 750v in pairs in series in parallel they worked directly off the 1500v DC supply. The lighting was powered at 110v by a generator on the train driven from the 1500v. The third-class compartments had two ceiling lights wired in parallel; the first-class had one ceiling light and four bracket lights, switched on by the passengers. The result of this parallel wiring was that if one heating or lighting element failed the other one was unaffected.

Each motor coach had four 328-hp motors wound for 750 volts, the two on each bogie being connected permanently in series. The motor coach developed a maximum tractive effort of 23,000 lb. producing an acceleration of 1.43 mph/sec. with a fully-loaded 3-coach train weighing 134 tons on straight, level track. The trains were designed for a maximum speed of 60 mph. Starting was by the usual series-parallel method, all four motors being connected in series at the start, the two series pairs being re-connected in parallel halfway through the initial acceleration period. The starting resistances were cut out in sections automatically during acceleration under the control of a current-limiting relay. These resistances were at first placed in the equipment compartment but were soon re-located on the underframes on account of heating problems.

The control equipment consisted of electro-pneumatic contactors and reversing switch contained in a compartment behind the driving cab in each motor coach. The door into this compartment from the cab was so interlocked that it could not be opened with the equipment 'live'. The main circuit breaker, also in the compartment, had to be closed by hand by means of a cord from the adjacent driver's cab. It tripped (i.e. opened) automatically on overload and could also be tripped electrically from any cab. Power was taken from the overhead wire by means of a pantograph over the equipment compartment, raised and held up by compressed air. A handpump was provided for raising the pantograph when no air was available. Apparently, the original pantographs had copper contacts, which required lubricating. When a train arrived at London Road, the pantograph was lowered, and a man on the platform dipped a long pole into a wheelbarrow full of graphite grease, and rolled the grease onto the pantograph. This operation became unnecessary when carbon contacts were fitted. The original pantographs were replaced (around 1958 to 1960) by a slightly different type of dc pantograph; then, from 1968, these were replaced by ac-type pantographs, to facilitate the conversion work.

Compressed air for the Westinghouse brake and the contactors was obtained from a reciprocating compressor driven by a 1500-volt motor, and the 110-volt DC supply for the lighting and control gear was provided by a 12 kW motor-generator set. Both these were mounted on the motor coach underframe.

The driving cab had its own independent heating and lighting, for economy when moving empty trains in winter. The drum-type master controller had the usual 'dead man's handle' and a starting bell was provided, operated from the guard's compartment by a loose key.

A lightning arrester was mounted on the roof adjacent to the pantograph.

East of Cornbrook Junction, 1932 with the CLC into Central on the left and the MSJA to Knott Mill on the right, showing the special supports used there for the overhead catenary. *National Railway Museum*

Just north of Dane Road station in 1932, showing the standard overhead support used on the quadruple-track section of the line. *National Railway Museum*

(Not as superfluous as you might think. A train was struck by lightning in Altrincham station in June 1970. Holes were made in the roof, the pantograph fell off, and the equipment compartment caught fire. The guard was unhurt.)

The overhead equipment was compound catenary, with suspension insulators. The suspended copper conducting wire had a cross-sectional area of 0.85 square inches and the whole thing was flexible enough to allow perfect pickup at 60 mph. The overhead circuit could be split up into sections using switches positioned along the line; thus repairs could be made to one section in safety while the trains used the rest, a steam or bus service bridging the 'dead' gap.

The normal height of the wire above rail-level was 16 ft, with a minimum of 13 ft 10 in. under bridges (under some, and in Old Trafford tunnel, the track had to be lowered to give this clearance, and so the platforms at Old Trafford station were lowered also). At level crossings there was intended to be 18 ft clearance; at Deansgate Lane, however, only 16 ft could be obtained without steepening the wire gradient beyond the maximum permitted 1 in 100 (because of the bridge just north of the crossing). Gauge-boards were erected beside the roadway.

The maximum distance between supports of the overhead catenary system was 220 ft and anchoring supports were provided at approximately 1 mile intervals. The standard support was made of rolled steel sections and spanned two tracks, and the same construction was used for four track sections where there was room for a centre support. Otherwise a lattice girder cross-member was used. A number of special structures were to be found however, for anchoring the conductors and where the CLC ran alongside at Cornbrook. In Old Trafford tunnel and under some bridges the catenary system was supported on span wires of bowstring form.

The power supplied to the overhead cables came from the two substations at Old Trafford and Timperley. Power for these was obtained from the Stretford and District Electricity Board's Longford Bridge substation at 11,000v 50 c/s 3 phase ac and turned into 1,500v DC.

Old Trafford substation contained two rotary converter units, each consisting of two 750v 750kw machines working at 750 rpm, connected in series and supplied by a common 1,650 kvA transformer with a secondary winding for each converter; and one 1,500v mercury arc rectifier. This rectifier was of considerable interest, being the first one to be installed in this country for 1,500-volt railway service and was put in to obtain experience in this field. The experiment can only be described as a resounding success, the rectifier giving no trouble and carrying peaks of up to five times full load without difficulty. In addition its 'all-day' efficiency was well above that of the rotary converters. Timperley substation contained three rotary converter sets identical with those at Old Trafford.

Timperley was unmanned and controlled by Midworth distance-control equipment from Old Trafford. Operations performed by remote control were the switching on and off of Timperley's converters, varying their output, and various circuit making and breaking. The results of these operations were shown on dials at Old Trafford. In the event of malfunction at Timperley the equipment concerned was automatically shut off and alarm bells automatically rung at Old Trafford. Three cables connected Old Trafford and Timperley: one 110v pilot cable and two EHT. The HT compartments in the substations were protected by safety doors.

Automatic cleaning equipment was installed in all the substations: vacuum tubes or air blowers were situated at strategic spots in the machinery and, when turned on, removed dust and dirt. The sub-stations were heated and lit by transformed power; however in the case of failure each had a stand-by 110v 220 amp-hour battery to provide emergency lighting to repair the machine by.

The repair shop was established on the site of the old Bowdon station, fitted with a 25 ton travelling crane, two electrically operated bogie traversers and all the equipment necessary to maintain, repair and modify the rolling-stock and electrical equipment. The power was taken from the 1500v and converted to 110v, where necessary, for shop use. The overhead wires in the shop were normally dead to permit safe roof working and walking; switches existed whereby individual sections of track could be energised to permit shunting and other operations.

The substation at Timperley was on the left of the down line, south of Timperley station and the one at Old Trafford was on the left of the up line, north of Old Trafford tunnel.

The line was electrified from London Road to the carriage sheds at Bowdon. Between Sale and Old Trafford all four tracks were electrified, as were the through loops between Altrincham and Navigation Road. A short stretch of the CLC was electrified through platforms 3 and 4 at Altrincham and a little way towards Hale. Certain sidings were also electrified.

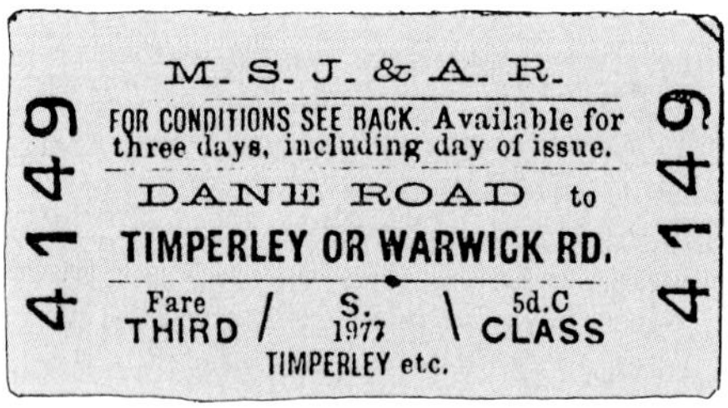

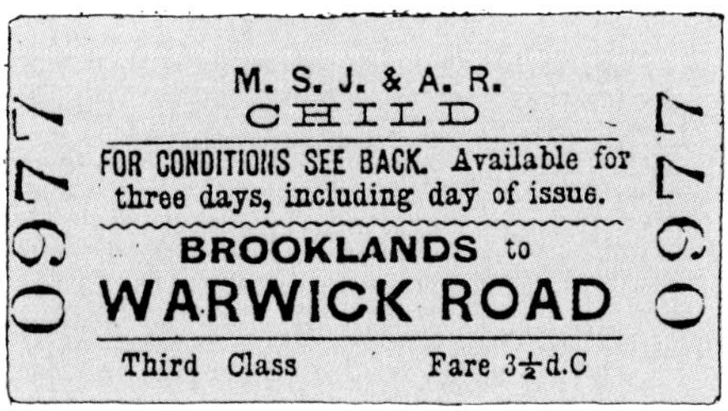

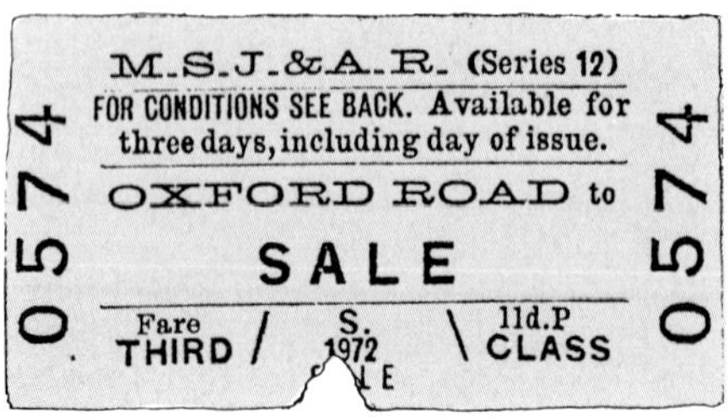

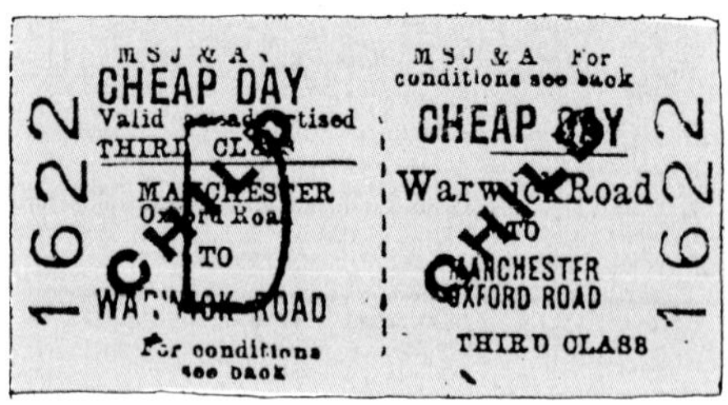

Overhead Construction and Maintenance Unit

In 1938 the LMS built an experimental three-car articulated diesel unit, numbered 80000/1/2, which was in passenger-carrying service at Bedford for some 6 months before the 1939–45 war. Subsequently it was stored, out of use, until in 1949 the two end cars were practically rebuilt to become a wire wagon, which carried drums of wire for the overhead cables, and a motive unit-cum-work platform-cum-mess unit, which had several functions. Diesel-powered, with a driving compartment at each end, it had a flat roof about 12 feet above rail level, on which the men could stand while fiddling with the overhead equipment. To reach positions wide of the wagon, 4 ft wide side flaps were provided on each side of the wagon. To reach high structures a lift could be operated which would give the worker another 6 ft reach. These extensions were hand-operated, from inside the wagon. Communication between roof, driver and lift/side-flap operator was by a tannoy system, with microphones that could be plugged in at many strategic positions. For the safety of men working on the wire, an earthing trolley was provided. Rollers were fitted at each end of the unit to carry wire.

Recognising that the workers might be stranded far from a canteen at dinner-time and that tea must be available at all times, the designers incorporated food lockers, fresh water supply, calor gas cooker and boiling ring. For similar reasons a chemical toilet and wash-basin were also built in.

The unit could travel anywhere on the MSJA, apart from certain sidings (mostly cattle docks). Numbered M 198895/6, it was generally kept at Stretford, and left the MSJA to assist with the electrification of the lines to Crewe, on which work began in 1958. It was seen in a derelict state at Longsight in September 1967, and a photograph taken then was apparently used in the 1969 Stock Book of the Railway Correspondence and Travel Society.

Overhead Construction & Maintenance Unit, photographed in 1949 after refurbishment. *National Railway Museum*

MANCHESTER, SALE, BROOKLANDS and ALTRINCHAM.—G. C. and N. W. Joint and C. L.

Down. — **Week Days.**

Miles	HOUR	6	6	6	6	6	7	7	7	7	7	7	8	8	8	8	8	8	8	8	8	8	8	8	9	9	9	9	9	9	9	9	9	10	10	10
	London Road A ......dep.	.	25	45	50	55	10	.	25	40	45	53	0	10	.	16	20	25	32	38	43	47	.	57	2	7	10	15	.	22	30	36	45	0	11	15
	Central .... "	15	.	.	.	.	.	17	.	.	.	.	.	.	.	.	.	.	.	.	.	.	50	.	.	.	.	.	25	.	.	.	.	.	.	.
¾	Oxford Road	.	27	47	52	57	11	.	28	42	47	55	2	12	14	18	21	27	34	40	44	49	.	59	4	9	13	17	.	24	32	38	47	2	13	17
1	Knott Mill and Deansgate	.	28	48	54	58	13	.	29	43	49	56	3	.	15	19	23	28	35	41	.	50	.	**0**	5	10	.	18	.	25	33	39	48	3	.	18
2½	Old Trafford	.	32	51	.	**0**	16	.	32	46	53	59	6	.	18	22	26	31	38	44	.	53	56	3	8	13	.	21	.	28	36	42	51	6	.	21
3	Warwick Rd. (O. Trafford)	.	34	53	.	2	17	.	34	47	.	**0**	7	.	19	23	27	.	39	.	.	54	.	4	9	.	.	22	.	29	37	.	52	7	.	22
4	Stretford	.	37	55	.	4	20	.	36	50	57	3	10	.	22	26	30	34	42	47	50	57	**0**	7	12	16	.	25	.	32	40	45	55	10	.	25
5¼	Dane Road (Sale)	.	39	58	.	7	22	.	39	52	.	5	12	18	.	28	32	.	44	.	52	59	.	9	14	18	.	27	.	34	42	.	57	12	.	27
5¾	Sale	23	42	59	**3**	8	24	26	42	54	**1**	7	14	.	25	30	34	37	46	50	54	**1**	5	11	16	20	23	29	.	36	44	48	59	14	23	29
6¾	Brooklands	.	44	**1**	.	10	25	.	43	55	3	8	15	.	26	31	35	.	47	51	55	2	.	.	17	21	.	30	.	37	45	.	**0**	15	.	30
7¾	Timperley	.	46	3	7	12	27	.	45	57	6	10	17	22	.	33	37	.	49	53	57	4	.	.	19	23	28	32	.	39	47	51	2	17	28	32
8	Navigation Road B	.	47	4	.	13	29	.	47	59	.	12	.	.	29	35	39	.	51	.	59	6	.	.	21	.	.	34	.	41	49	.	4	19	.	34
8½	Altrincham C ......arr.	30	50	7	.	16	31	34	49	**1**	.	14	20	25	32	37	41	.	53	57	**2**	8	12	.	23	26	.	36	40	43	51	54	6	21	.	36

HOUR	E 10	10	10	11	11	11	11	11	S 12	E 12	S 12	S 12	12	E 12	S 12	S 12	S 12	E 12	S 12	E 12	S 12	E 12	S 12	E 12	S 12	S 12	12	S 12	S 1	E 1	S 1	S 1	E 1	S 1	S 1	E 1	S 1	1
London Road A ......dep.	23	30	45	0	15	30	45	.	.	0	0	5	8	12	12	20	.	25	28	.	.	36	.	40	41	.	50	57	2	2	6	13	15	.	21	.	26	30
Central .... "	.	.	.	.	.	.	.	56	.	.	.	.	.	.	.	.	.	.	.	34	34	.	.	.	.	.	.	.	.	.	.	.	.	20	.	29	.	.
Oxford Road	26	32	47	2	17	32	47	.	0	2	2	7	10	14	13	22	27	27	30	.	.	38	40	42	43	50	52	59	4	4	8	15	17	.	23	.	29	32
Knott Mill and Deansgate	27	33	48	3	18	33	48	.	1	3	3	8	.	15	15	23	28	28	31	.	.	39	41	43	44	51	53	**0**	.	5	9	16	18	.	24	.	30	33
Old Trafford	31	36	51	6	21	36	51	.	.	6	6	11	.	18	18	26	.	31	34	.	.	.	44	46	47	.	56	.	.	8	12	19	21	.	27	.	.	36
Warwick Rd. (O. Trafford)	.	37	52	7	22	37	52	.	.	7	8	.	.	19	19	.	32	32	35	.	.	.	.	47	48	.	57	4	.	9	13	.	22	.	28	.	34	37
Stretford	34	40	55	10	25	40	55	.	6	10	10	14	.	22	22	29	.	35	38	.	41	.	47	50	51	56	**0**	.	.	12	16	22	25	27	31	.	36	40
Dane Road (Sale)	.	42	57	12	27	42	57	.	.	12	13	.	.	24	24	.	35	37	40	.	.	.	49	52	53	.	2	7	.	14	18	24	27	.	33	.	.	42
Sale	33	44	59	14	29	44	59	.	9	14	14	17	19	26	26	32	37	39	42	.	45	46	51	54	55	59	4	9	.	16	20	26	29	.	35	37	39	44
Brooklands	40	45	**0**	15	30	45	**0**	.	.	15	16	18	.	27	27	33	38	40	43	.	.	47	52	55	56	**0**	5	.	.	17	21	27	30	.	36	.	41	45
Timperley	42	47	2	17	32	47	2	.	12	17	18	20	23	29	29	35	40	42	45	.	.	49	54	57	58	2	7	12	17	19	23	29	32	.	38	.	43	47
Navigation Road B	.	49	4	19	34	49	4	.	.	19	19	23	.	31	31	37	.	44	47	.	.	51	.	59	**0**	4	9	13	.	21	25	31	34	.	40	.	.	49
Altrincham C ......arr.	46	51	6	21	36	51	6	**10**	15	21	22	25	.	34	33	39	43	46	49	48	52	53	57	**1**	2	6	11	16	.	23	27	33	36	.	42	44	46	51

HOUR	E 1	S 1	S 1	1	S 1	2	S 2	2	2	S 2	2	3	3	3	3	3	3	4	4	S 4	E 4	4	4	E 4	E 4	4	S 5	E 5	E 5	5	E 5	S 5	E 5	E 5	E 5	S 5	E 5
London Road A ......dep.	35	.	41	45	53	0	3	15	30	.	45	0	15	30	33	45	.	0	15	30	30	.	45	55	.	58	1	3	9	.	14	15	.	22	26	30	.
Central .... "	.	41	.	.	.	.	.	.	.	44	.	.	.	.	.	.	52	.	.	.	.	42	.	.	59	.	.	.	.	10	.	.	.	.	.	.	40
Oxford Road	39	.	44	47	55	2	5	17	32	.	47	2	17	32	36	47	.	2	17	32	33	.	47	57	.	**0**	3	5	11	.	15	17	22	25	28	32	.
Knott Mill and Deansgate	.	.	45	48	56	3	7	18	33	.	48	3	18	33	.	48	.	3	18	33	34	.	48	58	.	.	4	6	13	.	16	18	23	26	29	33	.
Old Trafford	.	.	48	51	59	6	11	21	36	.	51	6	21	36	41	51	.	6	21	36	37	.	51	.	.	.	7	9	16	.	19	21	.	.	31	36	.
Warwick Rd. (O. Trafford)	.	.	.	52	**0**	7	.	22	37	.	52	7	22	37	.	52	.	7	22	37	39	.	52	.	.	.	9	.	18	.	21	22	.	.	33	37	.
Stretford	.	.	51	55	3	10	15	25	40	.	55	10	25	40	.	55	59	10	25	40	42	.	55	.	**6**	.	11	12	19	.	23	25	28	31	35	40	.
Dane Road (Sale)	.	.	53	57	5	12	.	27	42	.	57	12	27	42	.	57	.	12	27	42	44	.	57	.	.	.	14	14	22	.	26	27	.	.	38	42	.
Sale	.	.	55	59	7	14	20	29	44	.	59	14	29	44	48	59	.	14	29	44	47	.	59	**5**	.	.	15	16	23	.	27	29	31	34	40	44	.
Brooklands	.	.	56	**0**	8	15	22	30	45	.	**0**	15	30	45	.	**0**	.	15	30	45	49	.	**0**	.	.	.	17	18	25	.	28	30	32	35	41	45	.
Timperley	52	.	58	2	10	17	25	32	47	.	2	17	32	47	53	2	.	17	32	47	51	.	2	.	.	12	19	20	27	.	31	32	34	37	43	47	.
Navigation Road B	.	.	.	4	12	19	.	34	49	.	4	19	34	49	.	4	.	19	34	49	53	.	4	.	.	.	20	.	28	.	32	34	.	39	45	49	.
Altrincham C ......arr.	.	55	**1**	6	14	21	.	36	51	58	6	21	36	51	.	6	**9**	21	36	51	55	58	6	10	15	.	22	23	31	25	35	36	37	41	47	51	48

HOUR	E 5	S 5	E 5	E 5	S 5	E 5	E 5	6	6	E 6	E 6	6	E 6	6	E 6	6	S 6	7	7	7	7	7	8	8	8	8	8	N 8	8	9	9	9	9	9	9	10	10	10
London Road A ......dep.	30	32	35	40	45	45	52	0	.	8	11	15	22	30	.	45	.	0	4	15	30	45	0	.	15	22	30	.	45	0	5	15	30	.	45	0	15	30
Central .... "	.	.	.	.	.	.	.	.	8	.	.	.	.	.	39	.	58	.	.	.	.	.	.	13	.	.	.	44	.	.	.	.	.	40	.	.	.	.
Oxford Road	32	35	37	42	47	47	54	2	.	11	13	17	24	32	.	47	.	2	7	17	32	47	2	.	17	24	32	.	47	2	8	17	32	.	47	2	17	32
Knott Mill and Deansgate	34	37	38	43	48	48	55	3	.	12	15	18	25	33	.	48	.	3	.	18	33	48	3	.	18	.	33	.	48	3	.	18	33	.	48	3	18	33
Old Trafford	.	.	.	46	51	51	58	6	.	.	.	21	28	36	.	51	.	6	.	21	36	51	6	.	21	.	36	.	51	6	.	21	36	45	51	6	21	36
Warwick Rd. (O. Trafford)	.	.	.	.	52	53	**0**	7	.	.	.	23	29	37	.	52	.	7	.	22	37	52	7	.	22	.	37	.	52	7	.	22	37	.	52	7	22	37
Stretford	.	.	43	49	55	55	2	10	.	17	.	25	32	40	.	55	.	10	.	25	40	55	10	20	25	.	40	.	55	10	16	25	40	.	55	10	25	40
Dane Road (Sale)	.	.	.	52	57	58	5	12	.	.	.	28	34	42	.	57	.	12	.	27	42	57	12	.	27	.	42	.	57	12	.	27	42	.	57	12	27	42
Sale	.	.	46	53	58	59	6	14	.	20	.	29	36	44	.	59	.	14	.	29	44	59	14	.	29	34	44	.	59	14	21	29	44	.	59	14	29	44
Brooklands	.	.	48	55	**0**	**1**	8	15	.	21	.	31	37	45	.	**0**	.	15	.	30	45	**0**	15	.	30	.	45	.	**0**	15	.	30	45	.	**0**	15	30	45
Timperley	46	53	.	57	2	3	10	17	.	23	26	33	39	47	.	2	.	17	20	32	47	2	17	.	32	39	47	.	2	17	26	32	47	.	2	17	32	47
Navigation Road B	.	.	.	58	4	4	11	19	.	.	.	34	41	49	.	4	.	19	.	34	49	4	19	.	34	.	49	.	4	19	.	34	49	.	4	19	34	49
Altrincham C ......arr.	.	.	52	**1**	6	7	14	21	24	26	.	37	43	51	54	6	**13**	21	.	36	51	6	21	29	36	.	51	58	6	21	.	36	51	57	6	21	36	51

Week Days.—Continued. — **Sundays.**

HOUR	10	10	E 10	10	S 11	11	11	11	Every 20 minutes until 11 10 aft.	8	8	9	And at	9	10	1	2	3	6	6	10
London Road A ......dep.	40	45	.	55	.	10	25	45		30	50	10		.	.	15	.	.	.	35	.
Central .... "	.	.	51	.	5	.	.	.		.	.	.		25	36	.	0	5	25	.	0
Oxford Road	42	47	.	57	.	12	27	47		32	52	12		.	.	18	.	.	.	39	.
Knott Mill and Deansgate	43	.	.	58	.	13	28	48		.	.	.		.	.	.	.	.	.	.	.
Old Trafford	46	.	56	**1**	.	16	31	51		35	55	15		30	41	23	5	.	.	.	.
Warwick Rd. (O. Trafford)	47	.	.	2	.	17	32	52		37	57	17		.	.	.	.	.	.	.	.
Stretford	50	.	.	5	.	20	35	55		39	59	19		.	46	27	11	.	.	.	.
Dane Road (Sale)	52	.	.	7	.	22	37	57		42	**2**	22		.	.	.	.	.	.	.	.
Sale	54	.	.	9	.	24	39	59		43	3	23		35	51	32	16	.	.	.	.
Brooklands	55	.	.	10	.	25	40	**0**		45	5	25		.	.	.	.	.	.	.	.
Timperley	57	**2**	.	12	.	27	42	2		47	7	27		.	54	37	.	.	.	54	.
Navigation Road B	59	.	.	14	.	29	44	4		48	8	28		.	.	.	.	.	.	.	.
Altrincham C ......arr.	**1**	.	**8**	16	19	31	46	6		51	11	31		42	58	.	23	19	39	.	16

A South Junction Platform.
B Navigation Rd. (Altrincham).
C Altrincham and Bowdon.
E Except Sats.
N Mons., Weds., and Sats.
S Sats. only.

[204

Where the MINUTES under the Hours change to a LOWER figure and DARKER type it indicates the NEXT HOUR.

From Bradshaw's Manchester ABC, March 1933.

205

ALTRINCHAM, BROOKLANDS, SALE, and MANCHESTER.—G.C. & N. W. Joint and C.L.

Up. — Week Days.

Miles	HOUR	5	6	6	6	6		7	7	7	7	7	7	7	7	7	7		8	8	8	8	8	8	8	8	8	8	8	8	8	9	8		9	9	9	9	9	9	9
—	**Altrincham C** ....dep.	55	15	25	45	56	.	.	4	15	25	35	.	45	49	55	58	.	.	0	7	15	19	24	.	30	32	.	36	43	48	.	58	.	3	.	10	20	30	33	.
½	Navigation Road **B**	56	16	26	46	57	.	.	.	16	26	36	.	46	50	.	.	.	.	1	8	16	20	.	.	31	.	.	37	.	49	.	59	.	.	.	11	21	31	.	.
1⅜	Timperley	57	17	27	47	58	.	2	.	17	27	37	.	47	51	57	.	.	.	2	9	18	21	26	.	32	.	.	38	45	50	.	**0**	.	.	.	12	22	32	.	.
2⅛	Brooklands	59	19	29	49	**0**	.	.	.	19	29	39	.	49	53	59	.	.	.	4	11	20	.	28	30	.	.	.	40	46	52	.	2	.	.	.	14	24	34	.	.
2¾	Sale	**1**	21	31	51	2	.	7	11	21	31	41	.	51	55	.	.	.	0	6	13	21	24	29	.	35	.	41	.	48	54	.	4	.	.	.	16	26	36	.	.
3¼	Dane Road (Sale)	2	22	32	52	3	.	.	.	22	32	42	.	52	56	**1**	.	.	1	7	14	23	26	31	.	.	.	.	43	50	55	.	5	.	.	.	17	27	37	.	.
4⅜	Stretford	5	25	35	55	6	.	12	18	25	35	45	.	55	59	.	**6**	.	4	10	17	25	28	33	.	.	.	43	45	52	58	.	8	.	.	.	20	30	40	.	50
5¼	Warwick Rd. (O. Trafford)	7	27	37	57	8	.	.	.	27	37	47	.	57	**1**	.	.	.	7	12	19	.	31	.	.	.	.	46	48	.	**0**	.	10	.	.	.	22	32	42	.	.
6	Old Trafford	9	29	39	59	10	.	17	23	29	39	49	51	59	3	5	.	.	8	14	21	28	32	.	.	40	.	.	49	55	2	6	12	.	.	.	24	34	44	.	.
7½	Knott Mill & Deansgate ..	12	32	42	**2**	13	.	22	.	32	42	52	55	**2**	6	9	.	.	12	17	24	32	36	38	41	44	.	50	53	59	5	.	15	.	12	21	27	37	47	.	.
7⅞	Oxford Road	14	34	44	4	15	.	25	.	34	44	54	58	4	8	11	.	.	13	19	26	34	37	40	43	45	.	51	**54**	**1**	7	.	17	.	14	24	29	39	49	.	.
—	**Central** ....arr.	.	.	.	.	.	.	.	35	.	.	.	.	.	.	.	16	.	.	.	.	.	.	.	.	.	49	.	.	.	.	13	.	.	.	.	.	.	.	47	**0**
8½	**London Road A** ..... „	16	36	46	6	17	.	29	.	36	46	56	**2**	6	.	13	.	.	16	21	28	35	40	42	46	49	.	54	58	3	9	.	19	.	16	28	31	41	51	.	.

HOUR	9		10	10	10	10	10	10	10		11	11	S 11	11	S 11	S 11	E 11	S 11		12	S 12	S 12	S 12	E 12		S 12	E 12	S 12	E 12	S 12	E 12	S 12	S 12	12	E 12	S 12	S 12		S 1	E 1	S 1	E 1
Altrincham C ....dep.	45	.	0	15	.	30	45	.	52	.	0	15	20	30	.	40	45	50	.	0	8	11	.	15	.	20	25	27	29	30	33	35	40	45	.	.	55	.	0	2	5	12
Navigation Road **B**	46	.	1	16	.	31	46	.	.	.	1	16	21	31	.	41	46	51	.	1	9	12	.	16	.	21	26	28	.	31	34	.	41	46	.	.	56	.	1	3	6	13
Timperley	47	.	2	17	.	32	47	45	.	.	2	17	22	32	.	42	47	52	.	2	10	13	16	17	.	22	27	29	.	32	35	.	42	47	51	51	57	.	2	4	7	14
Brooklands	49	.	4	19	.	34	49	.	.	.	4	19	25	34	.	44	49	54	.	4	12	15	19	19	.	24	29	31	.	34	37	.	44	49	.	.	59	.	4	6	9	16
Sale	51	.	6	21	30	36	51	.	.	.	6	21	26	36	42	46	51	56	.	6	14	17	21	21	.	26	31	33	.	36	39	41	46	51	.	55	**1**	.	6	8	11	18
Dane Road (Sale)	52	.	7	22	.	37	52	.	.	.	7	22	27	37	.	47	52	57	.	7	15	18	.	22	.	27	32	34	.	37	40	.	47	52	.	.	2	.	7	9	12	19
Stretford	55	.	10	25	34	40	55	.	.	.	10	25	30	40	.	50	55	**0**	.	10	18	21	25	25	.	30	35	37	.	40	43	46	50	55	.	**0**	5	.	10	12	15	22
Warwick Rd. (O. Trafford)	57	.	12	27	.	42	57	.	.	.	12	27	32	42	.	52	57	2	.	12	21	23	.	27	.	32	37	.	.	42	45	.	52	57	.	.	7	.	12	14	17	24
Old Trafford	59	.	14	29	.	44	59	.	**3**	.	14	29	34	44	.	54	59	4	.	14	22	25	29	29	.	34	39	40	41	44	47	50	54	59	.	4	9	.	14	16	19	26
Knott Mill & Deansgate ..	**2**	.	17	32	.	47	**2**	56	.	.	17	32	37	47	51	57	**2**	7	.	17	25	28	33	32	.	37	42	43	.	47	50	.	58	**2**	**6**	8	12	.	17	19	22	29
Oxford Road	4	.	19	34	.	49	4	59	.	.	19	34	39	49	52	59	4	10	.	19	27	30	36	34	.	39	44	45	.	49	52	.	59	4	9	11	14	.	19	21	24	31
Central ....arr.	.	.	.	.	43	.	.	.	9	.	.	.	.	.	.	.	.	.	.	.	.	.	.	.	.	.	.	.	47	.	.	58	.	.	.	.	.	.	.	.	.	.
London Road A ..... „	6	.	21	36	.	51	6	**2**	.	.	21	36	41	51	.	**1**	6	12	.	21	.	32	39	36	.	41	46	.	.	51	54	.	**1**	6	12	14	16	.	22	23	27	33

HOUR	S 1	S 1	E 1	S 1	1	E 1	S 1	1	1	S 2	E 2	2	2	S 2	2	2	E 2		3	3	3	3		4	4	4	E 4	S 4	E 4	E 4	E 4	S 4	E 4	S 4		E 4	S 5	E 5	E 5	S 5
Altrincham C ....dep.	15	20	25	27	35	.	.	45	53	0	2	15	30	39	45	.	57	.	0	15	30	45	.	0	4	15	25	30	35	.	.	45	48	.	.	55	0	1	9	15
Navigation Road **B**	16	21	26	28	36	.	.	46	.	1	3	16	31	.	46	.	.	.	1	16	31	46	.	1	.	16	26	31	36	.	.	46	49	.	.	56	1	2	10	16
Timperley	17	22	27	29	37	.	.	47	.	2	4	17	32	.	47	52	.	.	2	17	32	47	.	2	.	17	27	32	37	.	48	47	50	53	.	57	2	3	11	17
Brooklands	19	24	29	31	39	42	44	49	.	4	5	19	34	.	49	.	.	.	4	19	34	49	.	4	.	19	29	34	39	.	.	49	52	.	.	59	4	5	13	19
Sale	21	26	31	33	41	45	47	51	.	6	8	21	36	.	51	.	.	.	6	21	36	51	.	6	10	21	31	36	41	48	52	51	54	57	.	**1**	6	7	14	21
Dane Road (Sale)	22	27	32	34	42	.	.	52	.	7	9	22	37	.	52	.	.	.	7	22	37	52	.	7	.	22	32	37	42	.	.	52	55	.	.	2	7	8	16	22
Stretford	25	30	35	37	45	49	51	55	.	10	12	25	40	.	55		.	.	10	25	40	55	.	10	.	25	35	40	45	.	.	55	58	.	.	5	10	11	21	25
Warwick Rd. (O. Trafford)	27	32	37	39	47	.	.	57	.	12	14	27	42	.	57	..	.	.	12	27	42	57	.	12	.	27	37	42	47	.	.	57	**0**	.	.	7	12	13	22	27
Old Trafford	29	34	39	41	49	.	.	59	.	14	16	29	44	.	59	.	.	.	14	29	44	59	.	14	.	29	39	44	49	.	.	59	2	.	.	9	14	15	23	29
Knott Mill & Deansgate ..	32	37	42	44	52	56	58	**2**	.	17	19	32	47	.	**2**	**5**	.	.	17	32	47	**2**	.	17	.	32	42	47	52	56	**1**	**2**	5	**8**	.	12	17	18	26	32
Oxford Road	34	39	44	46	54	59	**0**	4	.	19	21	34	49	.	4	8	.	.	19	34	49	4	.	19	.	34	44	49	54	58	4	4	7	11	.	14	19	20	28	34
Central ....arr.	.	.	.	.	.	.	.	.	**10**	.	.	.	.	54	.	.	**14**	.	.	.	.	.	.	.	25	.	.	.	.	.	.	.	.	.	.	.	.	.	.	.
London Road A ..... „	36	42	46	48	56	**3**	4	6	.	21	23	36	51	.	6	12	.	.	21	36	51	6	.	21	.	36	46	51	56	**1**	7	6	9	15	.	17	21	23	31	36

HOUR	E 5	E 5	E 5	S 5	E 5	E 5	5	E 5	S 5	E 5	S 5	E 5	S 6	E 6	6	6	6	6	E 6	6		E 6	7	7	7	7	7	7		8	8	8	8	8	9	9	9	9	9	9	9	9
Altrincham C ....dep.	16	.	26	30	34	39	41	44	45	.	.	54	0	2	.	15	21	30	40	45	.	50	0	.	15	30	45	54	.	0	.	15	30	45	0	8	15	.	30	32	45	53
Navigation Road **B**	17	.	27	31	:	40	.	45	46	.	.	55	1	3	.	16	.	31	.	46	.	.	1	.	16	31	46	.	.	1	.	16	31	46	1	.	16	.	31	.	46	.
Timperley	19	.	28	32	36	41	.	47	47	51	51	56	2	4	9	17	.	32	.	47	.	52	2	13	17	32	47	.	.	2	22	17	32	47	2	.	17	26	32	.	47	.
Brooklands	20	23	30	34	.	43	.	49	49	.	54	58	4	6	.	19	.	34	.	49	.	.	4	.	19	34	49	.	.	4	.	19	34	49	4	.	19	.	34	.	49	.
Sale	22	25	32	36	39	45	48	51	51	55	57	**0**	6	8	13	21	.	36	.	51	.	55	6	17	21	36	51	.	.	6	27	21	36	51	6	.	21	31	36	.	51	
Dane Road (Sale)	23	.	33	37	.	46	.	53	52	.	.	1	7	9	.	22	.	37	.	52	.	.	7	.	22	37	52	.	.	7	.	22	37	52	7	.	22	.	37	.	52	.
Stretford	26	30	36	40	42	49	.	55	55	.	**1**	4	10	12	17	25	.	40	.	55	.	.	10	.	25	40	55	.	.	10	.	25	40	55	10	.	25	.	40	.	55	.
Warwick Rd. (O. Trafford)	28	.	38	42	.	51	.	57	57	.	.	6	12	14	.	27	.	42	.	57	.	.	12	.	27	42	57	.	.	12	.	27	42	57	12	.	27	.	42	.	57	.
Old Trafford	30	34	40	44	45	53	55	58	59	.	5	8	14	16	21	29	.	44	51	59	.	**5**	14	24	29	44	59	**5**	.	14	34	29	44	59	14	.	29	.	44	.	59	.
Knott Mill & Deansgate ..	33	38	43	47	48	56	.	**2**	**2**	**5**	9	11	17	19	26	32	.	47	.	2	.	.	17	28	32	47	**2**	.	.	17	38	32	47	**2**	17	.	32	41	47	51	**2**	.
Oxford Road	35	41	45	49	50	58	.	4	4	8	12	13	19	21	29	34	.	49	.	4	.	10	19	31	34	49	4	.	.	19	41	34	49	4	19	.	34	44	49	54	4	.
Central ....arr.	.	.	.	.	.	.	**2**	.	.	.	.	.	.	.	.	.	40	.	57	.	.	.	.	.	.	.	.	11	.	.	.	.	.	.	.	25	.	.	.	.	.	**9**
London Road A ..... „	37	45	47	51	53	**1**	.	6	6	12	17	16	22	24	34	36	.	51	.	6	.	14	22	34	36	51	6	.	.	22	44	36	51	6	21	.	36	48	51	57	6	.

Week Days—*Continued.*

HOUR	10	10	10	10	10	N 10	11	11	
Altrincham C ....dep.	0	15	30	.	45	53	0	15	.
Navigation Road **B**	1	16	31	.	46	.	1	16	.
Timperley	2	17	32	40	47	.	2	17	.
Brooklands	4	19	34	43	49	.	4	19	.
Sale	6	21	36	46	51	.	6	21	.
Dane Road (Sale)	7	22	37	.	52	.	7	22	.
Stretford	10	24	40	50	55	.	10	25	.
Warwick Rd. (O. Trafford)	12	27	42	.	57	.	12	27	.
Old Trafford	14	29	44	54	59	.	14	29	.
Knott Mill & Deansgate ..	17	32	47	.	**2**	.	17	32	.
Oxford Road	19	34	49	**0**	4	.	19	34	.
Central ....arr.	.	.	.	.	.	**10**	.	.	.
London Road A ..... „	21	36	51	3	6	.	21	36	.

Sundays.

HOUR	7	Every 20 minutes until 10 40 aft.	8	8	8		And at	9	2	3	4		8		9		9
Altrincham C ....dep.	40		0	20	40	.		8	14	.	51	.	24	.	.	.	53
Navigation Road **B**	.		1	21	41	.		.	.	.	.	.	.	.	.	.	.
Timperley	.		2	22	42	.		.	.	33	.	.	.	.	7	.	.
Brooklands	.		4	24	44	.		.	.	.	.	.	.	.	.	.	.
Sale	47		6	26	46	.		15	.	.	.	.	31	.	12	.	.
Dane Road (Sale)	.		7	27	47	.		.	.	.	.	.	.	.	.	.	.
Stretford	55		10	30	50	.		.	.	.	**0**	.	35	.	16	.	.
Warwick Rd. (O. Trafford)	.		12	32	52	.		.	.	.	.	.	.	.	.	.	.
Old Trafford	**1**		14	34	54	.		22	.	.	4	.	39	.	21	.	.
Knott Mill & Deansgate ..	.		.	.	.	.		.	.	.	.	.	.	.	.	.	.
Oxford Road	.		19	39	59	.		.	.	50	.	.	.	.	27	.	.
Central ....arr.	10		.	.	.	.		33	30	.	10	.	45	.	.	.	**9**
London Road A ..... „	.		21	41	**1**	.		.	.	53	.	.	.	.	31	.	.

A South Junction Platform.
B Navigation Rd. (Altrincham).
C Altrincham and Bowdon.
E Except Sats.
N Mons., Weds., and Sats.
S Sats. only.

[205

Where the MINUTES under the Hours change to a LOWER figure and DARKER type it indicates the NEXT HOUR.

From Bradshaw's Manchester ABC, March 1933.

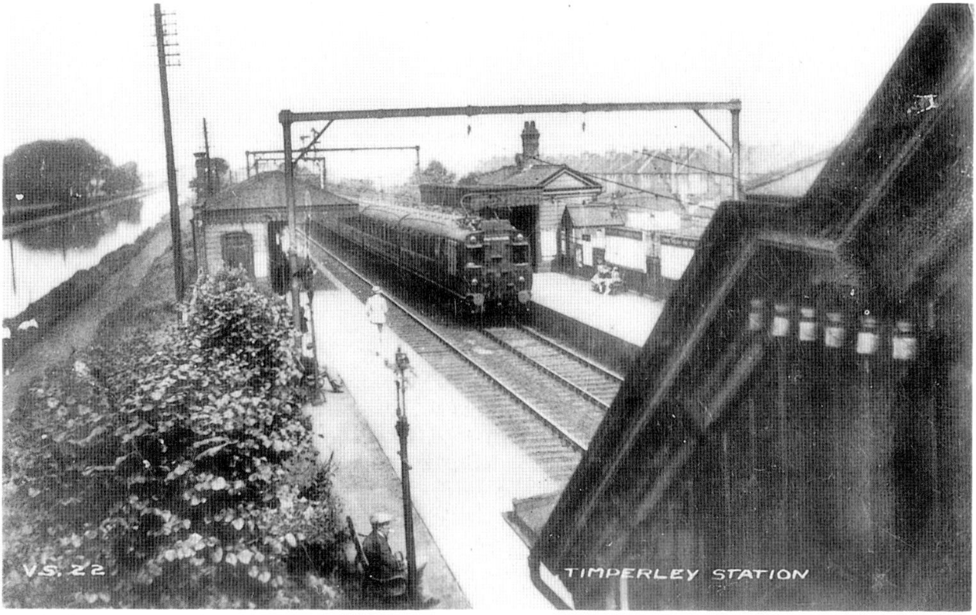

Two views of Timperley station, the top one showing an electric service in 1933 whilst the lower photograph is of a similar scene in 1952. *Lens of Sutton and R.E. Gee*

Chapter Eleven

'Electric Railways Can End Traffic Chaos'

Following the MSJA electrification, there was a rash of schemes for electrifying the Manchester lines. Many inches of newspaper columns were filled with speculation and suggestion: replace the Timperley curve lifted in 1903 and electrify the CLC line to Northenden; build a new line from the MSJA at Dane Road through Sale Moor, Wythenshawe and Hale Barns to join the CLC to Knutsford near the Wolf; and so on. It was all journalese, but poignant in a way (1936 headline: 'ELECTRIC RAILWAYS CAN END TRAFFIC CHAOS').

Another suggestion was that a station or a halt be provided by Woodhouse Lane East, midway between Timperley and Brooklands stations. The idea was first mooted about the time of the electrification, and in subsequent years it was considered, the possibilities of building a bridge over the Canal to enable people living on the other side of the canal to use it discussed, and its potential earning power strictly scrutinised. The proposal was on and off the table for many years.

On Wednesday 6th December, 1933, with visibility limited by thick fog, the 8.45 am electric from London Road was allowed, by a signalman's error, to run into the back of the 8.35 am from London Road which was standing at No. 2 platform at Altrincham station. The driver of the moving train was killed instantly, and several passengers taken to hospital suffering from shock. The two electrics were locked together: three steam engines were needed to pull them apart.

In 1939 eight extra trailer cars were obtained to deal with increased passenger traffic. Two of them were built for the MSJA at Wolverton, five were displacements from the Liverpool–Southport line (after that line was restocked in 1938–1940), and the eighth was imported from the London–Watford line. The last six needed their electrical equipment changing from 630v to 1500v before they could be brought into use.

The extra stock was used to run 7-coach trains in peak hours. However, the extra weight reduced accelerations and increased the journey time between Altrincham and London Road by three minutes. The 7-coach trains were soon abandoned and six of the extra coaches disposed of; the other two remained on the MSJA.

In 1940 there were two nasty accidents, both in January. On Wednesday, 10th, during the blackout, the 5.01 pm ex-Altrincham ran into the 4.55 ex-Altrincham as the latter was standing at the up slow-line platform of Stretford station. Two coaches, one in each train, were severely telescoped, and 16 people had to be taken to hospital. One passenger died from his injuries. On Tuesday, 25th, a goods train from London Road to Cross Lane (on the ex-L&M line) was derailed at Castlefield Junction. It demolished the signal box there (which was positioned between the 'up' side of the Altrincham branch and the 'down' side of the South Junction line to Ordsall Lane) and completely blocked the MSJA. The signalman was catapulted out of his box and landed on the track, unharmed. While the line was being cleared, MSJA traffic was handled by steam services into Central. The replacement signal box was situated on the other side of the South Junction line (i.e. beside the 'up' track).

However, the most disastrous event on the MSJA in 1940 was the bombing of the viaduct. During the blitz on Manchester (21st–23rd December) the MSJA viaduct was breached near Cornbrook. The adjacent line into Central was unaffected so it was decided to stop the electric trains at Warwick Road and run a steam service from there into Central.

Warwick Road (rather than Old Trafford) was used for the electric-to-steam interchange because it had four platforms. The steam trains used the cricket-ground side of the station, arriving from Central at the island (platform 2) whenever possible. The electric trains used the other side of the station, and the island (platform 3) as much as possible, and thus changing from steam to electric was just a matter of crossing the island platform.

The other advantages of Warwick Road were its sidings (for storing trains) and its crossover roads (which enabled engines to run round their trains). As there was no turntable there, tender engines working the shuttle service had to make the journey in one direction tender first.

At first the shuttle service was ad hoc and not timetabled; later, once the necessary arrangements had been made, it was run to schedules that appeared on time-sheets and in national timetables. The shuttle service used platform 9 of Central exclusively. On weekdays there were 60 shuttles each way, and on Sundays 34. Steam services using the MSJA into London Road were diverted into Central.

The shuttle was worked by any engines that came to hand. At first ex-GC Robinson 4–4–2 tanks were used; then came 'J39' 0–6–0s, 'K3' Moguls, 'J11' 0–6–0s and Robinson 'B9' 4–6–0s. Also observed were large-boilered Robinson 'D9' 4–4–0s, a Pollitt 'D6' 4–4–0 and an ex-GN 0–6–0. All these were supplied by the LNE, as were the coaches used in the shuttle service. Three 7-coach sets were supplied; off-peak two were rested while the third set was split into a three-coach train and a four-coach train.

The MSJA viaduct near Cornbrook which was breached during the Blitz in December 1940. The CLC lines (*left*) were untouched during the raid. *R.M. Dunne*

Two views of Oxford Road, photographed in March 1948 showing where part of the roof was destroyed in the Blitz. *J.I.C. Boyd*

The aftermath of the accident at Stretford on Monday 1st November, 1948 involving the 10.50 pm Altrincham to Manchester electric train.

Manchester Evening News, per C.E. Box

The shuttle service was run until 21st September, 1941, by which time the broken viaduct had been satisfactorily repaired. On Monday, 22nd September, the electric trains ran again into London Road.

With the viaduct down, no MSJA passenger trains used Knott Mill or Oxford Road stations. However, passenger trains still used the South Junction viaduct. Exchange was also bombed, and the LMS diverted some North Wales trains from Exchange to the MSJA London Road platforms. These ran over the South Junction line onto the ex-L&M at Ordsall Lane and then followed their normal route to North Wales, stopping at Cross Lane to pick up passengers from Exchange.

From 22nd–24th September, 1941 the MSJA was used for testing No. 6701, the first of the mixed-traffic electric Bo-Bos that were brought into use on the line to Sheffield via Woodhead when it was electrified at 1500v DC overhead in 1954. Apparently, an electricity meter was installed in the switchgear room of No. 6701, so that the LNE could be charged for the electricity its locomotive used! Further tests were carried out at the beginning of October, and in July 1947.

In the blackout, compartment blinds had to be pulled down. To prevent light leaking around their edges, a two inch wide band of black was painted around the edges of the windows.

Nationalisation came, and from 1st January, 1948 the MSJA was part of British Rail's London Midland Region (LMR). Goodbye individuality: coats of arms on carriages and the company name on tickets.

On 1st November, 1948 there was a nasty accident near Stretford station: an electric train hit some metal that had fallen off a goods train. No-one was killed, but the driving trailer involved had to be scrapped, and was replaced by modifying a trailer.

On Saturday 24th March, 1956, a goods train from the direction of Central ignored the signals against it and collided with the 10.45 passenger train to Warrington at Old Trafford Junction. An engine, a coach and several goods wagons were derailed, but no one was seriously injured. The line was cleared in time for the Monday morning rush-hour, but the nearby signal box was damaged and out of action for some weeks, during which time hand signals had to be used in the vicinity of the junction.

From June 1957 to September 1958, some Buxton (via Stockport Edgeley) services terminated at Oxford Road (rather than the main part of London Road), as did some Saturday trains for Crewe, Stafford and Wilmslow.

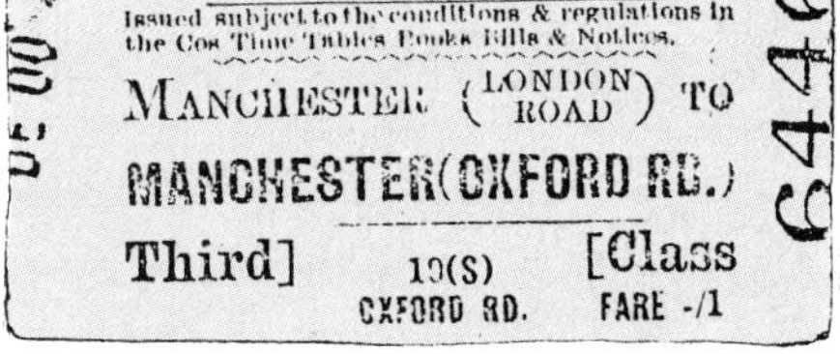

The 6.39 pm Manchester to Chester train passing through Brooklands station on 26th May, 1950 with class 'C13' 4–4–2T No. 67436 in charge. *J.D. Darby*

A fine view of the four platforms at Stretford. *Real Photographs*

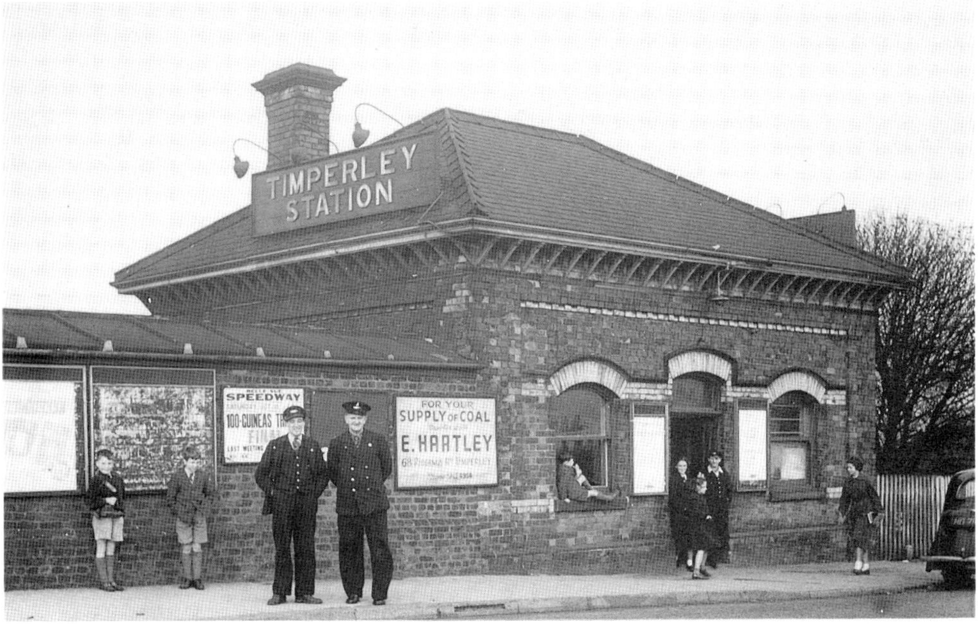

Timperley station entrance with staff posed for their photograph on 8th October, 1952. Note the advert for Belle Vue Speedway! *R.E. Gee*

London Road in 1958 showing platform 12, the bay platform used by the Altrincham trains (the through lines served platforms 10 and 11). Note the electric destination boards. *Manchester Public Libraries*

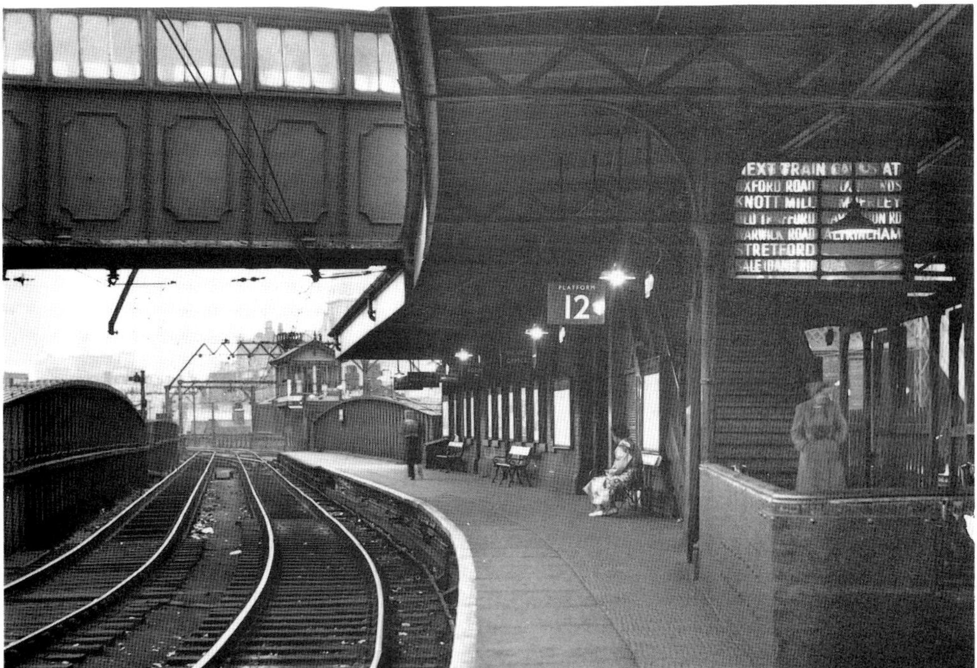

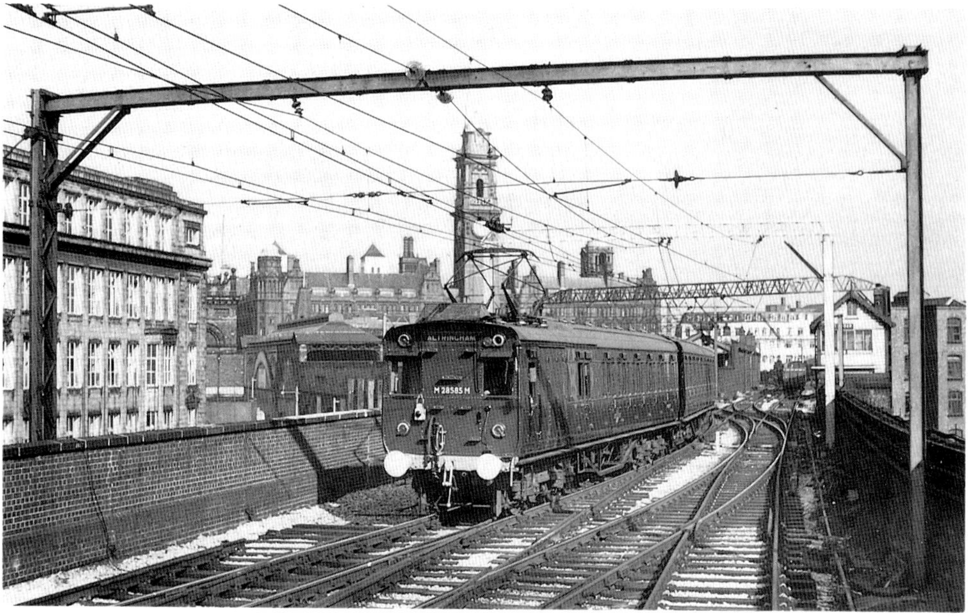

Seen near Oxford Road, on 9th September, 1958, a 3-car train which includes motor coach No. M 28585M. *R.E. Gee*

The same day showing track and permanent way work in progress at Oxford Road. *R.E. Gee*

Chapter Twelve

A Change of Terminus

In 1958 work began on electrifying the line from Manchester to Crewe at 25,000v ac as the first stage of the electrification of the main line south. As part of this £175 million scheme, London Road was modernised and re-christened Piccadilly, and the South Junction line between London Road/ Piccadilly and Oxford Road was re-electrified at 25kv ac, so that 25kv ac electric services could run between Oxford Road and Crewe. The work involved the demolition of London Road, and thus MSJA trains terminated at Oxford Road from 15th September, 1958, as did the trains over the Lymm line. The viaduct between Oxford Road and London Road was then closed.

London Road station was rebuilt (costing over £3M) and its MSJA platforms were demolished, as were the two bridges over Fairfield Street, after nearly 80 years' service. The two bridges were replaced by a single main prestressed concrete slab, with two subsidiary cantilevers, one on each side of the main slab. The new island platform is built on the main slab, giving it a depth of 8 feet, and the tracks are carried on the cantilevers, which are 16 feet wide. The maximum width of the big slab is 31 feet; and it tapers towards the end. The big slab is supported by two columns, one on each side of Fairfield Street, and the cantilevers are supported by the big slab and by abutments where their ends reach other elevated railway structures.

The structure is quite complex and claimed to be unique. It weighs about 3,000 tons and is designed to support 5,750 tons (including its own weight). The work was carried out under the direction of A.N. Butler, Chief Civil Engineer LMR, and finished in November 1959. The new island platform was then built; its buildings, the passage down to Fairfield Street and the new footbridge were erected; and the viaduct between London Road and Oxford Road re-electrified and track layouts were modified. By August 1960 all was complete.

Meanwhile, at Oxford Road, rebuilding was also going on, for £250,000 in all. The bridge over Oxford Road had to be widened and Oxford Road was closed between midnight of Saturday to 5 am on the Monday after, 20th June, 1959. Overhead electric equipment was taken down to give two 50 ft railway cranes room to work. Two 106 ft long, 68-ton prestressed concrete girders were laid over Great Marlboro Street, widening the existing bridge. The bridges over Oxford Road and Gloucester Street (now Whitworth Street) were also widened, the track layout changed, platforms extended and a new footbridge built, as well as lifts and a subway for heavy luggage.

The most noticeable change was the demolition of the old station buildings, and the construction of a new station building with a remarkable wooden roof (described by Rex Christiansen as 'almost a miniature look-alike of Sydney Opera House'). This roof consists of three 'concentric' conoids, varying in width from 97 ft 3 in. (max.) to 41 ft 6 in. (min.), waterproofed and glazed. After the roof was erected, extra supports were needed to strengthen it while men were working on it; the reason was to give it extra strength, but sceptics claimed the roof was sagging, pointing to the jacking up of supports and packing of foundations (July 1959) as proof.

The new platform canopies, too, were made of wood. These were pre-

Stretford station, 1962, showing its fine roof and pillar details on Platforms 2 and 3.
Manchester Public Libraries

An up train crossing to the down line before running into Brooklands station during single line working due to Sunday track relaying in October 1966. Note the second type of pantograph.
J.I.C. Boyd

fabricated in joinery shops for speedy erection and contained panels of transparent plastic to allow natural light to filter through onto the platform.

The first new platforms (4 and 5) were finished in July 1959 and the Altrincham trains started using these bay platforms immediately, allowing work to begin on improving platforms 1, 2 and 3. Meanwhile demolition gangs were moving in on the old station buildings, and from 5th November, 1959 business was conducted from temporary offices while the old buildings were demolished. By March 1960 all the southern part of the station was a mass of rubble. On 25th April, 1960 the line between Oxford Road and London Road re-opened to be used by a diesel shuttle service and by some trains to and from Macclesfield.

The whole station was re-opened on 12th September, 1960. The viaduct between Oxford Road and London Road was electrified at 25,000v ac and Oxford Road became the terminus for local services to Alderley Edge and Crewe, via both the Stockport line and the Styal line, using class AM4 electric multiple units (as they were then called). The Lymm line trains, too, ran from London Road (now renamed Piccadilly) and used the new platforms; the MSJA electric trains terminated in the bay platforms at Oxford Road. Unfortunately, at first the timetables of the two electric services did not allow for connections at Oxford Road – for example, a train from Altrincham would arrive just as a train to Crewe left – causing considerable annoyance to through passengers. Matters improved after complaints.

While all this had been going on BR closed the Northwich–Crewe line for passenger services, a line which had been used (between the early 1880s and the 1930s) for a direct LNW Oxford Road–Altrincham–Crewe service, including a through coach to London (and back) for part of the period.

The last passenger services over the Lymm line ran on Saturday 8th September, 1962; the stations on it were closed on and from Monday 10th September. This enabled several economies to be made. After the timetable was revised, with no 'overtaking' workings, from 9th September, 1963 platforms 1 and 2 at Dane Road, Stretford and Warwick Road were no longer needed; work began on lifting the slow lines. Also, the new timetable had no trains that started or terminated at Sale, so the Sale south siding could be taken out of use. The Timperley–Broadheath curve was only used by passenger trains; these were gone and it could be taken up. A good deal of this work was completed within the month, thus saving many thousands of pounds a year maintenance; but a third track was left between Stretford and Warwick Road, giving access to the Stretford sidings.

With the introduction of this new timetable, the frequency of off-peak evening trains was reduced from every 20 minutes to every half-hour.

On 16th January, 1963 the 8.30 am from Altrincham ran into the buffers at Oxford Road. The collision was mild, but with everyone standing up, about to get out, 42 people were hurt as the jerk caught them off-balance and they fell against doors, etc.

The next few years saw a gradual decline in services and facilities. The odd rush-hour train here and there disappeared; the Sunday services took a hammering. Through booking facilities were pruned. Parcels facilities were withdrawn from the 'minor' stations. With domestic coal sales falling, BR

Oxford Road station in 1961: 1500 v DC on the left (bay platforms 4 and 5); 25 kv ac on the right. *British Rail*

decided to concentrate its coal traffic in the Manchester area at a few large depots, none of which were on the MSJA. Thus the coal sidings disappeared up and down the line; and in like manner the goods traffic came to an end. Sidings were lifted and the surplus land used for parking cars or let go wild.

During the widening of the Edge Lane road bridge (at Stretford station) a sort of corrugated iron tunnel was built over the line and work progressed while the trains ran normally. Then a great mound of earth and concrete, a bank and a support for the widened bridge, covered up the path of the lifted tracks. Subsequently the redundant platform 1 and its buildings were demolished and the space between platforms 1 and 2 (where the lifted tracks once were) filled in, so that mail-vans could drive onto the ex-island platform.

Before Central station closed in 1969, £500,000 was spent to enable its services to be transferred to Oxford Road and Piccadilly (ex-London Road). New junctions with the CLC Liverpool line were laid at Cornbrook Junction, and once again Oxford Road was rebuilt. Sidings were lifted and a new platform was built: the new platform 1. The other platforms were re-numbered and the old platform 5 had its track lifted, so that Oxford Road station gained a through platform and lost a bay platform. The old uncovered footbridge was demolished (after 10 years) and a new, covered bridge built, linking the new platform with the main station (but not with the old platform 5). The track layout was altered once again. Colour light signals were installed, controlled from London Road box, to enable the closure of the signal boxes at Oxford Road, Castlefield Junction and the two boxes at Cornbrook Junction. A train-indicator was installed at Oxford Road.

Very little was done at Piccadilly, apart from installing an indicator on the MSJA platforms 13 and 14 to indicate where the next train from each platform is bound for. This is necessary, as trains are liable to leave from both platforms in both directions for many different destinations; not, of course, simultaneously.

Central was closed. The last trains to use it did so on Saturday 3rd May, 1969; Sunday, 4th, was taken up with relaying track at Cornbrook, and on Monday, May 5th, all the trains previously using Central were diverted to Oxford Road and Piccadilly. Oxford Road now had an extra 118 trains a day to handle.

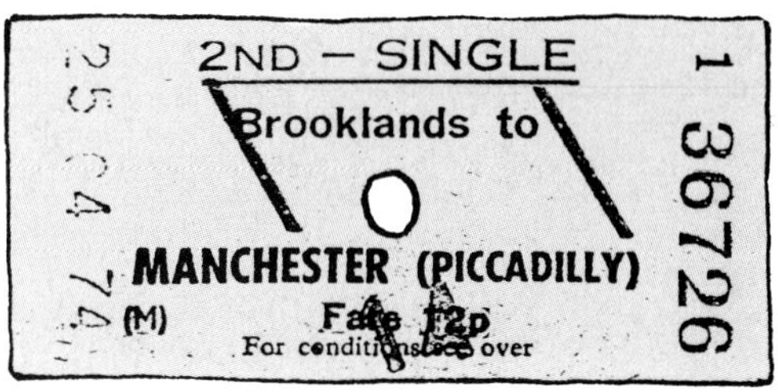

MANCHESTER–ALTRINCHAM LINE MODERNISATION 1970–1971

Until approximately April 1971 extensive engineering work will be undertaken between Manchester and Altrincham. The main work will be carried out on Sundays and will consist of : —

(a) the conversion of the overhead electrification system from 1200 volts D.C. to 25 kv. A.C.

(b) the installation of modern signalling.

On completion in 1971, the present rolling stock will be replaced by modern electric multiple units and through trains may be operated between Altrincham and Crewe.

Until then, however, it will be necessary on some Sundays to operate special buses instead of trains between certain stations. On other days the journey times may be slightly extended.

PASSENGERS TRAVELLING ON SUNDAYS ON THIS LINE ARE ADVISED TO CHECK THEIR TRAVEL ARRANGEMENTS IN ADVANCE.

Every effort will be made to keep alterations to a minimum and any inconvenience is regretted.

British Rail

Note the error in this official poster, which should read 1500 volts DC, not 1200 volts!

Chapter Thirteen

The 1971 Re-electrification (25kv ac)

With the stock approaching the end of its working life, and some of the electrical equipment on its last legs, it was time to think about the re-electrification of the line between Oxford Road and Altrincham. BR also considered extending the new electric services to Hale, but unfortunately concluded that ¾ mile of extra electrification would not pay, and abandoned the idea. In 1968 the first motor coaches had their old dc pantographs removed and replaced by ac-type pantographs, which are smaller; this enabled clearances to be increased during the changeover to 25kv ac, the system already used for the services between Oxford Road and Crewe. When the re-electrification was completed, there would be through electric services between Altrincham and stations on the lines to Crewe.

Work started in earnest in June 1969 on the £1 million re-electrification. This involved removing what few redundant sidings there were left (odd bits of track at Stretford and Warwick Road) and resignalling the line. Already the northern end was controlled by colour-lights, operated from London Road box; now the rest of the line was re-signalled. A good deal of lineside equipment had to be installed. In December 1970 colour-light signals, operated from Altrincham, Navigation Road and Deansgate Lane boxes, were brought into use over the line between Altrincham and Deansgate Junction. On 1st February, 1971 the remaining section of the line (Warwick Road to Deansgate Junction) saw its colour-light signals brought into operation, controlled from London Road box. The signal boxes at Warwick Road, Stretford, Mersey Bridge, Sale and Brooklands were 'abolished'. The crossover roads at Warwick Road and Brooklands were then worked by ground frames, electrically released from London Road box. (A telephone link to London Road was provided at each ground frame.) Thus, all the line from Piccadilly to Deansgate Junction was controlled from London Road box.

To supply the 25,000v ac a new relay power supply building (itself supplied from Heaton Norris feeder station) was constructed beside the up line between Navigation Road and Deansgate Junction. This looked after the southern part of the line; the northern part was (electrically-speaking) an extension of the line from Wilmslow.

Various redundant overhead structures were cut down and removed, and where necessary new supports erected. Much of the old overhead equipment remained, modified if necessary.

The line also enjoyed a face-lift. This involved the demolition of existing waiting-rooms, shelters, canopies and so on at certain of the stations (Warwick Road being the outstanding example) and their replacement by bus-shelters. Everything was repainted, even the facings of the steps of the footbridge at Altrincham station. Patches of greenery on the platforms of some stations were tarmacked over. Down came the old totem station signs in the LMR maroon, and up went rectangular black-and-white ones. The net result may have been cheaper to maintain, but it was bleaker, drearier, and disastrous when raining.

The siding at the un-numbered north bay platform at Altrincham station, used for occasional mail-coaches and for storing track-inspection units, was

Manchester→Altrincham

Mondays to Fridays

Oxford Rd.*	Altrincham
06 50	07 10
07 10	07 30
07 30	07 51
07 50	08 10
08 00	08 22
08 15	08 35
08 27	08 47
08 33	08 53
08 41	09 01
08 47	09 07
08 55	09 15
09 10	09 32
09 18	09 41
09 30	09 50
and every 20 minutes until	
16 30	16 51
16 45	17 05
16 55	17 15
17 03	17 24
17 11	17 32
17 17	17 37
17 25	17 45
17 36	17 56
17 44	18 04
17 50	18 10
18 00	18 20
18 20	18 40
18 45	19 06
19 05	19 25
and every 30 minutes until	
23 35	23 55

Saturdays

Oxford Rd.*	Altrincham
07 10	07 30
07 40	08 00
08 12	08 32
08 30	08 50
08 50	09 10
09 10	09 30
09 30	09 50
and every 20 minutes until	
20 10	20 31
20 35	20 56
and every 30 minutes until	
23 35	23 55

Sundays

Oxford Rd.*	Altrincham
14 10	14 30
14 40	15 00
and every 30 minutes until	
23 10	23 30

* For other station departures add:—Knott Mill (1 min). Old Trafford (4 mins), Warwick Road (6 mins) Stretford (8 mins), Dane Road (11 mins). Sale (12 mins), Brooklands (14 mins), Timperley (16 mins), Navigation Road (18 mins)

Altrincham→Manchester

Mondays to Fridays

Altrincham*	Oxford Rd.
06 20	06 40
06 40	07 00
07 00	07 20
07 20	07 41
07 35	07 55
07 50	08 10
08 02	08 22
08 09	08 29
08 15	08 35
08 23	08 43
08 29	08 49
08 38	08 58
08 51	09 12
09 00	09 20
and every 20 minutes until	
16 00	16 21
16 12	16 32
16 27	16 47
16 37	16 57
16 45	17 05
16 53	17 14
16 58	17 19
17 12	17 32
17 19	17 39
17 26	17 46
17 36	17 56
17 53	18 13
18 10	18 30
18 35	18 55
and every 30 minutes until	
23 05	23 25

Saturdays

Altrincham*	Oxford Rd.
06 40	07 00
07 10	07 30
07 40	08 00
08 00	08 20
08 23	08 43
08 41	09 01
09 00	09 20
and every 20 minutes until	
16 40	17 00
16 58	17 19
17 20	17 40
and every 20 minutes until	
20 00	20 20
And every 30 minutes until	
22 30	22 50
23 05	23 26

Sundays

Altrincham*	Oxford Rd.
13 40	14 00
14 10	14 30
and every 30 minutes until	
22 40	23 00

* For other station departures add:—Navigation Road (1 min). Timperley (3 mins). Brooklands (5 mins), Sale (7 mins), Dane Road (8 mins), Stretford (11 mins), Warwick Road (14 mins), Old Trafford (15 mins), Knott Mill (19 mins)

For other trains between Manchester and Altrincham see separate folder

information subject to alteration without notice

The last 'old' electric timetable 4th May, 1970–2nd May, 1971.

lifted in September 1970. At Sale the track layout south of the station was modified. The up line was relaid on its old course parallel to the down line, over where the south siding had been.

The completion of the conversion involved replacing the dc catenary with ac catenary, connecting the overhead wires to the 25kv system, and replacing the trains. The 'new' trains were class 304 electric multiple units (formerly referred to as 'AM4' units), which had been built in 1960–61. They were new to the Altrincham branch, but not new to the MSJA, having been used for the services between Oxford Road and Crewe. As the new 25kv service involved considerable changes to the timetable, with the introduction of through services between Altrincham and the lines to Crewe, the completion of the work was scheduled for the beginning of May, when the new LMR timetable would be introduced.

The new timetable had both good news and bad news. The good news was that the basic daytime electric service on the Altrincham branch was increased from three trains per hour each way to four trains per hour: one 'Crewe via Stockport', one 'Alderley Edge via Stockport', and two 'Alderley Edge via Styal' services. (The evening service remained at two per hour: one 'Crewe via Stockport', and one 'Alderley Edge via Stockport'.) And the through running benefited all the passengers who previously had had to change at Oxford Road to get to Piccadilly, or Stockport (say). The bad news was that the 'new' trains would take 22 minutes for the trip from Altrincham to Oxford Road, stopping at all stations, compared with only 20 minutes for the 40-year-old electrics. There was also one small 'presentational' improvement: for the first time for several years, the diesel service between Manchester and Altrincham was shown in the same table as the electric service! The table showed all the stations to Chester, as if the ex-CLC line were an extension of the MSJA. However, this approach had the disadvantage of splitting the through electric service between two tables: one showing Altrincham–Manchester, the other showing Manchester–Crewe. The May 1973 timetable put the complete service between Altrincham and Crewe into one table (including all the diesels between Altrincham and Manchester) and showed the ex-CLC Chester line service in a separate table.

The last of the old trains ran on 30th April, 1971, withdrawn after 40 years' service. The very last train to run, the 11.35 pm ex-Oxford Road, arrived at Altrincham decorated with 'last 1500v dc train' signs provided by the Altrincham Electric Railway Preservation Society. There followed celebrations (or, rather, a wake), and everyone went home to bed.

The next day, Saturday 1st May, a diesel service ran. On the Sunday there were no trains at all, to allow the completion of the conversion work. Then came Monday 3rd May, 1971. The first of the 25kv trains from Altrincham was the 6.10 am, and this carried a few passengers plus a couple of railway enthusiasts. Services ran smoothly all morning until, at 11 o'clock, the Mayor of Altrincham arrived to perform an opening ceremony. He waved a flag, and the 11.10 pulled out, cut through a white tape stretched across the track, and the conversion was complete.

Although much more modern than the old ('compartment-style') electrics, the 'new' class 304 trains were not welcomed by commuters. As well as

The first morning of 25 kv ac working at Altrincham. The passengers have just alighted from a dmu at platform 3. Note all the bicycles on platform 1. *B. Avery*

Class 'AL6' No. E3155 stands in Altrincham's platform No. 2 in May 1971; waiting to depart with a special to London Euston to celebrate the new service. *B. Avery*

being slower than the 'old' electrics, they offered far fewer seats at rush-hours. The class 304s then operated only as 4-car units, and seated only 337 people, compared with the 552 seats of an 'old' electric 6-coach train. The number of trains at rush-hours was not increased to compensate for the reduced seating. Apparently, when the post-re-electrification timetable was approved in principle, it was recognised that 'restraints on service provision' caused mainly by a 'shortage of suitable rolling stock' would result in a 'deterioration in comfort levels'. Passengers complained about overcrowding, and petitioned for improvements. Unfortunately, BR said, extra carriages could only be added in multiples of four. This would be uneconomic, and anyway no extra carriages were available. BR added that 'up to 40 per cent standing should be expected at peak hours' on commuter services, a remark that was doubtless appreciated by its customers.

'This is a convenient place to end the MSJA's history', I wrote in 1972. 'It has lost what little identity it had left: its rolling stock (with sepia prints, matchstrikers, 'ladies only' compartments, patchwork seats and brass-barred windows) is gone. The Bowdon carriage sheds are demolished, their sidings lifted, their overhead equipment cut down: no more local maintenance. It is now just an extension of the line to Crewe.' How wrong I was . . .

The way it used to be: an 'old' electric train heads south from Stretford in 1962 on the fast lines. *D. Morgan/N. Dodson Collection*

Altrincham station from the north on 29th May, 1976. *N.D. Mundy*

Amid many interested on-lookers, 'The Red Rose' departs Altrincham on 28th April, 1979, with the Hereford to Guide Bridge special hauled by 'Merchant Navy' class 4–6–2 No. 35028 *Clan Line*. *T. Heavyside*

Chapter Fourteen

What Happened Next

A million pounds had been spent re-electrifying the MSJA. Its future was secure (as long as £266,000 per year was found for grant aid): the line was needed to keep people off the roads. And better days were ahead: the South East Lancashire and North East Cheshire (SELNEC) Passenger Transport Executive was considering co-ordinating the buses and trains from Altrincham, Sale, Stretford, etc. into Manchester: the 63–64 bus route, parallel to and competing with the MSJA, might be turned into a series of feeder buses, connecting with trains at various stations along the line. Another suggestion was for a new station to replace Warwick Road, with a busway to the Trafford Park industrial estate. There was talk of obtaining additional 4-car units, and of lengthening station platforms to take 8-car trains, which would run every 5 minutes at peak times. The passenger capacity would be tripled (from eight 4-car trains in one direction in a peak hour to twelve 8-car trains an hour). Investment of some £7.5 million was envisaged (including the cost of the new rolling stock and extra car parking), but even with this the line would still lose £250,000 a year. SELNEC also noted that 'now that financial viability is no longer the only factor' electrification beyond Altrincham might be re-considered, the maximum benefit possibly coming from electrification to Knutsford, subject to reaching satisfactory arrangements with the new Cheshire County Council. Unfortunately, little came of all this.

However, the main railway development envisaged by SELNEC (e.g. 1971's 'A Broad Plan for 1984') was the construction of a subterranean route between Piccadilly and Victoria. This would connect the lines from Alderley Edge, Macclesfield and Hazel Grove, on the one hand, with the lines to Bury and Bolton (the latter via a reinstated link from Radcliffe). Following conversion work electric services from these lines would run through this 'Picc-Vic' tunnel, via underground stations at Princess Street, Albert Square and Market Street (an indirect route was chosen, to serve the city centre better). The report also thought that passenger conveyor (travelator) systems had great potential, and suggested that (subject to the results of a more detailed study) such systems might be installed between Oxford Road station and St Peter's Square, and between Piccadilly station and Piccadilly Gardens. In 1972, Parliamentary approval was obtained for the 'Picc-Vic' scheme, but not sufficient funds for the project to go ahead; the plan was eventually abandoned in 1977, a fate shared by many other SELNEC proposals.

In 1979, another method of linking Piccadilly and Victoria was proposed: the construction of a 'Castlefield Curve'. This would have been a short connection, from the South Junction line towards Salford, enabling trains from Piccadilly to run through to Victoria via Oxford Road, Deansgate (formerly Knott Mill & Deansgate) and Salford. However, BR had reservations about the capacity of the South Junction line between Piccadilly and Castlefield Junction, and the scheme was also opposed by the City Council (who wanted trains to run into the city centre, not around it). This proposal also made no progress.

Class '303' 'up' and class '304' 'down' services pass at Brooklands on 9th May, 1989.
J.D. Darby

Unit 303036 between Oxford Road and Piccadilly on 24th May, 1984. *T. Heavyside*

Some developments did go ahead, including the provision of 'bus/rail interchange facilities' at Altrincham (i.e. the return of Altrincham bus station to the railway station forecourt, which it had left in the early 1960s for the other side of Stamford New Road). Work started in April 1975. A new booking-office was opened on platform 4, serving passengers arriving from the car park on the site of the former goods yard. Platforms, awnings and some buildings were restored and renovated, and a curious pendulum clock in a see-through case was installed in the booking-hall. The Victorian canopy at the front of the station was dismantled to make way for the new £400,000 bus station. (These changes were not appreciated by everyone. An article in the newsletter of the Victorian Society's Manchester Group commented: 'Unfortunately, the appearance of the station from the street has been largely spoilt in recent years by the removal of an iron and glass *porte cochère* and its replacement by a large canopy intended to give shelter to passengers waiting to board buses. The concern for bus passengers is estimable, but it is a pity that the arrangements for keeping them dry could not have been made in a more sympathetic manner.') The interchange began full operation in November 1976.

Another important development at Altrincham was the opening, in autumn 1972, of a £500,000 flyover bridging the line north of the level crossing. This reduced considerably the road traffic over the level crossing. The large level crossing gates were finally taken out of use by a court order dated 20th October, 1978; the wicket gates for pedestrian use were retained after public protests about their proposed removal.

Work also took place at a number of other stations. In some cases, old buildings were demolished and new ones (e.g. booking offices) constructed; in other cases, existing buildings were renovated. Examples included a rebuilding of Deansgate station, and the replacement of Stretford's platform buildings by bus shelters. Sometimes services to passengers were improved (e.g. the installation of a tannoy at Altrincham) at the same time as others were lost (e.g. the closure of the parcels office at Sale, both early in 1981).

First class was abolished on the Altrincham line in two stages: on the services to Chester from 1st June, 1981, and on the electric trains from 17th May, 1982.

The electric services had been provided by class 304 electric multiple units since the re-electrification in 1971. In addition, class 310 emus were used occasionally during the 1970s. In 1982 some class 303 units (ex-Glasgow Blue Trains) began to join them, and by 1984 there were a dozen class 303s based at Crewe and used regularly on services between Crewe, Manchester and Altrincham. (The class 303s were later withdrawn from the North West of England due to their unreliability.) Towards the end of 1991, several class 305 emus visited the line, on crew training runs. These refurbished units (from the London–Tilbury–Southend line) were subsequently used on services between Deansgate and Crewe, but never ran in passenger service to Altrincham.

One of the MSJA's connections was electrified in 1980: a short stretch of the ex-CLC line towards Warrington Central. The mile and a half from Cornbrook Junction on the MSJA to Trafford Park Freightliner depot and Trafford Park exchange sidings was electrified so that electric-hauled

New electric and diesel services between Oxford Road and Piccadilly in 1979.
N. Dodson

MSJA viaduct near Castlefield in 1979 with the Rochdale Canal in the foreground and the viaduct carrying the former CLC into Central in the background. *N. Dodson*

container trains could work through to Trafford Park. This also enabled the use of electric units for the match day shuttle service between Oxford Road and the platform at United's ground.

Following the electrification of the line between Stockport and Hazel Grove, a regular through service between Altrincham and Hazel Grove began on 1st June, 1981. The basic pattern of daytime electric services on the MSJA remained four trains per hour each way, but now with one 'Crewe via Stockport', one 'Alderley Edge via Stockport', one Alderley Edge via Styal', and one 'Hazel Grove'. 'Hazel Grove' replaced 'Alderley Edge via Styal' as the destination of some trains from Altrincham. Subsequently, electric trains from Altrincham began to venture further afield. From 16th May, 1983, some of the evening 'Alderley Edge' services were replaced by trains that ran to Macclesfield, some of which continued to Stoke or even to Stafford. A couple of years later, one of these workings was extended to Wolverhampton. Later still, for a while, one electric train per day ran all the way from Altrincham to Birmingham. This left Altrincham at 7.35 pm, and proceeded via Piccadilly, Stockport, Macclesfield, Stoke, Stafford and Wolverhampton to Birmingham New Street, where it arrived at 10.29 pm, having travelled over 90 miles and stopped at 35 intermediate stations. (It did not call at only two of the stations on its route: Levenshulme and Heaton Chapel.) And, for a time, an evening service ran through to Walsall. In the other direction, the passenger timetable did not show any through workings from Birmingham to Altrincham, but there was one train a day from Wolverhampton, and a few from Stoke or from Macclesfield.

Since its closure in 1969, Central station had passed through a number of hands, including those of 'an Anglo-Irish property and race horse owner from County Meath' and those of a 'demolition and scrap recovery company'. The great building stood, empty and increasingly derelict, until work started on its £22 million conversion to form the Greater Manchester Exhibition and Events Centre (G-Mex), which was formally opened by the Queen on 21st March, 1986. This brought more passengers onto the MSJA, as Deansgate was the closest station to G-Mex. A footbridge was built to link Deansgate station and the G-Mex site, and various improvements made to Deansgate station, to handle the extra traffic generated by G-Mex.

There was an unusual accident in February 1986. At about 6 am one morning, a class 303 emu made an unscheduled departure from Altrincham station, where it had been stabled overnight. It had neither driver nor passengers on board. Apparently, its brakes had not been applied properly. The signalman in the Altrincham North box diverted this runaway train onto the down loop line, and it derailed itself on the points at the Navigation Road end of the loop.

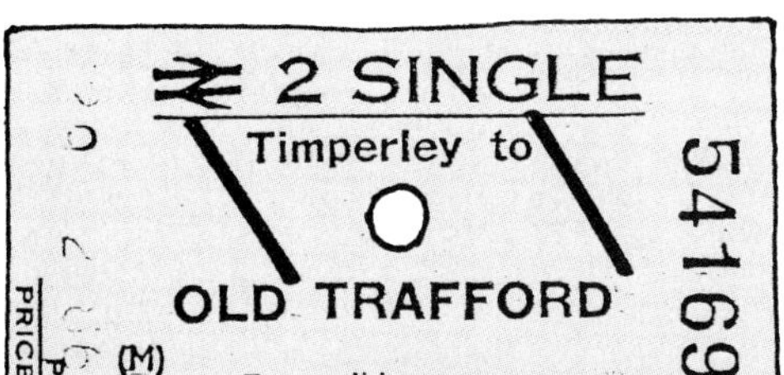

Unit No. 304030 waiting to depart from Old Trafford on 6th March, 1985. *J.D. Darby*

Unit 304004 departing Altrincham on the 13.50 Alderley Edge service on 27th September, 1985. *T. Heavyside*

Chapter Fifteen

The Windsor Link

In 1980, BR published proposals to concentrate InterCity and Express services at Piccadilly, to improve passengers' connections and to reduce operating costs. These proposals would have significant implications for the MSJA: the South Junction line would once again be an important link for through services. However, new connections elsewhere were required before any services using Victoria were diverted to run via the South Junction line and Piccadilly.

Most important was the building of the 'Windsor Link', a short stretch of new line running from a little to the west of Ordsall Lane to Windsor Bridge (on the ex-L&Y line to Bolton and Wigan). This enabled trains from Oxford Road to run to (e.g.) Bolton, Preston, Blackpool, Barrow, Wigan, and Southport. Another new link (the 'Hazel Grove chord', opened in 1986) allows services from Oxford Road to run to Sheffield via Stockport Edgeley. These developments enabled BR to introduce services between, say, Blackpool and Norwich, running via the South Junction line, calling at Oxford Road and the MSJA platforms at Piccadilly. Indeed, even some InterCity trains between Birmingham and Edinburgh or Glasgow began to run over the MSJA, calling at the through platforms at Piccadilly. Such InterCity trains (and the local services using these lines) would have been electric-hauled under the original plan, which was to electrify from Castlefield Junction to Preston and Blackpool, but the financial case for electrification was not strong enough: the economics of the new diesels ('Sprinters') were thought to make electrification unattractive. However, the benefits of the Windsor Link as a link were recognised, and it was built. So far, the most peculiar InterCity service using the South Junction line has been the 6 am from London Paddington to Edinburgh Waverley, which runs via Reading, Oxford, Birmingham, Macclesfield, Piccadilly, Bolton, Preston and Carlisle, and which takes about 8 hours to reach its destination.

The Windsor Link is, in spirit (but not in fact), an extension of the South Junction line: the two are separated by a short stretch of ex-LNW line between the southern end of the Windsor Link (a little west of Ordsall Lane) and the (post-1882) end of the South Junction line at the west end of the bridge over the Irwell. Work started in July 1986, and cost about £13 million. Salford Council met the £1.5 million cost of a new bridge carrying the ex-MSJA line between the bridge over the Irwell and Ordsall Lane over the intended route of Salford's new inner ring road. The bridge was built of steel clad in concrete, but disguised to look like a Victorian structure, with brick-faced abutments; it included a separate single-track line into the Museum of Science and Industry at Liverpool Road, At the same time, Ordsall Lane Junction was remodelled, and the Windsor Link connection was made. During the work, a turntable dating from 1905 was unearthed and presented to the museum. A new station was opened at Salford Cresent in May 1987, just to the north of the Windsor Link, to serve the area around the University of Salford and to provide connections to and from Victoria for the services using the Windsor Link. There were also changes to the South Junction line.

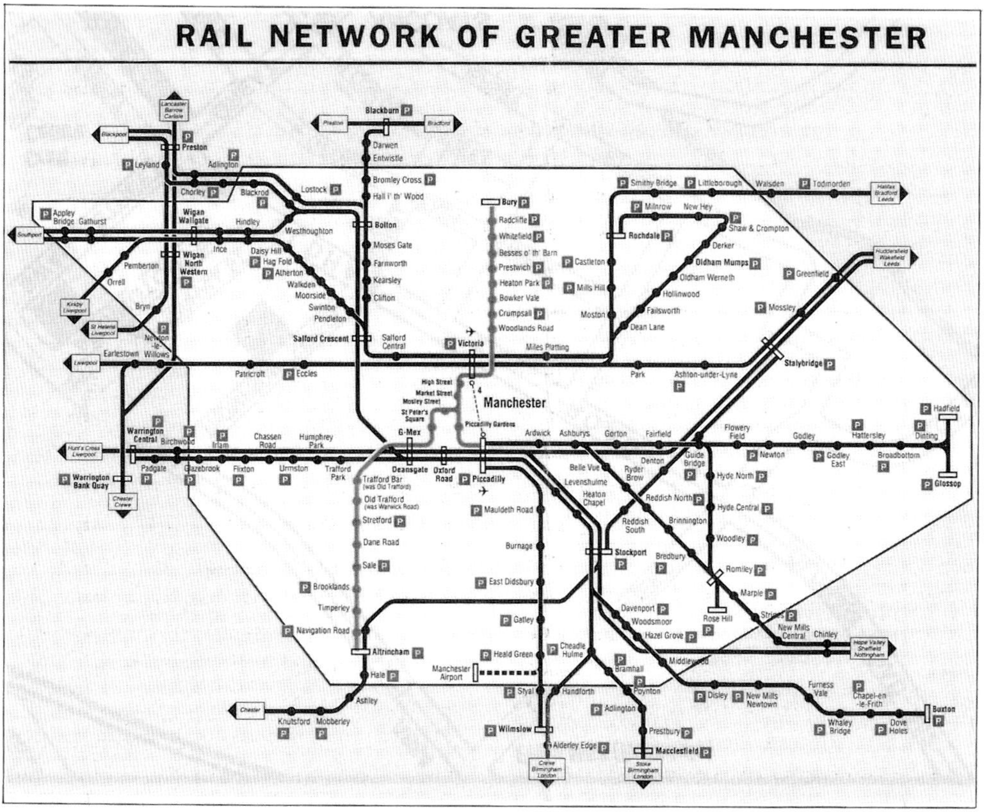

The city centre line as an important cross-country link: class '47' No. 47476 departing Piccadilly with the 8.25 Newcastle–Liverpool service on 5th September, 1989.

T. Heavyside

About £250,000 was spent on Oxford Road station, to update the building and prepare it for its new role as a city centre station with express services between, on the one hand, Merseyside and Lancashire and, on the other, the East Midlands and East Anglia. For example, computer screens displaying details of departures were installed.

When the link was opened in May 1988 only a few trains ran over the Windsor Link: a great deal of work was required at Piccadilly before the link's full potential could be realised. This started in June 1988, and included closures in October: e.g. for two weeks there were no trains between Piccadilly and Oxford Road. About £4 million was spent on the stations. The MSJA platforms at Piccadilly were lengthened to take two trains each at a time. The provision of improved waiting room, buffet and toilet facilities, and escalators and lifts for passengers took longer, unfortunately, and passengers huddled together by the stairs to shelter from strong winds, composing letters complaining about the delays in this work. Some £9 million was spent on track and signalling work. The track layout at Piccadilly was remodelled to cater for the new traffic, for example for running between the MSJA platforms and the line to Guide Bridge. The old London Road signal box closed in October 1988, a new 'Manchester Piccadilly' signalling centre was brought into use, and the signalling area controlled from Piccadilly was extended to, for example, Blackrod (between Bolton and Preston).

To mark my 37th birthday, the new timetable that came into effect on 15th May, 1989 made great use of the South Junction line. The Trans-Pennine services (e.g. between Liverpool and Newcastle) were transferred from running via Newton-le-Willows and Victoria to running via Warrington Central and Oxford Road, and thence via Guide Bridge to rejoin their original route at Stalybridge. The basic service over the Windsor Link was four trains per hour between Stockport and Bolton (alternately Blackpool and Wigan Wallgate services). In consequence, the number of passengers rose: for example, people living along the Bolton line could now catch trains to the South Junction stations as well as trains to Victoria. The wider choice of destinations made commuting by rail more attractive: there was a 40 per cent increase in the morning peak number of passengers into Manchester from Bolton southwards.

When some Windsor Link trains began to terminate at Hazel Grove, the electric service between there and Altrincham was withdrawn, and replaced (on the Altrincham branch) by additional 'Alderley Edge via Styal' trains. The basic day-time electric service remained four trains per hour each way, but returned to the pattern that had been introduced in 1971: one 'Crewe via Stockport', one 'Alderley Edge via Stockport', and two 'Alderley Edge via Styal'.

Also in May 1989, except on Sundays, the ex-CLC Chester line service stopped going via Sale and was transferred to run via the Baguley line and Stockport Edgeley. (The Sunday service was re-routed via Stockport from 20th May, 1990.) The benefits of a regular direct service between Altrincham and Stockport hardly justified the increased journey times into Manchester for passengers from Hale and beyond, but that was not the point: this 'heavy

Oxford Road station on 5th September, 1989. More through services. Some unusual: two car dmu, Nos. 54269 and 53929 with the 13.02 Warrington to Chester via Manchester, Stockport and Altrincham (!) . . . *T. Heavyside*

. . . others laudable: unit No. 156413 with the 11.25 Liverpool to Norwich. *T. Heavyside*

rail' service was taken off the MSJA between Timperley and Manchester, to make way for the 'Metrolink' light rail system. At first, the Chester trains were extended to take in Warrington, so giving a remarkable through service from Warrington Central to Chester via Oxford Road, Piccadilly, Stockport and Altrincham! This involved a lot of extra mileage for the 30-year old diesels then used for the service, and reliability suffered. The May 1990 timetable split it into two services: first, between Warrington and Oxford Road; second, between Piccadilly and Chester via Stockport and Altrincham. As both services could terminate in bay platforms, the change also reduced the pressure on the MSJA platforms at Piccadilly and on the line between Piccadilly and Oxford Road. However, with new stock, in May 1992 the ex-CLC Chester line trains started running through Oxford Road again: this time proceeding via the Windsor Link to Wigan Wallgate (mainly); some went to Blackpool or to Southport (from May 1993, most served Southport).

There were changes to the services over the South Junction line in May 1993. With the opening of the branch to Manchester Airport, on 17th May, some Windsor Link trains were reorganised to terminate at the new station, giving an hourly service between the Airport and Blackpool, via Oxford Road. (However, the basic Oxford Road–Windsor Link service was reduced from 4 per hour to 3 per hour.) Also, almost all the weekday services between Manchester and Chester/North Wales via Newton-le-Willows began to use Oxford Road rather than Victoria (the Sunday services had been transferred a few years earlier). These changes followed the announcement, earlier in the year, of a £473,000 'facelift' for Oxford Road.

Unit No. 304033 departs Navigation Road station with the 14.30 Crewe to Altrincham service on 4th May, 1991. *T. Heavyside*

Network NorthWest Day, 20th October, 1990 with class '90' No. 90049 arriving at Altrincham with the 08.45 from Crewe (No. 85109 is attached at the rear). At that time, the down through loop line had been lifted. A fourth track was subsequently reinstated as part of the preparation for Metrolink. *B. Avery*

Castlefield Junction on 20th October, 1990 with class '85' No. 85109 on the Altrincham–Crewe special train, and the former CLC into Central in the background. *B. Avery*

Chapter Sixteen

Metrolink

In 1982, the Greater Manchester Council, the Greater Manchester Passenger Transport Executive (PTE) and British Rail set up a Rail Strategy Group, to look at possible developments of the area's rail network and improved access to the city centre. The group concluded that a number of local rail routes should be converted to 'light rail' operation. The first stage would be the conversion of the Altrincham and Bury lines, and the construction of light rail routes, running over city centre streets, to link them together and to connect Victoria and Piccadilly stations. The total route length would be about 19 miles (31 km). It would bring 'trams' back to the centre of Manchester, where they had last been seen in 1949. The new 'Metrolink' system would be the first modern light rail system in the UK to include on-street running.

The possibility of running the light rail services south of Altrincham was considered, but not in detail. The options considered were to extend the line to the site of the old carriage sheds (and Bowdon terminus) at Lloyd Street, and to include Hale in the new system. Unfortunately, apparently there were major engineering and practical constraints, and the proposals did not even reach the stage at which their costs would have been estimated.

A Bill for the construction of the city centre section was put to Parliament in November 1984, with a Bill for the conversion of the Altrincham and Bury lines following in November 1985. In July 1985 the PTE applied to the Department of Transport for a grant (under Section 56 of the 1968 Transport Act) for the construction work. Progress was delayed by the abolition of the Greater Manchester Council (31st March, 1986) and the de-regulation of bus transport (from 26th October, 1986). De-regulation took away from the PTE responsibility for operating buses, and powers for determining bus fares and ensuring co-ordination of road and rail services. There were also changes to the rules governing the funding of projects like Metrolink. A revised application for 50 per cent Government grant was made in July 1987, and the Government gave a 'double yellow light' to the project in January 1988, subject to private sector involvement: a private contractor should design, build, operate and maintain the system. The network (including all the infrastructure and rolling stock) would be owned by the PTE; the contractor would have a 15 year concession to operate the system, using the revenue from fares and other income (e.g. advertising) to pay for the operation of the system, its maintenance and any profit. There was no guarantee that the operator would make a profit: the Greater Manchester PTE is not empowered to subsidise Metrolink.

It should be noted that the BR Altrincham services were making considerable losses. While precise figures for the amounts of 'Section 20' support for individual routes are not available, the Greater Manchester PTE suggest a 'guesstimate' of around £2.5 million per year for the Altrincham services.

The Bills received the Royal Assent on 9th February, 1988, and the process of selecting the contractor began. In May, suitable companies were invited to apply; in September eight were selected for the first stage of the

The entrance to Brooklands station on 8th December, 1984. *N.D. Mundy*

The station buildings at Brooklands from platform level on 9th May, 1989. *J.D. Darby*

The station buildings at Brooklands on 8th November, 1986 now being used as a Bistro Bar and Restaurant. *J.D. Darby*

tendering process. Five tenders were received by February 1989. These were evaluated, and three of the contenders were chosen for the second stage. They submitted their final tenders in July, these were evaluated, and in September 1989 it was announced that the chosen contractor was the GMA group, a consortium involving GEC Alsthom, Mowlem and AMEC. Their responsibilities (in some cases through sub-contractors) would be: GEC Alsthom – vehicles, power supply, signalling, telecommunications, ticketing; Mowlem – construction/modification of track, stations, viaducts, bridges, city centre link; AMEC – construction of the Operations and Maintenance depot and offices. In November, Greater Manchester Buses Ltd joined the consortium, to provide operating expertise. In January 1990, the enlarged consortium, together with the Greater Manchester PTE, set up Greater Manchester Metro Ltd (GMML) as the operating company. Each of GEC Alsthom, Mowlem and AMEC owns 25.1 per cent of GMML; GM Buses and GMPTE each own 12.35 per cent.

On 24th October, 1989, the Government announced that a 'Section 56' grant would be available for the project. The total capital costs were estimated (November 1992) to be £135 million, of which £5 million was, in effect, paid by the contractors, in return for the concession. Roughly half the remainder was covered by the Department of Transport's 'Section 56' grant. The PTE provided most of the rest, with some funds coming from the EC's European Regional Development Fund, the Central Manchester Development Corporation, and from Urban Programme money.

The selection of the contractors was a very expensive process. Preparation of the tenders required the contenders to research, design and cost their proposals; the PTE's evaluation of the tenders involved detailed consideration and discussion of the various bids. A great deal of work then went into the arrangements between the chosen consortium and the PTE, producing a pile of contracts about 30 inches high. The contracts include a specification of the level and quality of service to be provided (but not the fares: the operators can charge what they judge appropriate), and the penalties that will apply for poor performance. The legal complexities meant that the contracts took a long time to prepare and, because of the number of documents involved, signing alone took about 12 hours! Ideally, Manchester's experience would lead to simpler rules and procedures for subsequent projects: the *Metrolink Official Handbook* refers to a Greater Manchester PTE belief that this was one area that should not be a case of 'what Manchester does today, the rest of the world will do tomorrow'!

Work on Metrolink did not await the formal signing of the contract on 6th June, 1990. In March 1989, a £7 million scheme of work had started in the city centre streets that were on the Metrolink route, to divert public services (gas, electricity, water, etc.) away from where the tracks would run. Track-laying began in the city centre in April 1990: at a ceremony on the 5th, Councillor Jack Flanagan 'cut the first sod' with a JCB. The work had to be done while limiting the disruption to the city centre. For example, work in Mosley Street had to stop for the Christmas shopping period, work on the Piccadilly Gardens junction and station had to permit continued bus station services, and work at some important road crossings had to be done at

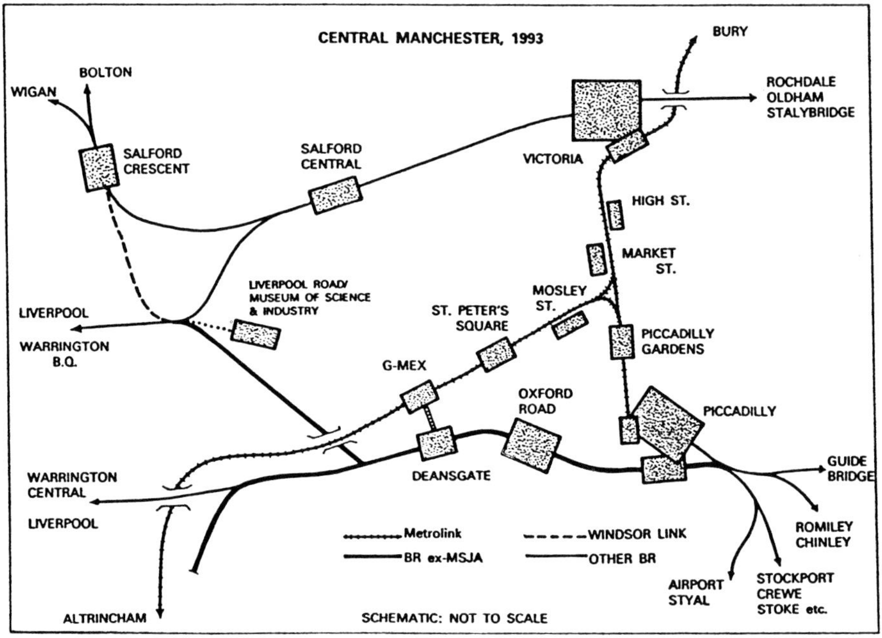

Looking from Altrincham towards Navigation Road on 19th July, 1991: the fortnight's engineer's possession was almost over. *J.D. Darby*

weekends, when traffic could be diverted. Unfortunately, there were problems with the polymer first used to bond the rails to the concrete trackbed: it would not set properly in Manchester's damp climate!

Changes to the MSJA

A number of changes to the MSJA were required so that Metrolink could run on separate tracks from 'heavy rail' BR trains. At the Altrincham end of the line, much of the work was completed when the MSJA south of Brooklands was closed for a complete engineer's possession from Sunday 7th to Sunday 21st July, 1991, for remodelling and resignalling. The trains reversed at Brooklands (using a crossover there, which was removed in mid-1992), and buses bridged the gap to Altrincham.

Between Altrincham station and Navigation Road level crossing Metrolink and BR each have a separate double-track route, following a realignment of the double-track main line and of the two through sidings that formerly ran alongside it between the Altrincham and Navigation Road level crossings. There is a connection between the BR track and the Metrolink track, just south of the Stockport Road flyover, for use for engineering purposes. From Navigation Road to Deansgate Junction, however, there is only room for a total of two tracks, so Metrolink and BR each run on a separate single track. Each single track line is signalled for working in either direction. Metrolink has one platform at Navigation Road station, that formerly used by BR services to Manchester. This platform is now used for tram services in both directions. BR Chester trains use the former 'down' platform, both for services to Stockport and for services to Altrincham. At Deansgate Junction, where the BR line turns off towards Stockport, Metrolink becomes the sole user of the MSJA route north. South of Timperley station, the up line was slewed towards the canal and a siding was put in between the two tracks, for stabling and reversing any Metrolink trams which terminate at Timperley.

In July 1991, the signal boxes at Altrincham North and Navigation Road were closed and demolished. Deansgate Junction signal box, with the first solid-state interlocking system in the North West of England, now controlled the lines from there to Northenden and to Mobberley (Skelton Junction and Hale signal boxes closed at the same time). The pedestrian level crossing at Altrincham was closed, leading to much public protest and eventually to a Public Inquiry (held in September 1992). The old pedestrian footbridge was demolished (in February 1991) and replaced by a new footbridge (with ramped access) built over the new four-track layout (previously there had been only two tracks over the level crossing). New arc lights and television cameras were installed at Navigation Road level crossing, so that it could be controlled from Deansgate Junction signal box (which also controls the level crossing at Hale station).

The MSJA stations all along the line were upgraded as necessary, for example with ramps and lifts where these were required to impove access to the platforms. Altrincham retained its booking offices, to cater for the many destinations available using BR services, but the other Metrolink stations would be unstaffed, with ticket vending machines, closed-circuit television surveillance and public address systems.

Towards the northern end of the Altrincham branch, about 6.5 miles (10.4 km) from Altrincham, the Metrolink route leaves the MSJA. Crossing the BR route between Oxford Road and Warrington Central on the level would not separate 'light' and 'heavy' rail. BR therefore built a £6 million 'dive-under' at Cornbrook, to take Metrolink under the BR route. Work began in January 1990. The Warrington line's alignment was altered so that space was left for possible future junctions to any subsequent extensions of Metrolink towards Trafford Park and towards Salford Quays.

After leaving the MSJA at Cornbrook, Metrolink runs for around 1.1 miles (1.7 km) towards G-Mex on the ex-CLC viaduct, which had not been used since Central closed in 1969. With little or no maintenance for over 20 years, metal sections had become corroded and some brickwork had decayed. Repairs included the replacement of the northern span of the Cornbrook Road bridge with a new steel box-girder deck bridge. Approaching a million square feet of brickwork required repointing, and thousands of damaged or missing bricks had to be replaced. The level of the bridge over the South Junction line at Castlefield was raised to improve clearances for the possible future electrification of the line from Castlefield Junction to Ordsall Lane (and beyond). The Metrolink station for G-Mex is at the end of the footbridge from Deansgate station, providing a very convenient interchange with the BR system.

The City Centre Route

The city centre section consists of around 1.2 miles (2.0 km) for the route between the G-Mex and Victoria stations, plus a further half mile or so (0.7 km) between Piccadilly Gardens and Piccadilly station. From the G-Mex station, the line descends to street level, using a new ramp viaduct running alongside the G-Mex site. This was constructed from reinforced concrete, then faced with bricks so that it would blend with existing structures, and includes a 44 metre long steel 'single bowstring arch girder bridge' over Great Bridgewater Street. This bridge was (it is claimed) 'designed to reflect its surroundings' and 'approved by the Royal Fine Art Commission'.

Metrolink then runs through the city streets via stations at St Peter's Square and Mosley Street (the latter a single platform, for southbound services only) to a triangular junction by Piccadilly Gardens. The route to Victoria proceeds past the Market Street (northbound) and High Street (southbound) platforms, and along Balloon Street to Victoria station. The route to Piccadilly station has an island platform at Piccadilly Gardens bus station, then runs via Aytoun Street into Piccadilly railway station's under-croft. Metrolink's concrete cavern is below the BR station concourse, with a 'mezzanine' level in between. This 'mezzanine' level is empty apart from a few advertisements on the walls: it is a cold, oppressive place, with brick arches and metal girders in the roof. It looks as if the Metrolink station is underground, but it is (of course) at ground level: it is the BR station that is high above ground. Lifts and escalators link the three levels. Thick concrete barriers were required by BR to prevent any runaway trams from damaging the columns that support the BR station above (and consequently causing it to collapse). The total cost of Metrolink's station was about £6 million.

Some parts of Metrolink's city centre routes are in separate lanes from other traffic, and some parts are shared by buses or by service vehicles. The system's electronics automatically seek priority for Metrolink at some traffic lights, but cannot always obtain it: the trams are often held up by traffic lights. While running through the city centre streets, Metrolink's drivers are often faced with pedestrians who are crossing the tracks as they cross the streets: the trams must therefore go carefully, often tooting to encourage people to get out of their way. Progress through the city centre is slow, with frequent halts for stations and for traffic lights, and accompanied by the trams' soft, mournful hoots.

The Royal Fine Art Commission did not approve of much of the city centre installation, claiming that 'a great city had been ruined by insufficient thought in design'. The Commission's Chairman, Lord St John of Fawsley, said that it had been 'appalled by the permanent devastation wrought by the system'. He felt that several city centre sites were 'filled with clumsy columns supporting untidy wirescape over streets laced by tram-devoted road surfaces and cluttered with signs, ticket machines and haphazard station platforms'. In response, a writer in *Modern Railways* wondered whether the commission would care to comment on the dozens of cities and towns in Britain which have been ruined by the motor car.

ALTRINCHAM TO TIMPERLEY, 1993

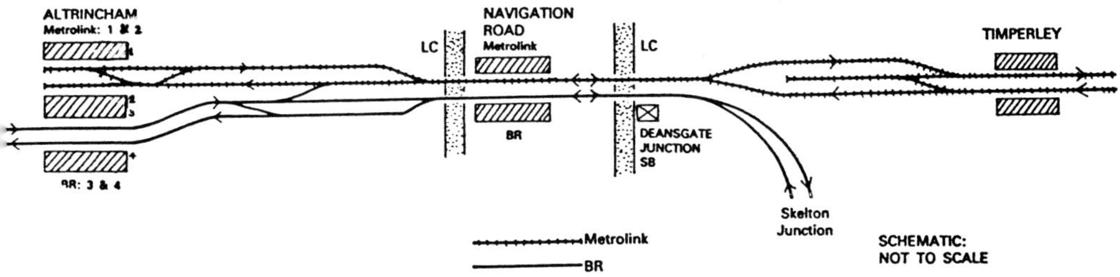

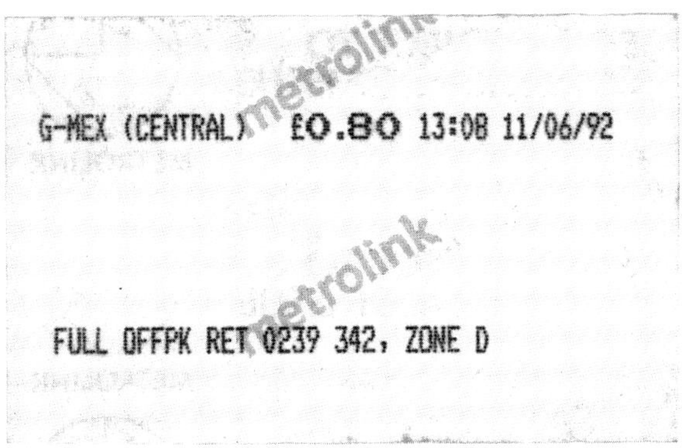

Metrolink's first type of ticket: from G-MEX (on the site of the former Central station) to 'Zone D' (City Centre Zone) and back again.

Two views of Navigation Road station in 1992 showing Metrolink trams Nos. 1026 and 1019. The upper picture is of a direct service to Bury whilst the lower one is of a tram to Altrincham. *N. Dodson*

Chapter Seventeen

The 1992 Re-electrification (750v DC)

The last 25 kv electric trains between Altrincham and Manchester ran on Christmas Eve 1991. The last passenger-carrying trains were the 9.05 pm from Altrincham and, in the other direction, the 9.05 pm from Oxford Road to Altrincham (which ran 'out of service' back to Manchester), with suitable commemorative decorations. These 30-year old trains remained in use at the Manchester end of the MSJA, on the Stockport and Styal line services.

At Cornbrook, the line to Altrincham was disconnected from BR on Sunday 5th January, 1992. An electrified siding was created, on a short stretch of the former route towards Altrincham, where trains from the Stockport and Styal lines, having called at Deansgate, wait until it is time for their return journey. This came into use on 27th January.

The original expectation had been that the remaining conversion work (e.g. rebuilding platform edges to align with the Metrolink trams, some repairs to the bridge over the Mersey, altering the overhead electric system and bringing the new signalling for Metrolink into use) would be completed quickly, and Metrolink services to Altrincham would start by the end of January 1992. This assumed that Metrolink services on the Bury line would start in Autumn 1991, and extend into the city centre by the end of the year. Unfortunately, this did not happen, because, for example, in mid-1991, it was discovered that additional engineering work was required on the Bury line; there was also the question of the availability of the rolling stock. The MSJA's customers were therefore faced with using replacement bus services (booked to take 45 minutes to an hour for journeys between Altrincham and Manchester) for several months rather than just a few weeks. (Some passengers, of course, could use the Chester line services between Altrincham and Manchester via Stockport, some of which started calling additionally at Navigation Road (from May, all did), but their capacity was limited.)

There were a lot of unhappy people: a GMPTE survey in March 1991 had found that, before 9.30 am on a weekday, about 1,500 people arrived at the Manchester stations on electric trains from Altrincham, and that, during the day as a whole, over 5,700 passenger journeys originated on the Altrincham branch. In addition, many passengers whose journeys started elsewhere would be inconvenienced. The MP for Altrincham and Sale wrote to the Transport Minister about the problems faced by his constituents, and raised the matter in the House of Commons, but without much success.

Metrolink opened for public services between Victoria and Bury on Monday 6th April, 1992. The modest opening ceremonies (trams driving through commemorative banners stretched across the tracks) were witnessed by the media, some of those involved in the construction and operation of Metrolink, enthusiasts and only a few members of the public – as the services began at about 6 o'clock in the morning. Public services were extended to G-Mex on Monday 27th April, with the introduction to the UK of a modern street-running light rail service marked by further modest ceremonies (at about 5.40 am!) and a tour of the system at 10 o'clock for some dignitaries. The first collisions between trams and other road vehicles occurred a little over a month later: with a car on 5th June, and with a bus on 15th June. The first passenger service derailment was on 14th September, when the front bogie of a tram came off the tracks just outside Piccadilly Gardens.

Trams had already started test running on the Altrincham branch, with the first one to run through to Altrincham doing so on 21st April. Driver training was complicated by the operation under BR control south of Timperley (because BR's Deansgate Junction signal box controls the level crossings at Deansgate Lane and Navigation Road, it also controls the Metrolink track at the south end of the MSJA): Metrolink drivers had to familiarise themselves with the BR rule book. The running of a 'ghost' service followed. On arrival at G-Mex, trams from Victoria and Bury unloaded all their passengers then proceeded to run empty onto the Altrincham line. The Railway Inspectorate visited the MSJA on 14th May, but were unhappy about a couple of technical points. It was not until the week beginning 8th June that they gave their approval for Metrolink passenger services on the Altrincham branch.

Metrolink services from Altrincham began on Monday 15th June, 1992. The first tram left Victoria at 5.26 am and arrived at Altrincham at 5.55, breaking yet another banner stretched across the tracks. It was greeted by a crowd that included Altrincham's Town Crier. A Trafford councillor 'cracked a bottle of bubbly to celebrate'. The tram set off at 6.05 am as the first Metrolink service from Altrincham to Manchester, and reached G-Mex in 18 minutes. Hundreds of carnations were handed out to passengers at stations along the line to mark the first day of Metrolink services from Altrincham.

The Royal opening of Metrolink was on Friday 17th July. The Queen unveiled a plaque on the platform of St Peter's Square station (after some 'technical' problems with the curtain in front of the plaque). The plaque was subsequently placed in the nearby Peace Garden, mounted on a block of sandstone that had been dug up during the laying of the foundations of Metrolink's tracks. The Queen then took tram number 1010 (which is called 'The Manchester Champion') to Bury. She did not travel on the Altrincham branch. The following Monday 20th July, again early in the morning, Metrolink services began running through to the Metrolink station in Piccadilly railway station undercroft, completing the system for the present. There was little publicity for this: in fact, the Piccadilly branch's formal opening ceremony took place a week later, on the mezzanine level of Metrolink's station at Piccadilly undercroft.

When Metrolink started running to Altrincham, Old Trafford station was renamed 'Trafford Bar', and Warwick Road station was renamed 'Old Trafford', as it is the best Metrolink station for the football and cricket grounds. There is talk of possible new stations: one at Cornbrook, one just south of Mersey Bridge (near Sale Water Park), and one at 'South Brooklands' (between Brooklands and Timperley). There has also been talk of an extension beyond Altrincham to a giant 'park and ride' station beside the M56 motorway, but there are no firm proposals at the time of writing (May 1993). Also possible is a Metrolink line to East Didsbury, which would start from a junction just south of Trafford Bar (formerly Old Trafford) station, where the trackbed of the ex-CLC Chorlton-cum-Hardy line runs under the MSJA, and use that route, and then the former Midland main line, to East Didsbury. A branch from this route could run south to serve the Airport. Other possible Metrolink extensions are being considered, such as lines to Rochdale via Oldham, and into East Manchester (if Manchester hosts the 2000 Olympic Games). The Trafford Park and Salford Quays extensions appear less likely, at the time of writing (May 1993), following a downturn in the property market. There is also talk of reviving the proposed 'Castlefield Curve', which would enable BR trains to run between Piccadilly and Victoria over the South Junction line, and which would, with the restoration of a curve at Ardwick, complete a circular railway line around the centre of Manchester.

The contracted level for Metrolink's 'off-peak frequency' weekday service was a minimum of six per hour between Altrincham and Piccadilly, with the trams from Altrincham starting at 6 am and the last tram arriving at Altrincham at midnight. The 'peak frequency' was to have one departure every 5 minutes, from Altrincham running alternately to Piccadilly and to Bury.

The Sunday service was to be four trams an hour, starting at 7 am and finishing at 11 pm. However, at first (while the system was settling down), the basic weekday service was only five trams an hour (and one every 6 minutes at peak times), and for several months there was no Sunday service at all. GMML did provide a special Sunday service between Victoria and Altrincham on 19th July, for a pop concert at Old Trafford Cricket Ground (carrying about 5,000 of the audience) and for the European Markets Festival held at Castlefield (served by the G-Mex station). GMML used 14 vehicles, running as seven coupled pairs. This was, apparently, the first time that a complete service had been provided using coupled pairs (prior to that, they had only been used occasionally).

A 'Manchester Metro News' comparison of journey times between Altrincham and Market Street in Manchester produced the following timings: Metrolink 26 minutes; car 43 minutes; and bus 62 minutes. A 'home to office/shops' comparison would show Metrolink in a less favourable light than these 'station to station' times.

Concern was expressed in some quarters about the level of Metrolink's fares, particularly where the fare zone system produces a high cost per mile. For example, the fare from Old Trafford to G-Mex is the same as that from Stretford to Victoria, as both journeys involve the same two fare zones. GMML argued that it was providing a premium level of service ('for example, the trams are always spotless: they are cleaned every 24 hours') 'and fares reflect this'. Whether standing passengers appreciate such arguments is another matter.

Another cause of complaints was a consequence of Metrolink being a completely separate commercial operation from BR. Some people were annoyed that GMML did not recognise BR Railcards, some were concerned about the loss of through ticketing from many BR stations, and others regretted that information about Metrolink did not appear in the BR national passenger timetable (GMML did not wish to pay for this, it seems). In

The new form of 'booking office': the Metrolink ticket machines at Navigation Road, 1992. *N. Dodson*

Metrolink tram crossing London Road at the entrance to Piccadilly Undercroft in 1992. *F.J. Dixon*

September 1992, GMPTE announced that new ticketing arrangements would be introduced to enable through booking from every BR station to every Metrolink station, and that, from May 1993, a page of information about Metrolink would appear in the BR national timetable.

Following the opening of the Piccadilly branch, the pattern of services changed. All trams now ran to Piccadilly station, except when the 'peak frequency' service was operating, when they alternated between 'Piccadilly' and 'Altrincham–Bury direct' services. This was not welcomed by those passengers who preferred the 'direct' G-Mex–Victoria route, nor by those who found themselves on a tram that was going the wrong way (for them). People changing trams at Piccadilly Gardens encountered problems, due to the number of passengers waiting on the platform, or due to the tannoy announcements (from the Metrolink Control Room) giving the wrong information about a tram, or due to disruptions of the service. And, given Manchester's climate, it is surprising that so little shelter is provided at Piccadilly Gardens, and at the other 'city street platforms'.

In July 1992, GMML announced that Metrolink was carrying 25,000 passengers a day. Helped by attractive fares after 9.30 am on working days, off-peak demand was greater than had been expected. On Saturdays, overtime working was required to provide a 'peak frequency' service of a tram every 6 minutes between about 10 am and about 4 pm; this was subsequently extended to run between about 9.30 am and about 5.30 pm. However, rush-hour usage was only building up slowly. There were fears that it would take a long time to win back commuters who made other travelling arrangements during the six month gap in MSJA services. Some 'replacement' bus services continued running, and were more convenient for some potential passengers; also, GMPTE bus and rail Travelcards were not valid on Metrolink, nor were certain other tickets.

Metrolink's first regular Sunday services began on 4th October, with trams running every half-hour from Piccadilly between 12.54 and 10.54 pm and from Altrincham between 1.25 and 11.25 pm. (Because of engineering work required on a bridge at Besses O'Th'Barn, Metrolink's Sunday service to Bury was not introduced until after the MSJA's Sunday service.) At the same time, following the withdrawal of GMPTE financial support for the BR Sunday service between Manchester and Altrincham, Altrincham became the Sunday terminus for the BR service to and from Chester via Northwich. For the benefit of BR passengers, who now had to use Metrolink for part of their journeys, BR tickets issued from Chester line stations became valid on Metrolink on Sundays, and BR's Manchester–Altrincham–Chester line timetable provided some information about Metrolink.

Because of high patronage of the 'off peak time' services, on 9th November, 1992, Metrolink started operating an all day 'peak frequency' service of a tram every 6 minutes between about 7.30 am and about 6.30 pm every weekday. 'Direct' services between Altrincham and Bury alternated with trams to Piccadilly during this period. (The 'off-peak' fare levels continued to apply after 9.30 am and at weekends, even when a 'peak frequency' service was operating.) At the same time, the Sunday service was much improved, to run between 7 am and 11 pm, with its frequency doubled to one every 15 minutes, with effect from 15th November.

In November 1992, Metrolink carried about 27,500 passengers per day, with more people travelling at 'off-peak times' than during the 'rush-hours'. Numbers increased considerably in December, when more than a million passengers were carried. On both Christmas Eve and Hogmanay, Bass Taverns sponsored an extension of the service, at reduced fares, after midnight. Apparently, these were very well patronised, with crowds of passengers cheering the trams into the stations.

By the beginning of February 1993, the GMML Chief Executive was talking in terms of Metrolink carrying over 10 million passengers in its first full year of operation, and of an operating profit of £1 million. The Altrincham Chamber of Commerce was reported to be delighted with the boost that Metrolink had given to local businesses, apparently more than counteracting the effects of a major recession. It is interesting to speculate how much of this was due to a 20 page booklet, entitled 'There's More To The Link Than You Think', produced by the GMML publicity department. This booklet described the delights to be found by alighting at each Metrolink station. Altrincham was said to be 'steeped in 700 years of history' and yet also 'right up to date with its wide choice of boutiques, bistros, restaurants and winebars' and a 'nationally acclaimed theatre'. The Chamber of Commerce, doubtless grateful for the booklet's picture of a smiling young couple 'Dining Out in Altrincham', was to sponsor a tram, which would (presumably) bring even more visitors to the town.

Shopping featured strongly in the list of attractions offered by the other stations along the line. The 'town' of Timperley, the booklet said, 'boasts a fine selection of shops and pubs', Sale has a 'thriving shopping area', and Stretford has an 'impressive Arndale Centre' [*sic*]. In contrast, Brooklands could only offer a pub and a barber's. The other attractions which, the copywriters hoped, would entice readers into sampling the delights of Metrolink included the bust of Dr James Prescott Joule (in Worthington Park, Sale) and the information that Frank Sidebottom lived in Timperley.

No doubt due to many people using it for shopping trips, or to get out of Timperley, Metrolink continued to carry more 'off-peak time' passengers than had been expected: almost 20,000 per day, on average. However, rush-hour usage, averaging around 9,500 per day, remained below target. It appeared that Metrolink had been able to attract many former bus users, but few car commuters. GMML admitted that many people considered that Metrolink's 'peak time' fares were too high, and it therefore reduced them (and the cost of its 'period passes') by 8 per cent from 26th April, 1993, with the aim of attracting more rush-hour passengers. At the same time, 'off-peak time' fares were increased by 8 per cent, because of the high usage. On the same day, coupled pairs of trams were introduced on a regular basis for some of the busiest services such as the 8.23 am Altrincham–Manchester. GMML also announced that, because some passengers had had problems with the single letter codes used for Metrolink's fare zones, the names of the stations would be used instead (e.g. beside the ticket machine buttons, and printed on the tickets).

The new BR national timetable introduced in May 1993 contained a page of information about Metrolink: a schematic route diagram, a summary of the service frequencies, and the times of departure and arrival of the first and last trams to and from Piccadilly, Altrincham and Bury. These suggested that a journey from Piccadilly (Undercroft) to Altrincham would normally take 26 minutes, but one should allow 28 minutes for the return trip. (Interestingly, the booked time for most BR services from Piccadilly to Altrincham (via Stockport) is also 26 minutes, but BR's scheduled time for Altrincham to Piccadilly is 31 minutes!) A journey from Victoria to Altrincham should take only 26 minutes by a direct service, and 40 minutes on a tram running via Piccadilly (Undercroft).

GMML has not published a detailed timetable, claiming that the frequency of the service makes one unnecessary. Hence, one must refer to the information displayed at each station to discover that the scheduled journey times to Altrincham are: 24 minutes from Piccadilly Gardens, 22 minutes from Mosley Street, 20 minutes from St Peter's Square, and 18 minutes from G-Mex. This last time appears better than the normal booked times of the former BR services to Altrincham from the adjacent Deansgate (formerly Knott Mill) station: the 'old' (1500v) electrics were timetabled to take 19 minutes, and the 'new' (25kv) electrics scheduled to take 21 minutes. Metrolink may be slightly faster than the old Altrincham electrics – the ride is certainly a lot bumpier!

Equipment and Further Details of Metrolink

The Metrolink trams are powered by an overhead 750v DC supply, from sub-stations at Altrincham, Timperley, Dane Road, Trafford Bar, G-Mex, and places on the Bury line. There are 26 trams (23 are required for the contracted peak level service of a tram every 5 minutes, and 20 are needed to run the current 6-minute peak service). They were built by Firema of Italy (with electrical equipment supplied by GEC Alsthom). They cost about £1 million each, are 29 metres long and weigh 45 tonnes when empty, 65 tonnes when full. Each consists of two halves joined by an articulation unit, and can negotiate 25 metre radius curves. Each tram has seating for 86 people and standing-room for at least 120 (the normally quoted carrying capacity of one tram is 206, but it is claimed that 'in high peak conditions' 270 people can be carried by one vehicle), and provision for wheelchairs, prams, etc. Each tram is powered by four 105 kW motors, and runs at up to 50 mph (80 km/hr) on the ex-BR lines, and at up to 30 mph (48 km/hr) in the city centre. The two outer bogies are powered (the third, under the articulation unit, is not), and the trams can be driven from either end and in either direction. Two trams can be coupled together and run as a single train, with a single driver. The driver can speak to the passengers over a public address system, and the passengers can contact the driver using an 'emergency call unit' or using low-level intercoms installed by the wheelchair etc. bays.

The trams have 'high' floors, for boarding from conventional platforms at the ex-BR stations. The Piccadilly Gardens station also has high platforms. However, the other city centre platforms are split-level, with a 'high' section,

Three views of Metrolink tram
running in Manchester's city centre i
1992. *Author's Collectio*

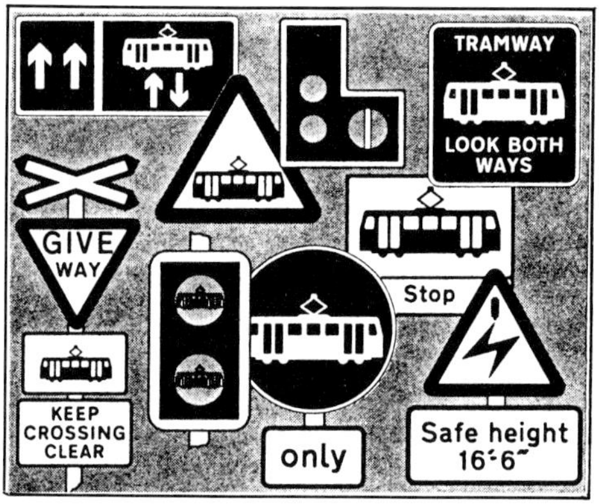

approached by ramps, towards one end, beside which the middle of the tram (or of the leading one of a coupled pair) stops, so that people in wheelchairs, with prams, etc. can board easily. The rest of the city centre platforms are at a lower level and there the trams automatically extend steps to help passengers climb aboard.

Each station has automatic ticket vending machines, which are connected to a computer system. The machines' tables of fares can be updated quickly by the computer system. The computer also receives reports from the machines, which are monitored from the Control Room (at the £8 million Operations and Maintenance centre, at Queens Road, Cheetham Hill, by the Bury line) in case problems arise (e.g. should a machine run out of change, or fail completely, or be 'molested'). It is the passenger's responsibility to obtain a ticket before boarding a tram; roving inspectors will check on this. (After a few months' operation it was reported that checks on 48,000 passengers had found only 0.6 per cent were 'fare evaders'.)

An optical fibre network links the Control Room with the stations, carrying speech, data and video signals. The controllers watch over the stations (which are unmanned) using closed-circuit television, can speak to passengers using the stations' public address systems, and can display messages on the computer screens which are installed at some of the main stations. Passengers can call the Control Room from the stations by pressing the 'passenger emergency call' buttons, which start a video recorder working. The controllers can also monitor the subways, tunnels, etc., using the closed-circuit television.

The system's electronics keep the Control Room informed of the location of each vehicle. The controller and the drivers can also radio each other. Hence, if problems arise, the controller can find out what has happened, where vehicles are, etc., and decide what to do. Should the city centre be blocked, the Altrincham line can be worked to the G-Mex station, with trams reversing there. Trams may also be turned at Timperley, or stabled in the siding there, and there is a trailing crossover at Old Trafford, for emergency use.

On the ex-BR lines, Metrolink's system will stop automatically any tram going through a red signal. In the city centre trams are driven 'on sight', with the driver in complete command, responding to other traffic and signals. Metrolink's electronics automatically inform the traffic lights that trams are approaching, to speed their flow through the streets. The city centre signals for Metrolink vehicles use a system of white bars to indicate 'stop' (horizontal), 'proceed' (vertical), 'proceed left' (inclined left), etc. The points at Piccadilly Gardens should change automatically as trams approach, according to their route codes, but it is apparently not unknown for the driver to have to get out to change the points manually, using an iron bar.

GMML has a Special Purpose Vehicle, which may be used for various engineering operations, and to 'rescue' broken down trams. This self-propelled unit has a hydraulic crane, a service deck which can carry up to 2 tonnes of equipment or materials, and a cab with seats for the driver plus a crew of three. The roof of the cab provides a platform for working on overhead wires and structures. The vehicle can bring with it a wagon carrying up to 10 tonnes of additional materials and equipment; it can also be coupled to a failed tram in order to haul it back to the Operations and Maintenance Centre for repairs.

Metrolink has roughly 200 staff, including about 60 drivers and some 20 Customer Service Inspectors (who check tickets and answer queries), plus people working on vehicle maintenance, track, signalling, office staff; etc. Most of the staff had not previously worked on the railways (for example, many were former bus drivers). The Brussels Public Transport Authority provided training for some of them, who then trained others. All operations staff, including the Operations Director, were trained as drivers, so that they would understand the equipment that they were dealing with and to provide a pool of 'reserve' drivers in case a shortage of regular drivers arose. Before Metrolink's public services started, a great deal of practice running was done on the Bury line, including running the full timetabled service, and simulating various incidents (e.g. breakdowns) to check that the system's procedures could cope with them. In February 1992, the Prime Minister, visiting the area shortly before announcing the date of the General Election, had a go at being a driver.

In the first of GMML's 'sponsorship' deals, tram number 1002 was named 'Manchester Arndale Voyager' (admittedly, not quite as bad as Harvey Smith's renaming a horse as 'Sanyo Music Centre') and put on display at the G-Mex station for the 'Light Rail '91' exhibition in November 1991. A number of other businesses subsequently entered into sponsorship arrangements with Metrolink. Also, one tram was later named 'Christie Metro Challenger', after the hospital was adopted as Metrolink's official charity.

* * * * *

Metrolink's trams run off an overhead 750v DC supply, so three different voltages have now been used for passenger services on the MSJA: 1500v DC, 25,000v ac and now 750v DC. This might be another MSJA 'claim to fame' – few lines have had three different overhead power systems; and fewer have had different systems operating at the same time on different parts of the line.

I have already said that I was wrong when, in 1972, I wrote 'This is a convenient place to end the MSJA's history.' No doubt it would be just as wrong to say the story ends here: who knows what the future will bring? The MSJA's 150th anniversary is in 1999, and what then? Manchester an Olympic city? Altrincham FC in the English Football League? Electrification to Hale? One dare not guess.

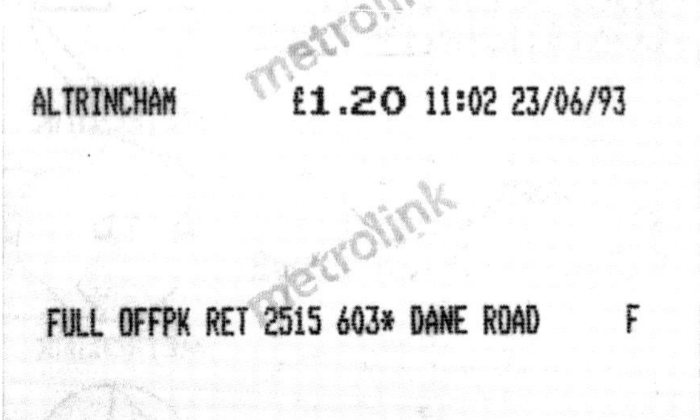

metrolink
ALTRINCHAM £1.20 11:02 23/06/93
metrolink
FULL OFFPK RET 2515 603* DANE ROAD F

Metrolink's second type of ticket: from Altrincham to Dane Road (which is in 'Zone F') and back again.

Chapter Eighteen

Signalling

(Information from Mr G.H. Platt and Mr A.D. Macfarlane)

What the earliest signals were like does not appear to be known, but it is almost certain that they would follow the contemporary practice of the MSL. The line appears to have been re-signalled with Saxby & Farmer equipment during the late 1870s, as the signal boxes known to be of this date were typical of this firm's products and contained their well-known rocker or 'grid-iron' locking frames. One of these boxes, Navigation Road, survived until 1991, with a later frame. Some of the original Saxby frames remained in use until quite recent years, the one at Brooklands only being taken out at the end of mechanical signalling in February 1971. This and the one removed from Deansgate Junction when the box was replaced in 1957 have been preserved, the latter in the Museum of British Transport. Signals of this period are visible in a photograph of the Old Trafford accident in 1889.

Later signalling work was carried out with the owning companies' equipment and by 1930 nearly all the signals were of the familiar LNW type (though some had mixed fittings) with a sprinkling of earlier survivors. Conversely, the majority of the signal boxes were of GC pattern, built by the Railway Signal Co.

When the line was electrified in 1930–31, many of the signals had to be resited before the overhead structures and wiring could be erected. This was especially the case between London Road and Knott Mill, where most of the signals were on gantries spanning the track. Oxford Road East signal box, which was similarly situated, was also removed and the whole of the station worked from the West box. The new signals were naturally of upper quadrant type, in the early LMS style, and some of them had very short arms and Corning-Adlake-Lebby electric lamps which were kept permanently lit, being in effect mechanical colour-light signals. One or two of the LNW signals managed to survive, however, right to the end of mechanical signalling. Perhaps the most notable of these was the tall 3-doll bracket signal at Old Trafford Junction.

In its earliest days the MSJA was worked on the time interval system, like other lines. The electric telegraph was introduced in 1855, making for much safer working. Subsequently the two portions of the line were worked in a different manner. On the South Junction the time interval system was retained with an important modification. If by the specified time after the last train had entered the section, the 'all clear' had not been received from the next box, then the following train would be allowed into the occupied section under caution. On the Altrincham branch a permissive block system was in use, any number of trains being allowed to enter the section, provided they were cautioned. This was an improvement, but the MSJA's signalling system was still far from perfect. After a collision by the site of the Agricultural Exhibition, on 16th July, 1869, between an LNW Lymm train and an MSL cattle train, the Board of Trade recommended, in its report, that the MSJA be worked on the absolute block system. The recommendation was accepted and the block system was brought into use on the Altrincham branch in 1870 and on the South Junction line in 1874. Just what type of

Warwick Road, up fast line home junction signal on 29th January, 1949. *J.D. Darby*

Warwick Road, up fast line starting signal, 29th January, 1949. *J.D. Darby*

Timperley station, up home and repeater, 27th March, 1952. *R.E. Gee*

Top left: Oxford Road, up starting signal, 9th September, 1958. *Top right*: Signals and signal box at London Road looking towards Stockport on 2nd July, 1956. *Bottom left*: Stretford station, up fast starting signal, 18th September, 1960. *Bottom right*: Stretford station, up slow home and the down slow signals mounted on the same post. *R.E. Gee*

Top left: London Road MSJA signal box, 1958. *Top right*: Altrincham South signal box, 1956. *Bottom*: Timperley Junction signal box, with signalman G. Jackson in charge, 1952.

R.E. Gee

instruments and working was employed at first does not seem to be recorded, but as with the signals, by the 1920s block working followed LNW rules and most of the instruments were of the LNW pattern.

The two terminal platforms at Altrincham were both worked as *down* lines between the North and South boxes, each with its own block instrument. Electric trains were offered to and accepted by the South box in the ordinary way, given 'on line', and then when they started back for Manchester, and the line was again clear, they were simply cancelled! A train which went into the sheds was signalled through and given 'out of section' in the ordinary way by the South box. The complication came when a train came out of the sheds and entered the platform at the South box. This was treated as a wrong direction movement and signalled on the block instruments accordingly.

With the closure of Manchester Central station in 1969, multiple aspect colour-light signalling, controlled from the panel at London Road, was brought into use over the northern end of the line as far as Warwick Road, and in February 1971 this was extended to Deansgate Junction. From there to Altrincham the mechanical boxes were retained on account of the level crossings, but they operated colour-light signals, and the line was track-circuited throughout. Absolute block working was retained between Deansgate Junction and Altrincham, including separate block instruments for the loop lines between Navigation Road and Altrincham North.

The road level crossing at Altrincham was taken out of use in October 1978, along with the (often ignored) road traffic lights, which were controlled from lever number 72 in the adjacent Altrincham North signal box. The pedestrian wicket gates were retained.

The signal boxes at Ordsall Lane were 'abolished', along with their semaphore signals, on 18th October, 1978. Control of the Ordsall Lane area passed to Deal Street signal box (situated between Salford and Victoria) and full track circuit block working was brought into use between London Road and Eccles (and hence over the whole South Junction line). Prior to this date, London Road box had used traditional bell codes for train description to Ordsall Lane No. 1 box.

The level crossing gates at Navigation Road and at Deansgate Lane were replaced by continental-style lifting barriers, with yellow and red warning lights, in the early 1980s.

As part of the resignalling associated with the opening of the Windsor Link, London Road signal box was taken out of use on 16th October, 1988, to be replaced by a new signalling centre situated in a tower block adjacent to Piccadilly station. The new box, known as 'Manchester Piccadilly', inherited control of the Altrincham branch as far as Deansgate Junction. All of the four-aspect colour light signals on the Altrincham branch which had been controlled from London Road were dutifully replated with an 'MP' prefix (instead of 'LR'). The new signalling centre also inherited control over the South Junction line and the ex-L&M to Eccles. Its area was extended over the Windsor Link towards Wigan (to Walkden and, via Lostock Junction, to Crow Nest Junction near Hindley), to Blackrod (between Bolton and Preston) and to Bromley Cross (between Bolton and Blackburn).

In preparation for Metrolink, the line between Deansgate Junction and Altrincham was remodelled and resignalled in July 1991. Altrincham North and Navigation Road signal boxes closed after the last train on Saturday 6th July, ending absolute block working on the MSJA. (That day's train service had been severely disrupted due to an electrical storm – 'the gods were angry' . . .!). The 72-lever LNW lever frame at Altrincham North survived to the end, as did the LNW pattern block instruments (which were placed in store for possible use in the Stockport area). The southern end of Deansgate Junction signal box was extended to accommodate a new control panel which was installed to control the new layout. The new control panel is a conventional one which interfaces with a solid-state interlocking system, the first of its type in the North West of England. Deansgate Junction signal box controls the level crossing at Navigation Road (and that at Hale), with closed-circuit television monitoring.

The resignalling removed the last semaphore signals at Altrincham (the platform 4 starter, with Hale's distant beneath it, and the up outer home) and 3- and 4-aspect colour-lights were installed on the BR lines. Two-aspect colour-lights were installed on what became the Metrolink lines. The BR lines between Altrincham and Navigation Road are bi-directionally signalled in the northbound direction, and the parallel Metrolink lines are bi-directionally signalled in a southbound direction. A tram can therefore leave Navigation Road on the 'wrong' line and run straight into platform 1 at Altrincham. Metrolink's single track between Navigation Road and Deansgate Junction is signalled for working in either direction, as is the parallel BR single track line.

Between 22nd July, 1991 and Christmas Eve, south of Timperley, the BR electric trains obeyed the new signals which had been installed for Metrolink. Following the withdrawal of the BR electric service, new 2-aspect colour-light signals for Metrolink were installed from Timperley northwards, and the BR 4-aspect signals removed. The Metrolink line north of Deansgate Junction is controlled by the Metrolink Operations Centre at Queens Road, Manchester. Fixed signals are provided as far as G-Mex. Driving in the city centre is 'on sight', although special tram signals are provided at traffic lights and at junctions.

The Manchester Piccadilly signalling centre controls the MSJA between Piccadilly and Cornbrook (where a junction was retained to give access to the turnback siding on a stretch of line towards Altrincham), and the line to Ordsall Lane. However, it is planned that a new Integrated Electronic Control Centre, to be located at Ardwick, will eventually control all BR lines in the Greater Manchester area.

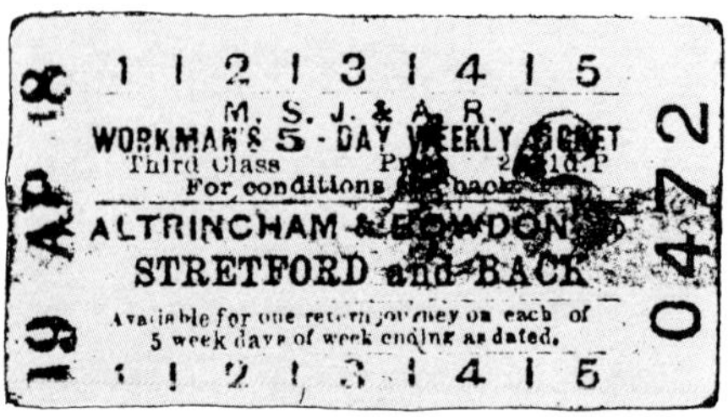

Chapter Nineteen

Goods Traffic

There were three main 'routes' using the MSJA. First, the South Junction line, which has always been heavily-used and is still an important east–west link; for example, freightliners rumble through Oxford Road on their way to the Trafford Park depot. The Gaythorn gas-works (which was a little to the west of Oxford Road station) used to be connected to the MSJA by a short length of line from the sidings at Oxford Road on a viaduct into the retort house, and was served by trains over the South Junction line which would drop off wagons at Oxford Road.

Second, there was the CLC traffic over the south end of the line (Deansgate Junction to Altrincham) which consisted of a fair amount of through goods traffic, such as the limestone trains from the Peak District to ICI near Northwich, which still run.

Third, there was the traffic over all or most of the Altrincham branch. There was a small amount of traffic from the Lymm line into Manchester and some off the CLC into Central. There was also the 'Ardwick goods' which served the stations on the Altrincham branch, running twice a day (morning and evening) from Ardwick to Altrincham and back, picking up and dropping off stuff at the stations along the line. There was also a morning milk-train from the lush Cheshire pastures served by the CLC which ran to Central, dropping trucks off at the major MSJA stations. At the time, Old Trafford was the distribution centre for much of south Manchester, and its morning milk was delivered by the milk-train stopping on the slow lines south of the station, detaching the trucks, backing them onto the down slow line, and moving off; the trucks trundling into the dock. When Altrincham boasted an abattoir, every Tuesday a cattle-train was run from Cross Lane cattle-markets to Altrincham. When Altrincham had its Altrincham Show, special trains would run bringing the cattle, from up and down the country. And, of course, there was always the coal and coke for the people and the gasworks.

Now, none of the MSJA stations has any form of goods yard and all the goods traffic of the third kind is gone.

The South Junction line at London Road with a freight train trundling through, hauled by a LNW Webb class '1P' 2–4–2T No. 6611. *H.C. Casserley*

Extract from the Shunting Engine and Local Trip notice – Manchester Divisional Manager's Area. 3rd October, 1966, until further notice.

T.48 Altrincham Trip Class 5 MT.

	arr.	SX	dep.	
Trafford Park M.P.D.			08.45	LE
Trafford Park Sidings	08.55		09.12	A
Cornbrook W. Junction	09.22		09.32	
Warwick Road	09.40		09.45	
Stretford	09.50		10.50	B
Warwick Road	10.55		11.00	
Sale	11.15		12.25	C
Altrincham	12.40		14.42	
Warwick Road	15.00		15.18	D
Cornbrook West	15.25		...	
Cornbrook Coal Yard	15.30	E	15.35	LE
Trafford Park M.P.D.	15.45			

A –*Marshalled*
Brakevan
1. Altrincham
2. Sale
Brakevan.
3. Stretford
Train engine.

At Stretford detach 3 and shunt.
At Sale detach 2 and shunt.

B –Take empties to Warwick Road.
C –Take empties to Altrincham for return working.
D –Attach Stretford empties.
E –Detach empties.

The LMR Working Timetable for the period 30th September, 1991 to 10th May, 1992 shows the position for freight services 'of a stable and regular nature' (i.e. the traffic was sufficiently stable and regular to warrant inclusion in the Working Timetable): 188 such freight trains were using some part of the MSJA each week.

Most ran over the section between Cornbrook Junction and Piccadilly, with 112 services timetabled (59 eastbound and 53 westbound). Most of these were Freightliners, linking the Freightliner terminal at Trafford Park with a variety of places, such as Felixstowe, Garston, Southampton and Stratford (in East London). In total, there were 74 Freightliner trains each week: 37 each way. The remaining freight services over the Cornbrook–Piccadilly stretch included five pet food trains per week from Melton Mowbray, plus return workings. (Unfortunately, this traffic was transferred to road at the end of 1992, apparently because of the cost of repairing or replacing the non-standard 'curtain-sided' containers used.) There were also five petrochemicals trains serving Glazebrook, plus return workings, plus others.

Between Deansgate Junction and Altrincham there were 76 freight trains timetabled per week (38 each way). Just over half were limestone trains, with three timetabled to run every day (including Sundays) from Tunstead sidings (near Buxton) to Oakleigh sidings (near Northwich), 'moving Derbyshire into Cheshire', as a freight manager once described his area's work. This traffic involves 21 workings each way each week. The hopper waggons used are, apparently, among the oldest vehicles running regularly on BR, having been built between 1938 and 1953. There was also a daily (except Sundays) rubbish train from Northenden Refuse Transfer Station to Appley Bridge (near Wigan), which ran via Northwich and Hartford Junction, again plus return workings. The remaining freight trains were involved in a number of through freight services, including a couple serving the petrochemical industry at Partington (these stopped at Skelton Junction for the locomotive to run round its train).

There were no services timetabled over the main part of the Altrincham branch (Deansgate Junction to Cornbrook) nor over the part of the South Junction line between Castlefield Junction and Ordsall Lane.

Class '47' No. 47438 heads a Tunstead to Oakleigh load of crushed limestone for ICI, seen here approaching Altrincham on 20th September, 1990. *B. Avery*

Chapter Twenty

Preservation

The Altrincham Electric Railway Preservation Society (AERPS) was formed in June 1970 to raise money to preserve one of the 1500v electric trains. Ultimately, only two trailer coaches (MSJA Nos. 117 and 121) were secured. They were taken to the Yorkshire Dales Railway (now the Embsay Steam Railway), a preserved line at Embsay near Skipton. There, hauled by steam engines, they carried passengers for a time. In 1983 they were moved to the Midland Railway Centre, at Butterley (near Alfreton and Ripley, between Nottingham and Chesterfield), where they are now kept under cover, and restoration work has much better prospects. At Butterley they joined a third trailer coach (MSJA No. 114), which had been preserved by the Midland Railway Project Group (now the Midland Railway Trust).

Another coach which saw service on the MSJA and has been preserved is an MSL 6-wheeler (No. 946). This was built at Gorton in 1888, and is preserved at the Buckinghamshire Railway Centre.

The AERPS has also preserved a number of MSJA 'railway relics', such as the illuminated track diagram board from Altrincham North signal box. The AERPS tried to have Altrincham North and Navigation Road signal boxes (along with other historical structures on the MSJA) listed by the Department of the Environment, but the request was turned down on the grounds that none of the structures was 'sufficiently unique'.

Manchester University Mechanical Engineering Department obtained the frame from Mersey Bridge signal box, together with semaphore signals from Altrincham station, one of which, the old 'starter' from platform 2, was an ex-LNW lower quadrant.

At Altrincham station in 1971, in the week following the introduction of the 'new' electrics to Crewe, BR sold £800 worth of old tickets, station signs, timetables, and various other 'relics' – so souvenirs are doubtless in many hands (including, for example, a Dane Road station totem preserved in British Columbia!). BR also produced a third MSJA souvenir booklet, with a print run of 500 copies.

Yorkshire Dales Railway 0–4–0ST *Fred* (ex-ICI at Dunstead) seen here with ex-MSJA coach No. 29670 at Embsay depot in 1972. *N. Dodson*

Appendix One

Acts of Parliament concerning the MSJA

Besides the following Acts, other Acts such as that of the Warrington & Altrincham Railway (3rd July, 1851) concern the MSJA inasmuch as they authorise connections with the MSJA; however these are too numerous to include. The date given is the date the Act received the Royal Assent.

Act of Incorporation, 21st July, 1845, 8 & 9 Vic. cap. cxi

The MSJA to be 'a Body Corporate, with Perpetual Succession and a Common Seal, and by that Name shall and may sue and be sued and also shall have Power and Authority to purchase, hold and sell lands . . . for the purposes of the said undertaking . . . and exercise such Powers and Authorities as are hereafter given or mentioned'.

Authorised capital was £400,000 of which the M&B and SA&M each supplied £175,000 and Lord Ellesmere the remaining £50,000. The MSJA could borrow up to £133,333 provided at least half the authorised capital had been paid up.

As a private company the MSJA did not have to hold meetings or declare dividends. Its accounts were to be kept half-yearly and were to be open to inspection by any of the owners. The dividends were paid half-yearly, the profits being split in proportion to the owners' investments. In the event of there not being sufficient profits to cover a 4 per cent return on investment, then the balance was to be made up by the M&B and the SA&M in proportions based on the revenues accruing to them from traffic between their systems and the MSJA; for which purposes they had to keep records of such traffic, these records being open to inspection. Thus Lord Ellesmere was guaranteed an 8 per cent p.a. return. The MSJA was to be run by a Board of Directors, three nominated by each owner. The MSJA was empowered to buy the necessary lands; however the Compulsory Purchase powers would lapse after three years. The MSJA had to be built within 5 years or the building powers would lapse.

The MSJA could be leased to either the M&B or the SA&M; provided that no such lease be granted to any parties interested in lines forming extensions of the MSJA south or west of Altrincham without the unanimous approval of the MSJA's Directors.

The MSJA to bear the costs of communication (altering track layout, etc.) with the L&M at Ordsall Lane.

Consideration to be given to a line connecting the MSJA and the Manchester, Bolton and Bury at New Bailey Street; and an application for an Act for this line to be in within two years. Various other general clauses covered maximum charges, etc.

LNW Act, 2nd July, 1847, 10 & 11 Vic. cap. lxxiii

Authorised the LNW to buy Lord Ellesmere's shares; the MSL had a month to decide whether it wished to participate in the purchase – during that month the LNW could not buy the shares without MSL permission.

If and when the MSL participated in the purchase it had to pay the LNW half the cost of getting this Act. Subsequently, Lord Ellesmere's Directors to be removed from the Board and each owner to provide the Chairman for Board meetings from its Directors at alternate meetings. The Chairman to have a casting-vote.

Act of 22nd July, 1848, 11 & 12 Vic. cap. lviii

Authorised capital increased by £250,000 to £650,000 and maximum borrowing allowed increased by £83,333 to £216,666; none of this extra borrowing could be used, however, until at least half the total authorised capital had been paid up. Each owner to provide half of the increase in capital.

Compulsory Purchase (C.P.) powers of 1845 Act extended by three years.

Various modifications to original plan of line authorised, together with necessary C.P. powers, etc. The work involved to be completed within five years or powers lapse.

Act of 23rd July, 1858, 21 & 22 Vic. cap. cxxxvi

The two owners to find an acceptable Arbitrator to attend MSJA Board meetings, where necessary, in order that contentious issues be speedily settled. In the event of disagreement (three Directors saying 'aye' and three saying 'nay') the Arbitrator's decision is final, and is entered in the minutes as if passed by a majority vote of the Directors.

Stockport, Timperley & Altrincham Junction Act 1861
Great Northern Act 1863
Midland Act 1865

The first of these gave the LNW, MSL and Cheshire Lines various running powers over the MSJA; the second gave the Great Northern the same; and the third the Midland. In all cases, the running company paid the MSJA a proportion of receipts based on the ratio of the mileage over MSJA to the mileage of the whole journey, after deduction of 20 per cent for terminal and haulage costs.

Incidentally, the GN Act also informs us that the Cheshire Midland terminated 'in the township of Witton-cum-Twambrooks in the parish of Great Budworth'.

MSL Act, 6th August, 1872, 35, 36 Vic. cap. clxxviii

The MSL was authorised to subscribe up to £50,000 more capital to the MSJA, thus increasing the authorised capital to £700,000. The MSL got the extra dividends, etc., that an increased stake implies; however, it did not obtain a controlling interest; it still had three Directors out of six and the Arbitrator still held the casting vote.

LNW Act, 30th July, 1874, 37, 38 Vic. cap. clix

The LNW could subscribe up to £50,000 more capital to the MSJA, increasing the authorised capital to £750,000. The LNW got more dividends, but no more votes.

LNW Act, 19th July, 1875, 38, 39 Vic. cap. cliii

LNW and MSL could divide amongst themselves, in proportions to be agreed upon, the MSJA's mortgage debts and borrowing powers and could use these as they saw fit, provided the total sums borrowed by the companies in this way when added to the MSJA's outstanding debts did not exceed the maximum allowed MSJA borrowing powers (£216,666).

Empowered improvement of the LNW approaches to London Road main line station. This involved the closure of a street and its replacement by a new street which had to underbridge the MSJA viaduct. The LNW to pay for this underbridging, and also to compensate the MSJA for delays, etc., to traffic resulting from the work authorised by this Act. If, at a later date, the MSJA viaduct were quadrupled; the LNW would have to pay the MSJA half the cost of the bridge required to carry the extra tracks over the new street.

MSL Act, 4th July, 1878, 41, 42 Vic. cap. xxx

MSJA authorised capital increased by £60,000 to £810,000; each owner to supply half.

Empowered rebuilding of MSJA platforms at London Road and modifying the track layout.

C.P. powers, lasting three years, for land south-west of Old Trafford station, north-east of Sale station and between Altrincham and Bowdon stations (site of the new A&B station).

MSL Act, 21st July, 1879, 42, 43 Vic. cap. cli

C.P. powers, lasting three years, for more land in Altrincham.

LNW Act, 3rd July, 1882, 45, 46 Vic. cap. lxxxviii

Empowered LNW modifications to Ordsall Lane station and to the MSJA between the junction with the ex-L&M and the east end of the Irwell bridge; all in all 275 yds of MSJA affected. On completion of the work, the 225-or-so yards of MSJA between the L&M junction and the west end of the Irwell bridge would be transferred to the LNW, the MSL getting running powers. The LNW to compensate the MSJA for inconveniences caused by these works.

LNW Act, 28th July, 1884, 47, 48 Vic. cap. ccvii

C.P. powers for land by London Road, Knott Mill, Navigation Road and Altrincham stations. C.P. powers to lapse after three years.

LNW Act, 16th July, 1885, 48, 49 Vic. cap. lxxxviii

Increased authorised MSJA capital by £50,000 to £860,000, each owner providing half.

MSL Act, 21st July, 1891, 54, 55 Vic. cap. cxiv

(a) Empowered building a 4 furlong link between the MSJA north of Old Trafford and the CLC line to Chorlton, driving a new tunnel under Chester Road at Old Trafford.

(b) C.P. powers for land at Knott Mill, needed for rebuilding of station there.

(c) Empowered widening the line between Warwick Road station and Timperley Junction, together with all necessary alterations to stations, platforms, sidings, approach roads, track, etc., etc., necessitated by (a), (b) and (c).

(d) Increased MSJA authorised capital by £200,000 to £1,060,000, each owner to provide half.

C.P. powers to lapse after three years.

The powers for the new railway and the widening to lapse after five years.

MSJA to make good any damage caused to anybody by these works.

MSL Act, 20th July, 1894, 57, 58 Vic. cap. lxxxi

Extended the time for the completion of the C.P. of land for (a) and (c) in the 1891 Act by two years. Confirmed purchase of certain land at Altrincham.

MSL Act, 7th August, 1896, 59, 60 Vic. cap. ccvii

C.P. of land near Sale; C.P. powers to lapse after three years.

Time-limit for completion of 1891-authorised widening extended by two years.

GC Act, 12th August, 1898, 61, 62 Vic. cap. ccliii

Deadline for completion of 1891-widening extended by three years.

MSJA might hold/sell superfluous lands adjoining the railway for 10 years; and might hold/sell superfluous lands not adjoining the railway for three years.

MSJA may C.P. land near Knott Mill.

LNW Act, 6th August, 1900, 63, 64 Vic. cap. ccliii

Authorised LNW building a footbridge from MSJA London Road platforms to Mayfield.

GC Act, 26th July, 1901, 1 Edw. cap. cvi

Deadline for completion of 1891-widening extended by three years.

More land adjoining the line could be held or sold for 10 years; not adjoining the line, for three years.

GC Act, 22nd July, 1904, 4 Edw. cap. xcvi
Extended time for completion of 1891-widening by two years.
C.P. powers, lapsing after three years, for land between Warwick Road and Old Trafford and south of Stretford station.
MSJA may hold/sell superfluous lands not adjoining line for a further three years.

GC Act, 4th August, 1905, 5 Edw. cap. clxxvii
C.P. powers, lasting three years, for land south of Warwick Road station.
MSJA incorporated into the LNW&GC Joint Committee together with the other joint LNW and GC properties. Henceforth there is no raising of capital specifically for the MSJA.

GC Act, 26th July, 1907, 7 Edw. cap. lxxviii and *GC Act, 16th August, 1909, 9 Edw. cap. lxxv* gave the MSJA further hold/sell powers.

LMS Act, 1st August, 1924, 14, 15 Geo. V. cap. liv
Vested the LNW&GC Joint Committee in the LMS-LNE Joint Committee.

Manchester, South Junction, and Altrincham Railway.
(B 23—1/93)
No. 202
Oxford Road Station, Manchester.
EXCESS LUGGAGE TICKET.
Received from Passenger £ : for Excess
Luggage to ______ on the ______ Ry.
per ______ Train. Date ______ 189__
Gross Weight ______ lbs.
Allowance for ______ Cl. Passenger ______ lbs.
Weight Chargeable ______ lbs. @ ______ per lb.
Clerk's Signature ______

Appendix Two

Opening Statistics

Fares Altrincham to Manchester: 6*d*. third class; 8*d*. second; 10*d*. first; 1*s*. express.

Passengers had to be at the principal station (Altrincham or Manchester) five minutes before the booked time of departure; and at intermediate stations 10 minutes before the train left. They could not be re-booked by the same train. Children under 3 travelled free; and those under 10 travelled half-fare. Luggage allowances: first and second class 100 lb. free; third class 56 lb.

The original staffing was: 8 station masters (one per station); 2 level-crossing gatemen; 5 pointsmen, 3 guards, 3 policemen, 1 carriage-cleaner; 1 inspector; 1 secretary/manager (James Kirkman who worked at Oxford Road, the line's HQ) and 13 porters (one of whom, R. Wardleworth, rose to be Sale station master, a position he held till he retired in 1903 with a £1/week pension from the MSJA). There were no engine drivers; these were provided, together with their engines, by the MSL. At that time signalmen had not been invented; when introduced, their numbers rose rapidly: in 1869 there were 13 of them; by 1899 this had grown to 57.

After 10 years' operations, the original staff of 37 had risen to 122, according to a Board of Trade Return of the numbers employed as at 30th June, 1859. The survey showed: 1 secretary/manager; 1 engineer; 1 station master, 2 ticket collectors; 27 clerks; 1 foreman; 4 engine drivers; 4 assistant engine drivers/firemen; 4 guards ('breaksmen'); 1 'artificer'; 8 'switchmen'; 3 gatekeepers; 1 policeman or watchman; 27 porters or messengers; 17 platelayers and 20 labourers.

Construction Costs:

Construction	£313,000
Land & Property	£200,000
Plant	£ 34,000
Law Charges	£ 14,000
Engineers' charges	£ 11,000
Parliamentary expenses	£ 3,000
	£575,000

Statistics Jan.–Dec. 1850 (first full year of operation):

Passengers booked	639,000	Passenger receipts	£19,227
Goods over line	114,600 tons	Merchandise receipts	£ 516
Season-ticket holders*	176	Parcels receipts	£ 335
PROFIT	£9,600		

* First and second class only. Third class not introduced until 1st January, 1883.

Appendix Three

Motive Power 1849–1931

For the first year or so tender engines, supplied by the LNW and MSL, were used.

October 1849 It was agreed that the MSL would provide engines and drivers, for a hire charge of 9*d*. per engine-mile; each engine to do at least 100 miles/day.

1850–early 1860s 2–2–2 WTs, MSL Nos. 72, 73 and 78, built 1849–1850, worked the line. In 1856 they were augmented by some 1840s-built Sharp 2–2–2s which had been turned into tank engines. They were phased out in the 1860s.

1860s–1880s 2–4–0 WTs, built by the MSL between 1860 and 1866, replaced the 2–2–2s in the early 1860s. The following MSL Numbers were used at some time or other: 9, 12, 20, 23, 24, 123* and 208, 209, 210, 211.

1882–1900s 2–4–0T engines, class '12AT', built by the MSL in 1881, were introduced onto the line in spring 1882, when the hiring charge was increased to 10*d*./mile, enabling the WTs to be withdrawn. Most of the class were used at some time and Nos. 23, 24† and 447, 448, 449, 450, 452 were known to have been at Altrincham. Incidentally, 'AT' stands for 'Altrincham Tank'.

1900–1931 In July 1899, with the pressing needs of its London branch the MSL, now the GC, was short of engines and agreed with the LNW to withdraw four of the GC tank engines, the LNW providing four 2–4–2 tanks in their place. Subsequently an agreement was reached whereby each company provided half the engines required.

Notes by Dudley Whitworth

The MSL's contribution, beside the 'AT' class tank engines, were 2–4–2 tanks of both classes, though the earlier class '3' were able to hold their own against other types right up to electrification. By the mid-1900s the 'AT' class had vanished and though one or two of the 776–785 batch made their appearance, by the end of World War I numbers 578, 590, 591, 593, 597, 599 and 600 were frequently performing from Altrincham shed. The number of engines from each company had by now increased to five and the LNW were using 4 ft 3 in. 0–6–2 'Coal Tank' engines, their numbers being 11, 443, 629, 766, 926, 1050, 2361, 2458, 3447, 3717 and 3770, and LMS numbers 7592, 7672, 7751, 7757 and 7777.

With the accelerated services of the summer of 1927, it was found that the 'Coal Tanks' were a little over-loaded with the trains of seven or eight bogies on the tight timings between the very close stations and in July–August, four of the North Staffordshire Railway's new 'L'-class 0–6–2 tanks were brought to Altrincham from six specially allocated to Longsight, LMS Nos. 2261–2266.

On odd occasions an 18 in. 0–6–2T of the LNW found its way to Altrincham, Nos. 115 (LNW) and 6919 (LMS) being brief visitors. In 1928, two of Longsight's LNW 4–6–2 superheated tanks Nos. 6977 and 6978 took their share of the turns. Though quite adequate for all the work they were called on to do, their drawback was that the superheater was practically useless, having been designed for fast main line work, and therefore barely getting going when they reached the end of their run.

The occasional 4–4–2 'Precursor' tank made an appearance but this was probably an emergency when Longsight could not lay hands on one of the usual types. In the first week of May 1930, Longsight received an allocation of seven Fowler 2–6–2 tanks, new ex-Derby works, Nos. 15505–15511, and four were sent to Altrincham shed, working the line until electrification. One 'Knotty' 0–6–2T, No. 2265, was kept at Altrincham to work the morning 'Ardwick Goods' because of a so-called 'tight' place by the Altrincham goods shed which the outside cylinder Derby 2–6–2T were supposed to foul.

---

* These were the second MSL engines to have these numbers.

† These were the third MSL engines to have these numbers, i.e. the 23, 24 here are *not* the same engines as the 23, 24 in the previous section which had been scrapped and their numbers passed on.

Appendix Four

Rolling Stock 1849–1931

As with the engines, the agreement of October 1849 provided for the MSL to supply the coaching stock. The rental charged per annum was 12⅓ per cent of the cost price for coaches and 15 per cent for guards' vans. This lasted until the MSJA started buying its own stock by tender from its owners; after which the LNW took more of an interest in supplying stock. From 1849 to the middle of the 1910s 4-wheeled coaches were in use on the MSJA, mostly provided and built by the MSL.

In 1875 the Smith vacuum brake was fitted to all trains.

In 1876 the first 6-wheelers were introduced to the MSJA: two built by the LNW at Wolverton. Over the next 25 years the MSL built several dozen 6-wheelers at Gorton. As these were brought into service on the MSJA the old 4-wheelers were phased out. By 1899 the standard MSJA train was twelve 6-wheelers seating 400 people, steam-heated and lit by Coligny gas-burners with gas supplied from collapsible reservoirs in the guard's van and in the middle of the train. The coaches were finished in varnished mahogany and embellished with the MSJA crest. At peak hours and such like, the 4-wheelers were brought into service.

In 1905 the LNW built the MSJA's first bogie coaches – two 8-car sets – which were soon introduced onto the line. By 1913, 35 more bogie coaches had been built and the 4-wheelers had vanished. With the introduction of the bogies the standard train became a 7-car bogie set seating 488, electrically lit and steam heated. When necessary these were strengthened by adding 6-wheelers as required.

The 1931 coaching stock was: about 25 'rather spartan' 6-wheelers of which the oldest were Nos. 107, 108 built by the LNW at Wolverton in 1876; the rest built by MSL at Gorton 1885–1901; two 8-car bogie sets built by the LNW at Wolverton in 1905; five 7-car bogie sets of which two were built by LNW at Wolverton in 1911, and the other three built by MSL at Dukinfield in 1915. After electrification the bogies were sold to the CLC and became CLC Nos. 621–628, 631–638, 641–647, 651–657, 661–667, 671–677, 681–687.

A steam service on the line just before electrification. *Courtesy D. Rendell*

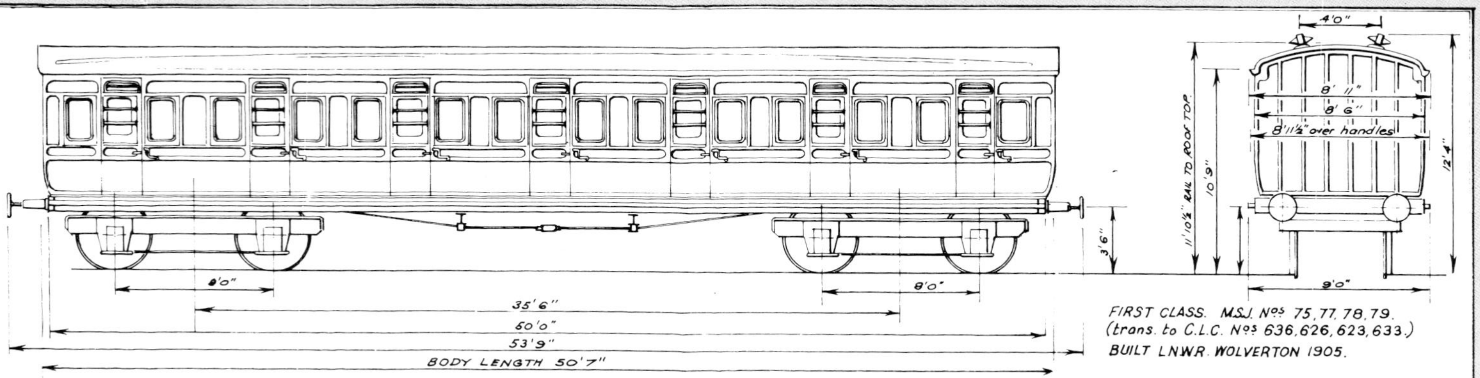

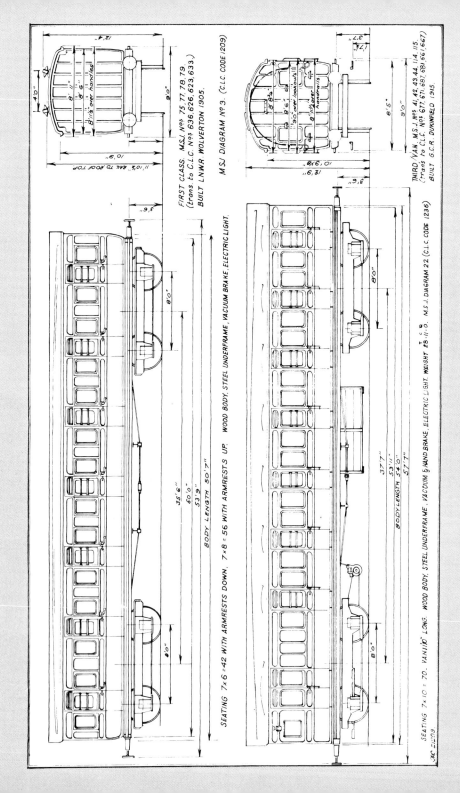

FIRST CLASS. M.S.J. Nos 75, 77, 78, 79.
(trans. to C.L.C. Nos 636, 626, 623, 633.)
BUILT L.N.W.R. WOLVERTON 1905.

SEATING 7×6 = 42 WITH ARMRESTS DOWN, 7×8 = 56 WITH ARMRESTS UP. WOOD BODY, STEEL UNDERFRAME, VACUUM BRAKE, ELECTRIC LIGHT.

MSJ DIAGRAM No 3. (C.L.C. CODE 1209)

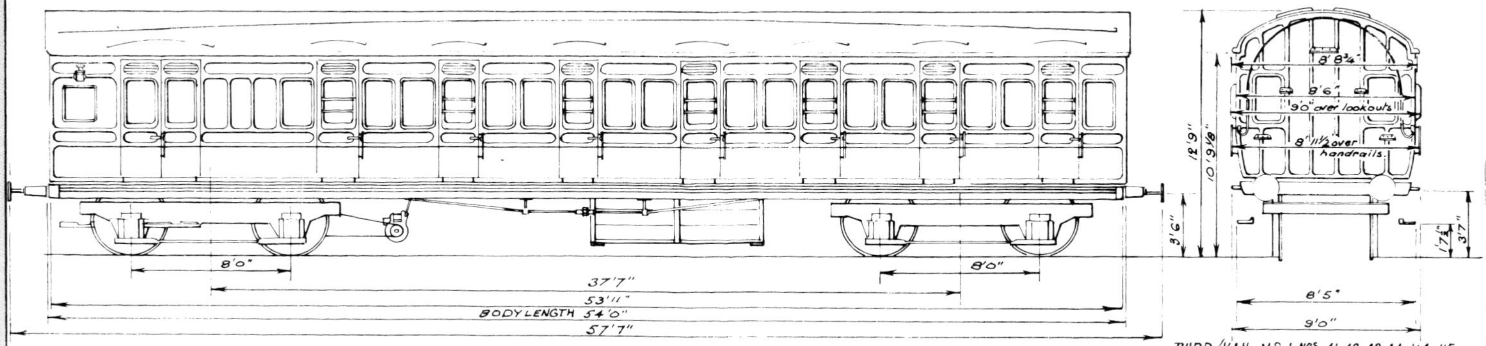

SEATING 7×10 = 70. VAN 11'10" LONG. WOOD BODY, STEEL UNDERFRAME. VACUUM & HAND BRAKE, ELECTRIC LIGHT. WEIGHT 28 T. 11 C. 0 Q. M.S.J. DIAGRAM 22 (C.L.C. CODE 1236)

THIRD/VAN. M.S.J. Nos 41, 42, 43, 44, 114, 115.
(trans to C.L.C. Nos 677, 671, 687, 681, 661, 667)
BUILT G.C.R. DUKINFIELD 1915.

JC 21209.

Appendix Five

Electric Stock 1931–1971

The odd-numbered motor coaches and driving trailers faced Altrincham, and the even-numbered motor coaches and driving trailers faced Manchester.

(a) *Motor Coaches*

24 built 1930–31 by the Metropolitan-Cammell Carriage, Wagon and Finance Company (MCC&W) under LMS lot No. 504.

MSJA No.	*LMR No.*	*When withdrawn*	*Notes*
1	M 28571	1971	'1971' means May 1971
2	72	1971	
3	73	1971	
4	74	1971	
5	M 28575	Jan. 1963	Involved in Oxford Road accident
6	76	1971	
7	77	1966	'1966' means July 1966
8	78	1971	
9	79	1971	
10	M 28580	1971	
11	81	1971	
12	82	1966	
13	83	June 1970	Cannibalised. See note *
14	84	1966	
15	M 28585	1971	
16	86	1966	
17	87	1971	
18	88	1971	
19	89	1971	
20	M 28590	1971	
21	91	1966	
22	92	1971	
23	93	1971	
24	M 28594	1971	Spare motor. See note *

* The initial MSJA stock was 22 units plus 2 spare motor coaches. In 1939/40 extra coaches were obtained. Accidents and withdrawals took their toll, and by the beginning of 1964 the stock was down to 22 units, plus one spare motor coach. One unit (13, 56, 112) was withdrawn from active service and kept at the carriage-sheds, where it was cannibalised to provide spares for units in active service; also, on at least one occasion, it was towed to Horwich works so that they could use it for parts while overhauling other MSJA electric units there. This unit was not completely withdrawn (i.e. towed off for scrapping) until June 1970. In July 1966 five units were withdrawn; and the stock was thus reduced to 16 units in active service plus the disintegrating unit plus the spare motor coach, MSJA No. 24. No. 24 was used for shunting in the carriage sheds and thus retained its dc pantograph till the end (from 1968 the other motor coaches had theirs replaced by ac pantographs) as there was no alteration to the catenary in the sheds.

MSJA motor coach No. 4, seen here at Altrincham on 18th October, 1946. Note the crest and lettering. *H.C. Casserley*

The same coach at Oxford Road on 30th April, 1971, now with the third type of pantograph fitted. *R.M. Casserley*

(b) *Driving Trailers*

22 (MSJA Nos. 51–72) built by MCC&W in 1930–31 under LMS lot No. 505. Augmented by the conversion of trailer No. 153 into driving trailer No. 74 to replace driving trailer No. 57 when 57 was withdrawn in 1948.

MSJA No.	*LMR No.*	*When withdrawn*	*Notes*
51	M 29231	1971	
52	32	1971	
53	33	1971	
54	34	1966	
55	M 29235	1971	
56	M 29236	June 1970	Cannibalised. See note * preceding table
57	–	Dec. 1948	Involved in Stretford accident, Nov. 1948
58	M 29237	1966	
59	M 29239	1971	
60	40	1971	
61	41	1971	
62	42	1971	
63	43	1971	
64	44	1971	
65	M 29245	1966	
66	46	1971	
67	47	1971	
68	48	1971	
69	49	1966	
70	M 29250	1971	
71	51	1971	
72	52	1966	
74	M 29238	1971	

Additional Notes: (1) There never was a (MSJA No.) 73. (2) The LMR renumbering took place in 1950; thus (MSJA No.) 57 never received a LMR number.

A posed pre-service photograph of driving trailer No. 64 at Oxford Road on 16th April, 1931. *National Railway Museum*

A 1950s view of Altrincham station from the south. *Lens of Sutton*

The carriage shed at Altrincham in 1947. *Lens of Sutton*

(c) *Trailers*

22 (MSJA Nos. 101–122) built MCC&W in 1930–31 under LMS lot 506. 1939–40: Augmented by Nos. 151, 152 built LMS at Wolverton in 1939, lot No. 1158; 153 imported from London–Watford line which had been built at Wolverton by the LMS under lot No. 464 in 1929; and 154–8 imported from Liverpool–Southport line. These had been built by Claytons in 1926 under LMS lot No. 237.

When the 7-coach electric trains were abandoned, six of the extra coaches imported onto the MSJA in 1939–40 became superfluous and were towed away to Lightbowne sidings, near Newton Heath. They languished there for some 10 years, as MSJA stock out of use, until they were converted into steam stock and renumbered in 1954, completing their withdrawal *from the MSJA*. They had been numbered M 29390–29395 in 1950; in 1954, as steam stock, they became M 12278–12283 and were withdrawn for scrapping in December 1966, December 1959, September 1962, July 1959, May 1962 and March 1962 respectively.

MSJA No.	*LMR No.*	*When withdrawn*	*Notes*
101	M 29650	1971	
102	51	1966	
103	52	1966	
104	53	1971	
105	54	1971	
106	M 29655	1971	
107	56	1971	
108	57	1971	
109	58	1971	
110	59	1966	
111	M 29660	1971	
112	61	Jun. 1970	Cannibalised
113	62	1971	
114	63	1971	Preserved by MRPG
115	64	Dec. 1963	Involved in Oxford Rd accident (Jan. 1963)
116	M 29665	1966	
117	66	1971	Preserved by AERPS
118	67	1971	
119	68	1971	
120	69	1971	
121	M 29670	1971	Preserved by AERPS
122	M 29671	1971	
151	M 29390	1954	Converted to steam stock and used on the ex-CL
152	M 29391	1954	As 151
153	–	–	Converted into a driving trailer and became (MSJA No.) 74
154	M 29392	1954	As 151
155	M 29393	1954	As 151
156	M 29394	1954	As 151
157	M 29395	1954	As 151
158	M 29396	1966	

Appendix Six

The Altrincham Gasworks Railway

Very little is known about this somewhat enigmatic tramway. The Altrincham Gas Company was registered in March 1846, and on 29th May, 1847 opened its gasworks off Moss Lane. Here it made gas using local fuels, until the opening of the MSJA and the rest of the railway system enabled it to import coal and coke from coalfields far distant. For a while these materials were detrained and loaded into carts in Altrincham goods yard, whence they travelled by road to the gasworks. However, the demand for gas was rising, and much larger quantities of fuel were needed, and as Moss Lane was 'circuitous in direction and parts thereof steep in gradient thereby causing the Company excessive expense for the hauling of their coals and other materials used or produced at their works' the gas company applied to build a tramway.

The company obtained an Act on 9th June, 1893 authorising it to build and maintain the tramway between Altrincham station and the gasworks, of length about a third of a mile, along the public highway, Moss Lane, and to carry out the street reconstruction required. This was done at a cost of £1,820, the standard gauge, single-track line laid, inspected by the Board of Trade and brought into use within two years. The 1893 Act authorised the use of animal power only; however this was no great handicap as the horses used could pull five times as much on the tramway as they could on the road; and there was no need to unload wagons; those destined for the gasworks were shunted into the south-eastern part of the goods yard for the horse to pick up.

Between the opening of the tramway and 1920, the sales of gas (and consequently the traffic on the line) more than doubled, and it became evident that more than 1 hp was needed to handle the traffic. Accordingly, the gas company obtained authority in 1924 to use other forms of motive power on the line.

A Sentinel steam lorry was purchased, and this drove along the road, pulling the wagons behind it on the rails. This was little more than a cab-and-chassis, and when not in use shunting or working on the line it was used to carry ammonia round a Manchester works. Following this, in 1943, a Peckett 0–4–0 saddletank was purchased, named *Arthur E. Potts* after a Director of the Company.

In 1946 a diesel was obtained to replace 'Potts'. However the diesel was repeatedly breaking down, and 'Potts' thus had to be kept in reserve.

Either 'Potts' or the diesel (depending which was in working condition) would make generally four, or occasionally five, trips a day each way between the station and the gasworks, and spend the rest of the time shunting.

The tramway was closed in 1958 when the company stopped making gas at the gasworks and the track disappeared under dirt and tarmac. 'Potts' was sold to Preston Docks.

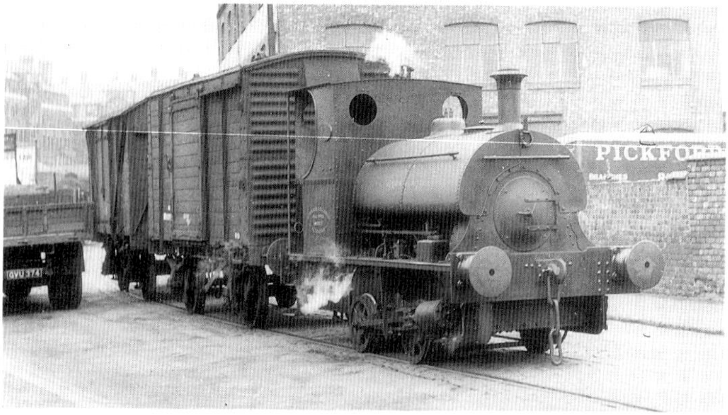

Arthur E. Potts, The Altrincham Gasworks Company 0–4–0ST locomotive, *en route* to the gasworks site in 1950. *F.R.M. Fysh*

Appendix Seven

Mileposts and Mileages

MSJA mileposts are made of cast-iron and consist of a tall pillar with a disc fixed to the top, yellow, formerly white. Nearly all are to be found on the down (Manchester–Altrincham) side of the line. The mileposts give the distance in miles and the reference-point (OR = Oxford Road; LR = London Road). For economy, fractions of a mile are indicated by ¼, ½ or ¾ as is appropriate, without the number of miles.

A few seem to be missing, or have been replaced by different types; two are on the up side of the line, two situated on station platforms and bolted to a wall, without a pillar.

In the table of mileages that follows, note:

(1) Mileages are approximate, to the nearest furlong (⅛ mile).
(2) Distances to stations measured from their booking offices.
(3) SB denotes signal box. Date in brackets is date of its closure.
(4) LC denotes Level Crossing.
(5) Sta. denotes Station.
(6) Jn denotes Junction.

0		Beginning of MSJA at London Road Sta. (Now called Piccadilly Sta.)
⅛		London Road MSJA SB (1958)
¾	0	Oxford Road East SB (1931), Sta. and West SB (1969)
1⅛	⅜	Knott Mill SB (1931) and Sta. (Now called Deansgate Sta.)
1¼	½	Castlefield Jn and SB (1969)
1⅝	–	Irwell Bridge and end of South Junction line near Liverpool Road and Ordsall Lane
	1¼	Cornbrook Jn East and SB (1969)
	1½	Old Trafford Jn and SB (1969)
	1⅞	Old Trafford Sta. (Now called Trafford Bar Sta.)
	2	Old Trafford SB (1963)
	2⅜	Warwick Road Sta. (Now called Old Trafford Sta.) and SB (1971)
	3¼	Stretford SB (1971)
	3½	Stretford Sta.
	4⅛	Mersey Bridge SB (1971)
	4⅝	Dane Road Sta.
	5	Sale Sta. and SB (1971)
	5⅝	Brooklands Sta.
	5¾	Brooklands SB (1971)
	6⅛	Site of proposed halt
	6¾	Timperley Sta.
	6⅞	Timperley Jn and SB (1963)
	7	Deansgate Jn, LC and SB
	7⅜	Navigation Road Sta., LC and SB (1991)
	7¾	Stockport Road LC and Altrincham North SB (1991). Altrincham Jn
	8	Altrincham & Bowdon Sta. and Altrincham South SB (1968)
	8¼	Former Bowdon terminus used as carriage sheds

The reason that the stations and signal boxes at Old Trafford (now called Trafford Bar), Stretford and Brooklands are shown at different mileages is because the SBs were at the other end of the station from the booking offices.

Ivatt class '2MT' No. 41212 derailed near Timperley junction in 1952. Note the MSJA electric sub station in the background. *G. Ellis*

A 1920s accident at Altrincham level crossing caused enormous interest, and then the photographer assembled all the spectators to capture the moment on a plate! *Courtesy Altrincham Library*

Appendix Eight

Extracts from the Accident Record Books of the 1890s

Extracts from the MS&LR Accident Record Book, Locomotive Engineer's Office, Gorton, concerning Altrincham shed.

		PARTICULARS OF STOCK				
Date	*Locality*	*No.*	*Type*	*Owner*	*Driver*	*Details*
1892						
May 6th	Oxford Road	555		MS&L	W. Pugh	Engine ran through points, no damage
May 19th	Between Sale & Manchester	449		MS&L	W. Pugh	Difficulty with automatic brake
June 17th	Cornbrook				W. Pugh	Platelayer narrowly missed injury
July 3rd	Bowden	5816	Wagon	MS&L	H. Taylor	Wagon off road and axle bent
July 25th	Castlefield Jn	447		MS&L	W. Pugh	Leading axle broke and engine off road
Sep. 7th	Bowden	449		MS&L	C. Williamson	Engine off road
Sep. 10th	Cornbrook Jn				W. Clarke	Man knocked down
Sep. 12th	Cornbrook				W. Savage	Man knocked down
Sep. 23rd	Bowden	113	Carriage	MSJA	C. Hindley	Carriage off road
Sep. 30th	Oxford Road	451		MS&L	C. Hindley	Engine off road
Oct. 3rd	Bowden	447		MS&L	W. Pugh & W. Clarke	Engine damaged in slight collision
Oct. 17th	Altrincham	451		MS&L	J. Redfern	Engine off road
Nov. 2nd	Bowden	88	Brake 3rd	MSJA	C. Hindley	Carriage off road
Nov. 5th	Timperley	3549	Wagon	GWR	J. Coffey	Wagon off road
Nov. 15th	Bowden				H. Taylor	Man killed; suicide
Dec. 7th	Bowden	40	Brake	MSJA	C. Hindley	Collided with a train standing in up platform, damaging brake and several passengers complained of injury
Dec. 24th	Bowden	452		MS&L	W. Clarke	Engine off road
Dec. 27th	Stretford	23		MS&L	R. Ridyard	Engine off road

Date	*Locality*	*No.*	*Type*	*Owner*	*Driver*	*Details*
1893						
Jan. 1st	Bowden	449		MS&L	J. Warburton	Fireman J. Berry caught between engine 449 and brake draw bar hooks and slightly injured his back and chest
Mar. 16th	Altrincham	11383	Wagon	MS&L	J. Coffey	Wagon off road
Mar. 20th	Oxford Road	451		MS&L	C. Hindley	Engine off road
Mar. 20th	Oxford Road	120	Brake 3rd	MSJA	C. Williamson	Quarter light broken
Mar. 29th	Cornbrook	448		MS&L	J. Warburton	Engine off road
May 3rd	Altrincham	75		MS&L	J. Coffey	Engine off road
June 28th	Oxford Road	452		MS&L	W. Clarke	Engine off road
July 3rd	Bowden	24		MS&L	J. Redfern	Engine off road
July 15th	Timperley				J. Warburton	Mr Bailey's child thrown off seat and injured
1897						
Apl 20th	Oxford Road	449	Engine	MS&L	J. Higson	Engine off road
Apl 22nd	Old Trafford	1	Ballast Wagon	MSJA	G. Coops	Wagon off road
June 11th	Cricket Gnd	72	3rd Cl.	MSJA	W. Pugh	Auto brake piston stuck
July 2nd	Stretford	5	Wagon	Ashley & Dunville	C. Williamson	Wagon off road
Aug. 19th	Cricket Gnd & Old Trafford	41	Brake	MSJA	Jas. Higson	Shackle broke
Aug. 20th	Stretford	4769	Wagon	L&NW	S. Pearson	Wagon off road
Sep. 10th	Altrincham	452	Engine	MS&L	J. Higson	Engine off road
Sep. 18th	Stretford	55356	Wagon	L&NW	J. Coffey	Wagon off road
Sep. 23rd	London Road				J. White	Porter Gregory caught between buffers and seriously injured
Oct. 8th	Altrincham	22557	Wagon	L&Y	S. Pearson	Wagons off road, and damaged and fence damaged
		314	Wagon	W&J Turner		
Oct. 16th	Oxford Road	575	Engine	MS&L	J. White	Engine ran through points and damaged them
Nov. 10th	Bowden	16	2nd Cl. Carriage	MSJA	G. Coops	Shackle broke
Nov. 12th	Oxford Road	77	1st Cl. Carriage	MSJA	W. Pugh	Wheel loose on axle
Nov. 14th	Altrincham	451	Engine	GC	J. Higson	Engine off road
Nov. 24th	Bowden				J. Redfern	Porter Booth knocked down, but was not injured

Date	Locality	No.	Type	Owner	Driver	Details
1898						
Jan. 21st	London Road S. Jn		Carriage	MSJA	H. Taylor	Side lamp of carriage knocked off and damaged
Feb. 8th	Bowden	118	3rd Brake	MSJA	W. Pugh	Heating apparatus pipe damaged
Feb. 12th	Old Trafford	21	3rd	MSJA	C.Williamson	Draw bars pulled out
Feb. 18th	Stretford	2377	Brake	L&NW	G. Brown	Ballast brake off road
Apl 15th	Bowden				W. Whitelegg (Fireman)	Fell off top step of eng. 449 and injured his elbow
Apl 25th	Altrincham	447	Engine	GCR	C. Williamson	Engines damaged and 447 off road through slight collision and fireman J. Howarth received slight injuries
		448	Engine		G. Brown	
May 31st	Stretford	25838	Wagon	L&Y	J. Redfern	Wagons off road
		95	Wagon	Tyldesley		
June 20th	Between Sale & Stretford				Wm Broome (Fireman)	1st finger rt hand injured with lid of locker
June 20th	Cornbrook	975	Wagon	Bridgewater	T.H. Taylor	Wagons off road
		1359	Wagon			
		654	Wagon			
		1200	Wagon			
		1007	Wagon			

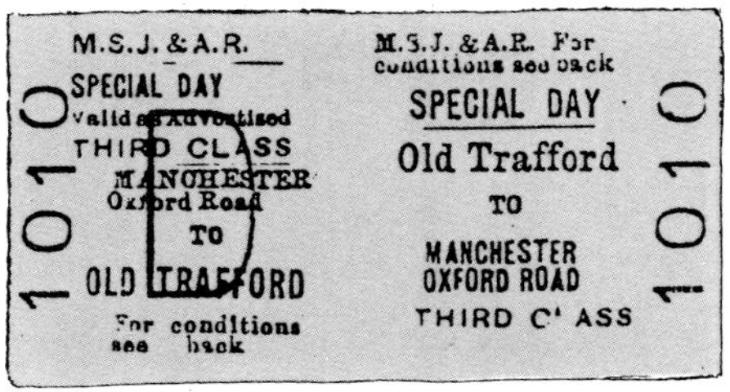

Appendix Nine

Statistics and Receipts

MSJA passenger services

	1850	1880s	*c.*1900	1930s	1970	1971
MSJA-only trains on a normal weekday (each way)	13	36	40	92	56	64
Passengers booked in year	639,000	2 mill.	5 mill.	8 mill.	2½ mill.	(estimated)

Traffic for the period 1st July, 1858 to 31st December, 1858

	South Jn line	*Altrincham branch line*	*Total*	*Percentage on Altrincham branch*
Passengers carried				
1st class	3,000	132,000	135,000	98
2nd class	4,000	117,000	122,000	96
3rd class and Parliamentary	9,000	443,000	452,000	98
Total	17,000	692,000	709,000	98
Season Ticket Holders	–	957	957	100
Goods Traffic (tons)				
Coal	30,800	5,400	36,200	15
Other minerals	15,700	4,300	20,100	21
Total minerals	46,500	9,700	56,200	17
General merchandise	74,500	20,300	94,700	21
Total Goods Traffic	121,000	30,000	151,000	20
Livestock carried				
Cattle	4,900	12,200	17,100	71
Sheep	24,100	6,100	30,200	20
Pigs	4,700	1,000	5,700	18
Total	33,700	19,400	53,100	37
Number of trains run				
Passenger	2,500	10,000	12,500	80
Goods	3,600	900	4,400	20
Total	6,100	10,900	16,900	64

Source: Board of Trade Railway Returns, at National Railway Museum. The numbers have been rounded for the purposes of this table, so some totals may differ from the apparent sum of their constituent parts.

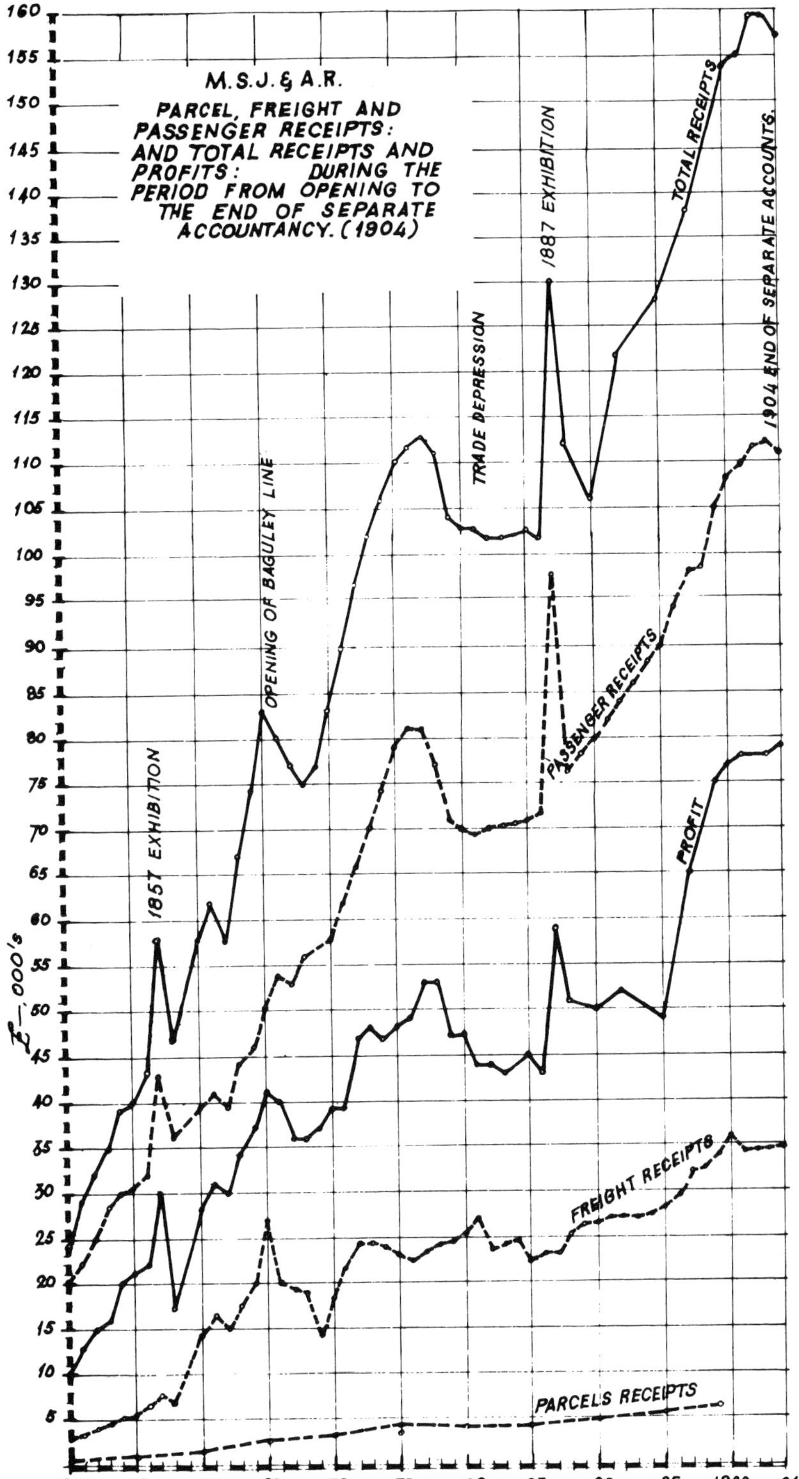
M.S.J. & A.R.
PARCEL, FREIGHT AND PASSENGER RECEIPTS: AND TOTAL RECEIPTS AND PROFITS: DURING THE PERIOD FROM OPENING TO THE END OF SEPARATE ACCOUNTANCY. (1904)
£ - ,000's
1857 EXHIBITION
OPENING OF BAGULEY LINE
TRADE DEPRESSION
1887 EXHIBITION
TOTAL RECEIPTS
1904 END OF SEPARATE ACCOUNTS.
PASSENGER RECEIPTS
PROFIT
FREIGHT RECEIPTS
PARCELS RECEIPTS
160
155
150
145
140
135
130
125
120
115
110
105
100
95
90
85
80
75
70
65
60
55
50
45
40
35
30
25
20
15
10
5
1850
55
60
65
70
75
80
85
90
95
1900
04

Numbers of Passengers on the MSJA's Services *Gross Receipts from Passengers*

	Passengers (excluding Season Ticket Holders) 1st class ('000)	2nd class ('000)	3rd class* ('000)	Total ('000)	Season Ticket Holders**	Total £	Of which: Season Tickets £	%
1861	310	228	1,054	1,592	2,521	42,400	8,100	19
1866	401	260	1,349	2,010	973	54,000	11,100	21
1871	438	338	1,528	2,305	1,445	61,700	15,200	25
1876	567	257	2,625	3,449	1,861	81,500	19,400	24
1881	345	337	2,350	3,032	2,299	68,700	18,100	26
1886	212	348	2,759	3,320	3,507	71,100	22,300	31
1887	338	486	5,110	5,934	3,812	98,000	23,500	24
1888	184	333	2,925	3,443	3,931	76,800	24,500	32
1891	184	331	3,201	3,717	4,571	81,700	27,000	33
1896	199	244	3,898	4,341	5,761	93,800	32,000	34
1901	211	326	4,419	4,955	7,386	109,100	39,400	36
1906	185	279	4,019	4,483	7,782	104,600	41,000	39
1911	143	168	3,591	3,901	7,484	90,800	40,400	44
1922	139	31	4,414	4,584	6,227	166,400	62,000	37

Notes:
* including Parliamentary and Workmen's
** Annual equivalent numbers, including Workmen's Weekly Tickets

Gross Receipts from Passengers on the MSJA's Services

	PASSENGERS (excl. season tickets) 1st class £	2nd class £	3rd class inc. Parliamentary £	Total £	SEASON TICKETS 1st class £	2nd class £	3rd class inc. Workmen's £	Total £
1861	9,600	4,800	19,800	34,300	na	na	na	8,100
1866	11,700	6,200	25,000	42,900	na	na	na	11,100
1871	12,200	7,300	27,000	46,400	na	na	na	15,200
1876	15,200	5,900	41,100	62,200	18,100	1,200	0	19,400
1881	9,400	7,300	34,000	50,600	10,400	7,600	100	18,100
1886	5,400	7,000	36,400	48,800	8,800	5,100	8,300	22,300
1887	7,500	9,100	57,900	74,500	9,100	5,100	9.400	23,500
1888	4,900	7,100	40,300	52,300	9,300	5,100	10,100	24,500
1891	5,000	7,000	42,800	54,800	9,100	5,200	12,700	27,000
1896	5,600	5,000	51,200	61,800	10,000	4,100	17,900	32,000
1901	6,100	6,700	57,000	69,700	11,800	5,600	22,000	39,400
1906	5,500	5,800	52,300	63,700	11,800	5,800	23,400	41,000
1911	4,200	3,400	42,900	50,500	11,900	4,800	23,700	40,400
1922	7,500	1,300	95,600	104,400	23,900	2,500	35,700	62,000

Notes:
na = not available

Source: Board of Trade Railway Returns, at National Railway Museum. Many of the numbers have been rounded for the purposes of these tables, so some totals may differ from the apparent sum of their constituent parts.

Goods Statistics and Total Receipts

	Volume of Goods Traffic		Receipts from Goods Traffic			Total	Total
	Coal, Coke and other minerals ('000 tons)	General merchandise ('000 tons)	Coal, Coke Minerals £	General merchandise £	Total (inc. livestock etc)* £	passenger train receipts** £	receipts (inc. misc.) *** £
1861	195	383	4,300	11,100	16,000	44,200	60,200
1866	400	353	8,400	11,600	20,900	56,700	77,600
1871	381	476	7,200	14,400	22,100	66,100	90,500
1876	882	382	9,300	12,900	22,800	86,600	112,300
1881	1,077	537	13,900	12,900	27,300	72,900	103,100
1886	1,100	515	11,100	12,000	23,600	75,500	102,300
1887	1,141	505	11,200	12,200	24,000	102,900	130,400
1888	1,205	611	11,900	13,400	25,900	81,700	112,200
1891	1,312	672	14,100	12,700	27,400	86,900	118,200
1896	1,552	780	14,600	15,300	30,700	99,700	134,100
1901	1,652	901	15,800	17,500	34,000	116,300	155,000
1906	1,769	1,102	16,900	18,400	35,900	112,200	154,000
1911	1,979	1,158	16,600	20,900	38,100	98,500	142,600
1922	na	na	35,500	40,200	76,900	175,700	254,300

Notes:

* This includes receipts for livestock etc., so is greater than the sum of 'Coal, Coke and Minerals' and 'General Merchandise'.

** This includes receipts for dogs, mails, etc., so is greater than the total receipts from passengers.

*** This includes Miscellaneous Receipts (e.g. Rents), so is greater than the sum of 'Goods Traffic' and 'Passenger Train' receipts.

Source: Board of Trade Railway Returns, at National Railway Museum. The numbers have been rounded for the purposes of this table, so some totals may differ from the apparent sum of their constituent parts.

Sale station looking towards Manchester on 8th December, 1984. *N.D. Mundy*

Numbers of passengers: 1922

	Total	*Of whom: originating on the MSJA* Number	*% of total*
Passengers (excl. season tickets)			
1st class	139,000	87,000	63
2nd class	31,000	31,000	100
3rd class	2.336.000	1,356,000	58
Workmen's ('single journey' basis)	2,078,000	1,503,000	72
Total	4,584,000	2,976,000	65
Season tickets (annual equiv.)			
1st class	1733	930	54
2nd class	219	219	100
3rd class	4275	2981	70
Total	6227	4130	66

Source: Board of Trade Railway Returns, in National Railway Museum. Some of the numbers have been rounded for the purposes of this table.

1939 pre-war weekday passenger arrivals in Manchester ex-MSJA

	7 to 8	*8 to 9*	*9 to 10*	*Total*	
Knott Mill	171	898	335	1404	
Oxford Road	211	1698	916	2825	
London Road	159	420	392	971	
Total	541	3016	1643	5200	10.8 per cent of the Manchester total

March 1991 Weekday Passengers alighting by 9.30 am from Altrincham to Manchester services

	Electric (via Sale)	*Diesel (via Stockport)*
Deansgate	410	12
Oxford Road	642	85
Piccadilly	419	232
Total	1471	329

Altrincham train at London Road, 9th September, 1958. *R.E. Gee*

Appendix Ten

Readers' Reminiscences

Following the publication of the First Edition, a number of readers wrote about some of their memories of the MSJA. This Appendix provides a selection of these reminiscences.

Mr E.K. Skelhorn, who had commuted on the line from 1926 to 1965, recalled the old 'rather spartan' 6-wheel coaches, and ex-LNW tanks having to reverse at Old Trafford station in order to start (when running to Altrincham). 'On more than one occasion they failed altogether, and were to be seen on the down slow line waiting for a "push", after being propelled there by the following train.'

Mr R.L. Harris had a very clear memory of the two years before the 1931 electrification. LMS tank engines and maroon coaches alternated with LNE engines and mahogany coaches. A guard, who lived in Altrincham, always had a flower in the button-hole, usually a rose in summer and a chrysanthemum in winter. Mr Harris used to spend hours beside Brooklands signal box, talking to the signalman and watching the trains, such as the local goods train, come with coal wagons for Brooklands, doing a quick shunt between passenger trains. He remembers the introduction of the practice of closing large doors to seal off the platforms, to prevent late-comers dashing after a moving train, and to prevent passengers off a crowded train from Manchester from rushing out without showing their tickets. (I remember that it was particularly galling, having hurried to Altrincham station only to see the platform doors being closed almost in your face, to have to listen to drawn-out preparations, and the eventual departure of the train, which seemed to take ages. The doors would then be opened, and you would be permitted onto the empty platform, to watch the train that you could have boarded accelerating away.)

A Lymm line train at London Road in the 1950s. *G.D. Whitworth*

The south-end of Altrincham station on 12th March, 1949 with Nos. 9276 and 69281 standing at the platforms when electric trains were replaced by steam during engineering works. *J.D. Darby*

Altrincham station with LNE class 'N5' 0–6–2T No. 9293 (ex 5536) on the 4.01 pm to Northwich on 28th April, 1948. *W.A. Camwell*

Mr J.D. Royle remembered the bars on the windows of the doors of the old electrics, and the loud sound of the compressors. (Mr Harris' memories included always travelling at the *other* end of a 3-car set from the motor coach, for a quieter and smoother trip.) In order to see more steam trains than the MSJA could offer, he had to pass through the territory of the 'much feared Norris Road gang' and then faced 'a lonely ride along the then rural Baguley Lane, through the marshes' to Baguley station.

Mr L.M. Hobdey recalled that the 'Lymm line' trains to Warrington and Liverpool were, at one time, 'practically all worked by the larger passenger engines. The 6 am from Liverpool was regularly hauled by "Princes", "Experiments", "Georges" and "Precursors".' Several other trains were hauled by "Jumbos", including an 8.10 pm Saturdays Only working. 'The engines on this train were always from strange sheds, and I think that it must have been a filling-in turn, as I have seen engines from Carlisle shed on it. The same applies to the 6 am from Liverpool. Engines from Crewe and Stafford sheds were also frequent visitors.' He remembered 'seeing the old "Cornwall" with the Inspection Saloon. It was a glorious day and her highly-polished brass dome was visible from a distance of over a mile.'

At one time, Dr R.S.B. Hamilton used to catch the 9.03 am express electric service from Altrincham every morning, to attend Manchester University. He remembers the MSJA's reputation for punctuality: 'the Altrincham electric line was one you could practically always rely on. However, one day I got the 9.03 from Altrincham, intending to catch the 9.45 am "Mancunian"' [from London Road to London Euston]. The 9.03 express from Altrincham was scheduled to arrive at London Road at 9.16 am, but 'for some reason was late, and we drew into London Road at 9.45 am, just in time to see the "Mancunian" leaving!'

Mr N.B.W. Thompson travelled on the MSJA in the late 1940s and early 1950s, and got to know 'a fair number of the staff at the time – particularly the two Brooklands signalmen' one of whom was 'Johnny Cogan, who subsequently became station master at Goostrey then Inspector at Altrincham'. He comments that 'in those days the traffic was much more interesting . . . the "Cheshireman" often headed by a "Director", the "North Western" to Warrington and Liverpool, the pick-up goods and the "hoppers" accelerating through Altrincham behind an 8F.'

Chester to Manchester train near Stretford about 1920 with a GC 4–4–2T at the head.
G.W. Smith, per A. Tyson

A view of the MSJA station at Stretford on 8th December, 1984. Part of the station is now a video shop!
N.D. Mundy

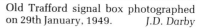

Old Trafford signal box photographed on 29th January, 1949. *J.D. Darby*

2–4–2T No. 5577 seen here at the Altrincham coaling stage in July 1929.
E.R. Whitworth

Appendix Eleven

Track Plans

drawn by J.M. Lloyd

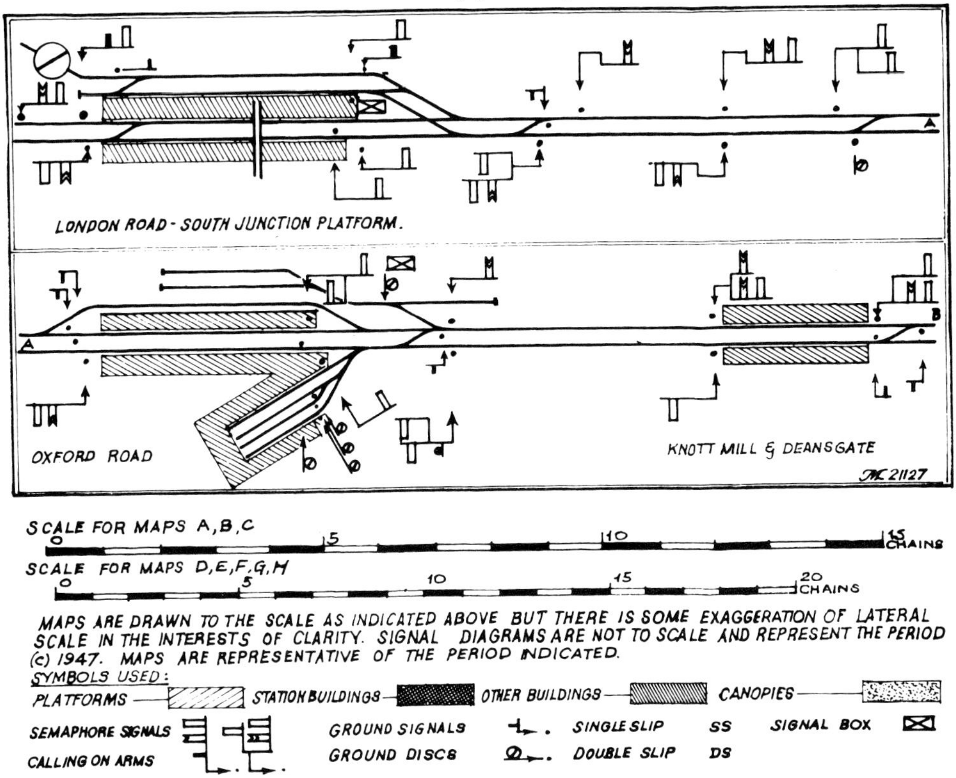

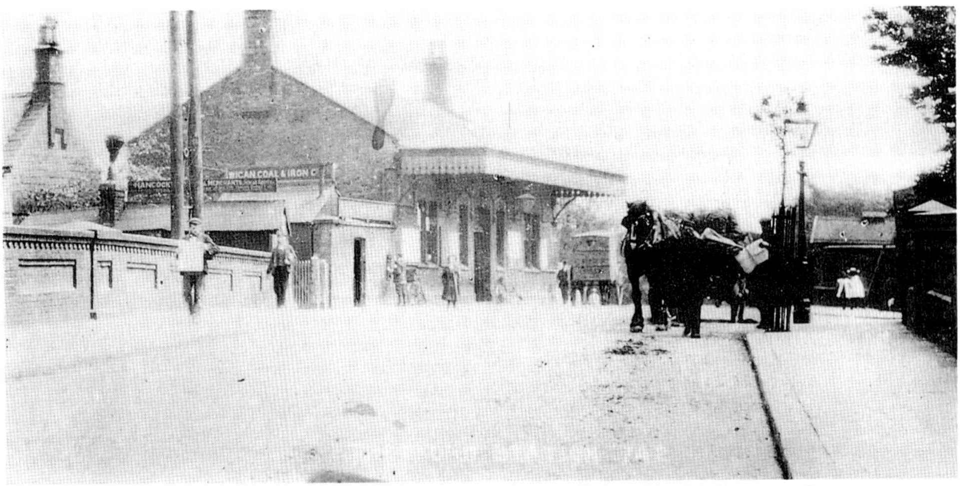

A 1920s view of Stretford station entrance. Compare this view with the opposite page: the chimneys and awning have been removed. *Lens of Sutton*

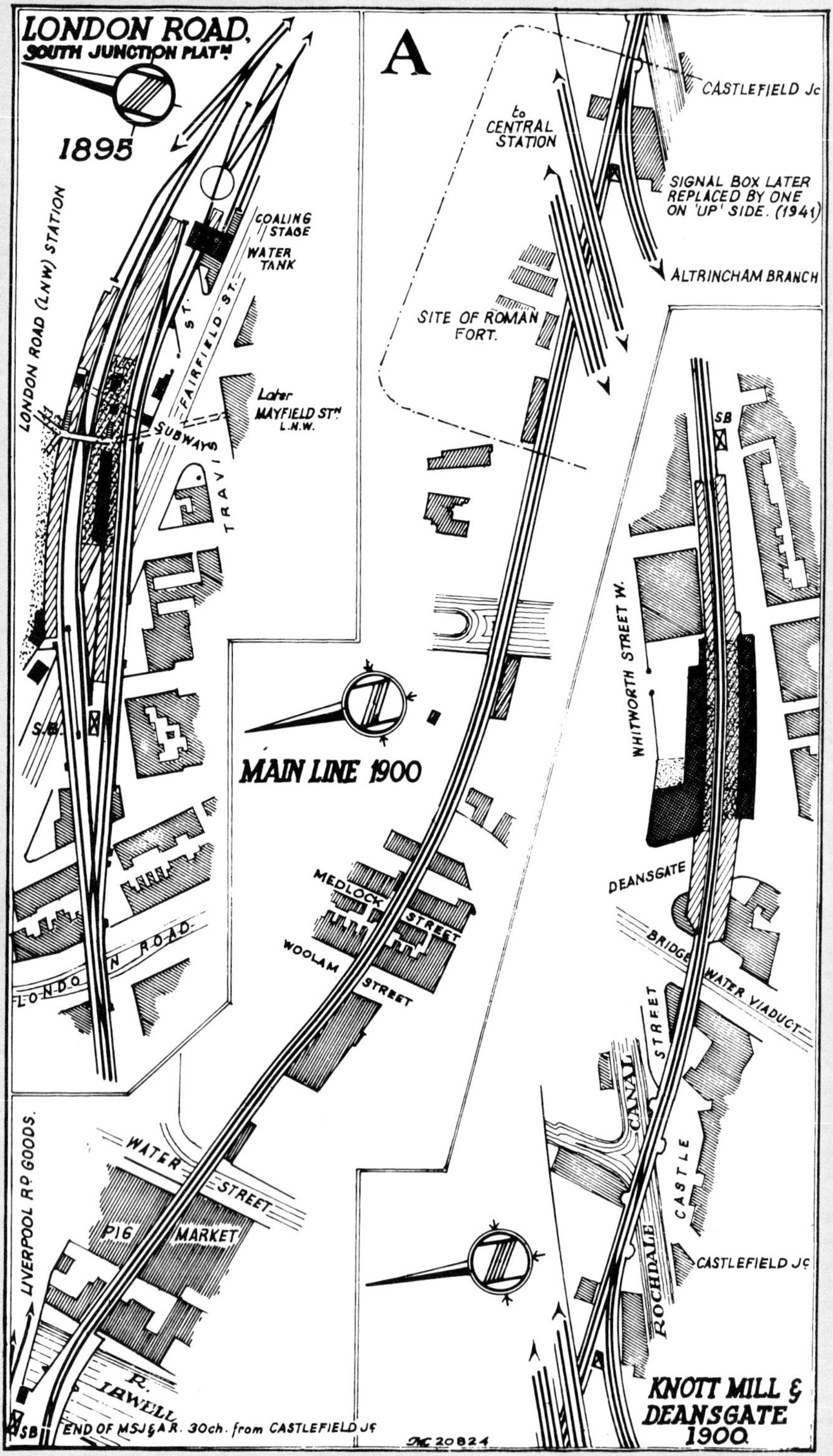
LONDON ROAD,
SOUTH JUNCTION PLATM
1895
LONDON ROAD (LNW) STATION
COALING STAGE
WATER TANK
ST
FAIRFIELD ST.
Later MAYFIELD STN L.N.W.
SUBWAYS
TRAVI
S.B.
LONDON ROAD
A
to CENTRAL STATION
CASTLEFIELD Jc
SIGNAL BOX LATER REPLACED BY ONE ON 'UP' SIDE. (1941)
ALTRINCHAM BRANCH
SITE OF ROMAN FORT.
MAIN LINE 1900
MEDLOCK STREET
WOOLAM STREET
WHITWORTH STREET W.
SB
DEANSGATE
BRIDGEWATER VIADUCT
CANAL STREET
CASTLE
ROCHDALE
CASTLEFIELD Jc
LIVERPOOL RD GOODS.
WATER STREET
PIG MARKET
R. IRWELL
SB
END OF MSJ&AR. 30ch. from CASTLEFIELD Jc
MC 20824
KNOTT MILL & DEANSGATE 1900

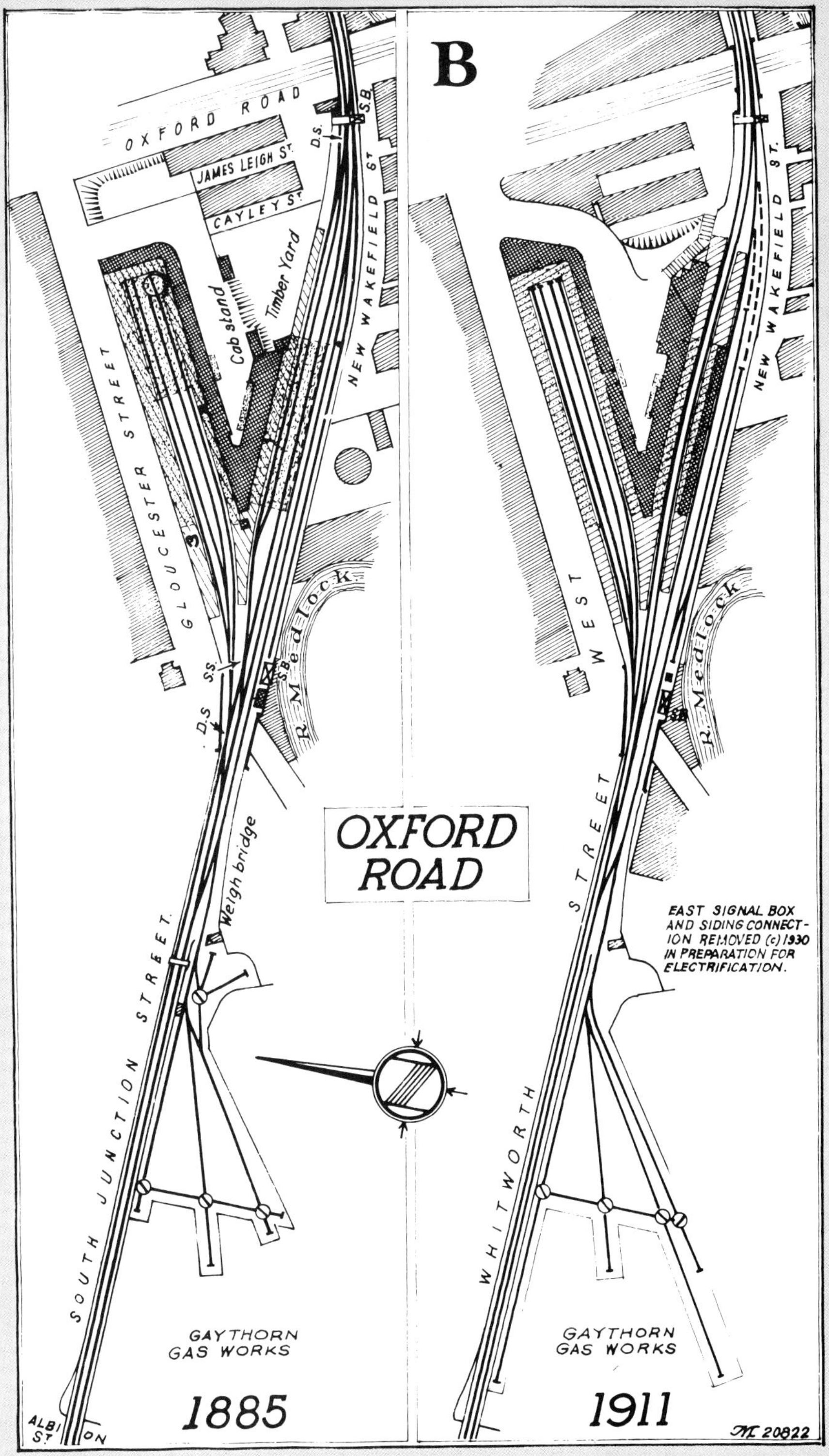
B
OXFORD ROAD
JAMES LEIGH ST.
CAYLEY ST.
Timber Yard
Cab stand
D.S.
S.B.
NEW WAKEFIELD ST.
GLOUCESTER STREET
3
R. Medlock
S.S.
D.S.
S.B.
Weigh bridge
SOUTH JUNCTION STREET
ALBION ST.
GAYTHORN GAS WORKS
1885
OXFORD ROAD
WEST STREET
WHITWORTH STREET
SB
EAST SIGNAL BOX AND SIDING CONNECTION REMOVED (c) 1930 IN PREPARATION FOR ELECTRIFICATION.
GAYTHORN GAS WORKS
1911
20822

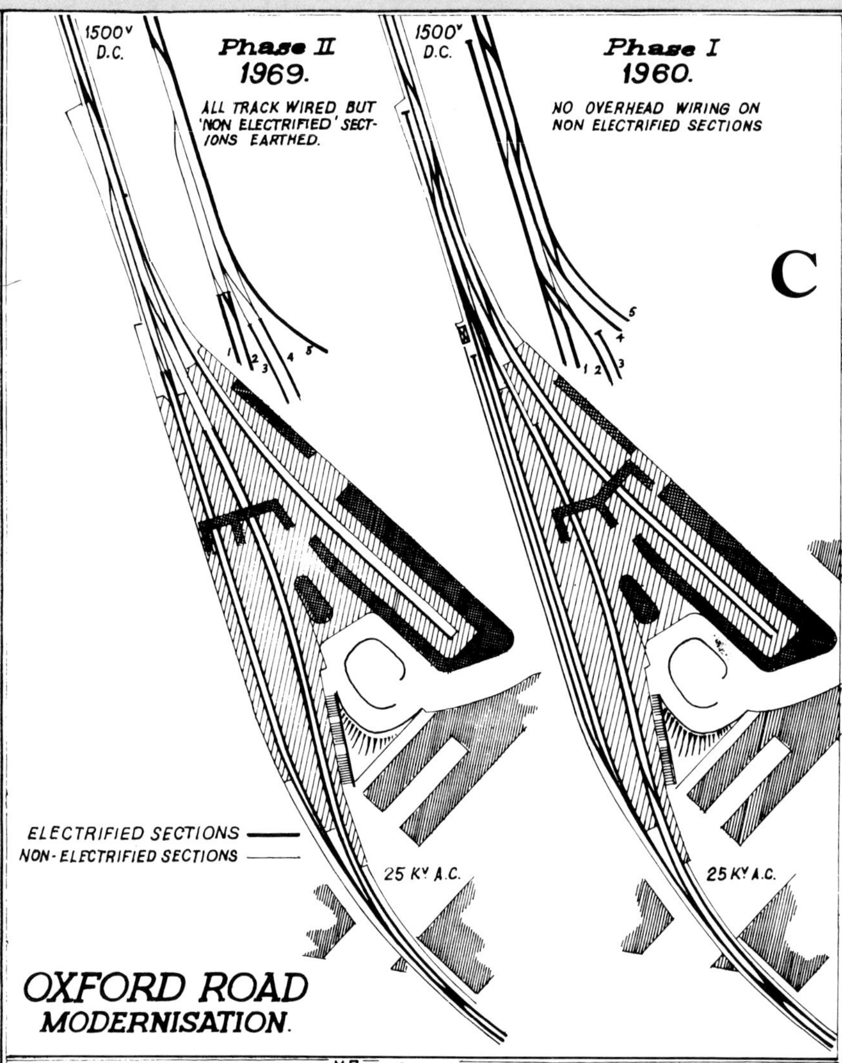
1500V D.C.
Phase II
1969.
ALL TRACK WIRED BUT 'NON ELECTRIFIED' SECTIONS EARTHED.
1500V D.C.
Phase I
1960.
NO OVERHEAD WIRING ON NON ELECTRIFIED SECTIONS
C
1 2 3 4 5
1 2 3 4 5
ELECTRIFIED SECTIONS
NON-ELECTRIFIED SECTIONS
25 KV A.C.
25 KV A.C.
OXFORD ROAD
MODERNISATION.

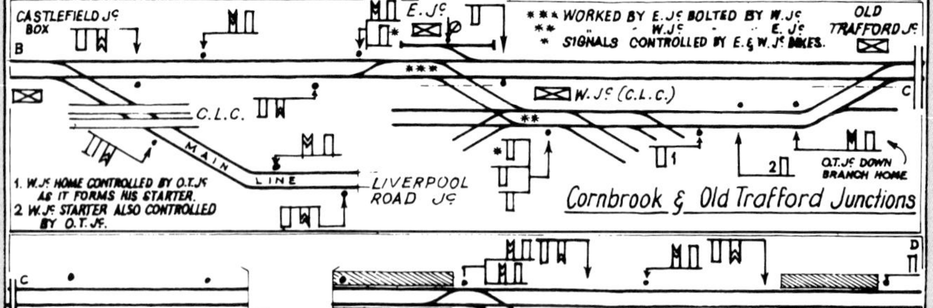
CASTLEFIELD Jc BOX
B
E. Jc
*** WORKED BY E. Jc BOLTED BY W. Jc
** " W. Jc " E. Jc
* SIGNALS CONTROLLED BY E. & W. Jc BOXES.
OLD TRAFFORD Jc
***
W. Jc (C.L.C.)
C
C.L.C.
**
MAIN LINE
1
2
O.T. Jc DOWN BRANCH HOME
1. W. Jc HOME CONTROLLED BY O.T. Jc AS IT FORMS HIS STARTER.
2. W. Jc STARTER ALSO CONTROLLED BY O.T. Jc.
LIVERPOOL ROAD Jc
Cornbrook & Old Trafford Junctions

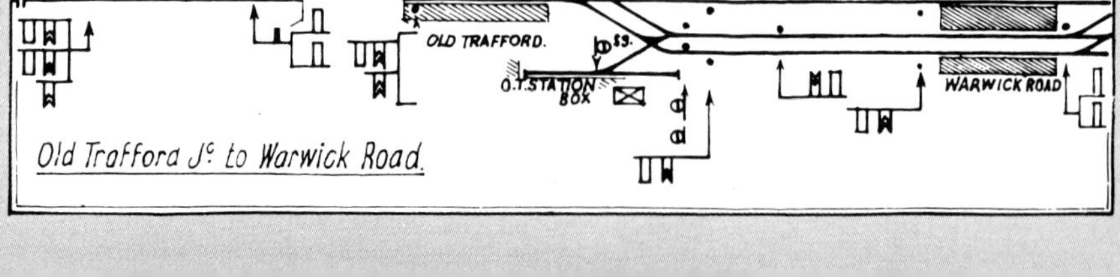
C
D
OLD TRAFFORD.
S.S.
O.T. STATION BOX
WARWICK ROAD
Old Traffora Jc to Warwick Road.

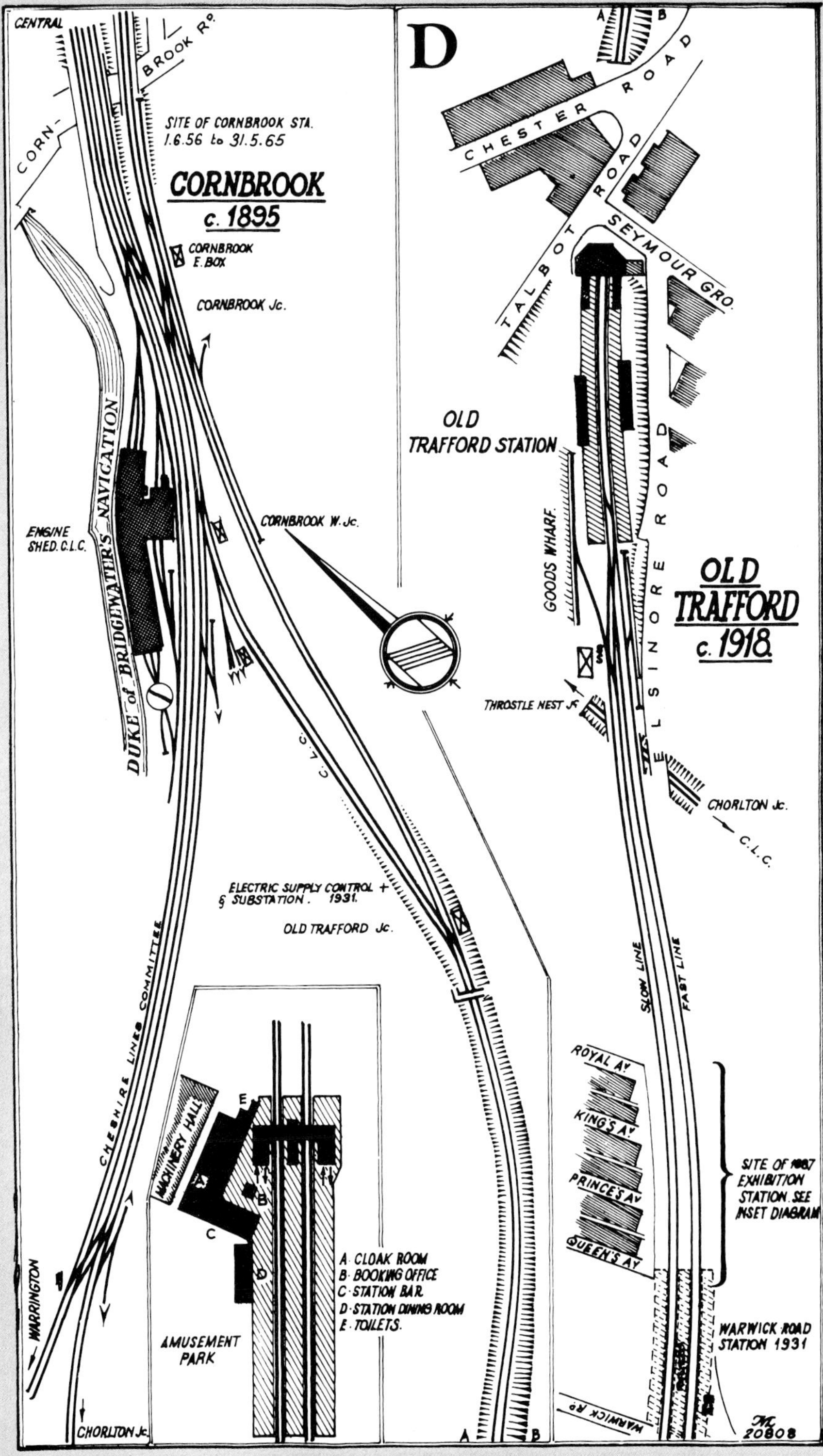
D
CORNBROOK
c. 1895
CENTRAL
BROOK Rd
CORN-
SITE OF CORNBROOK STA.
1.6.56 to 31.5.65
CORNBROOK
E. BOX
CORNBROOK Jc.
DUKE of BRIDGEWATER'S NAVIGATION
ENGINE
SHED. C.L.C.
CORNBROOK W. Jc.
C.L.C.
ELECTRIC SUPPLY CONTROL
§ SUBSTATION. 1931.
OLD TRAFFORD Jc.
CHESHIRE LINES COMMITTEE
WARRINGTON
CHORLTON Jc.
MACHINERY HALL
AMUSEMENT
PARK
A CLOAK ROOM
B BOOKING OFFICE
C STATION BAR
D STATION DINING ROOM
E TOILETS.
CHESTER ROAD
TALBOT ROAD
SEYMOUR GRO.
ELSINORE ROAD
OLD
TRAFFORD STATION
GOODS WHARF.
OLD
TRAFFORD
c. 1918
THROSTLE NEST Jc.
CHORLTON Jc.
C.L.C.
SLOW LINE
FAST LINE
ROYAL Av
KING'S Av
PRINCE'S Av
QUEEN'S Av
SITE OF 1887
EXHIBITION
STATION. SEE
INSET DIAGRAM
WARWICK ROAD
STATION 1931
WARWICK Rd
20808

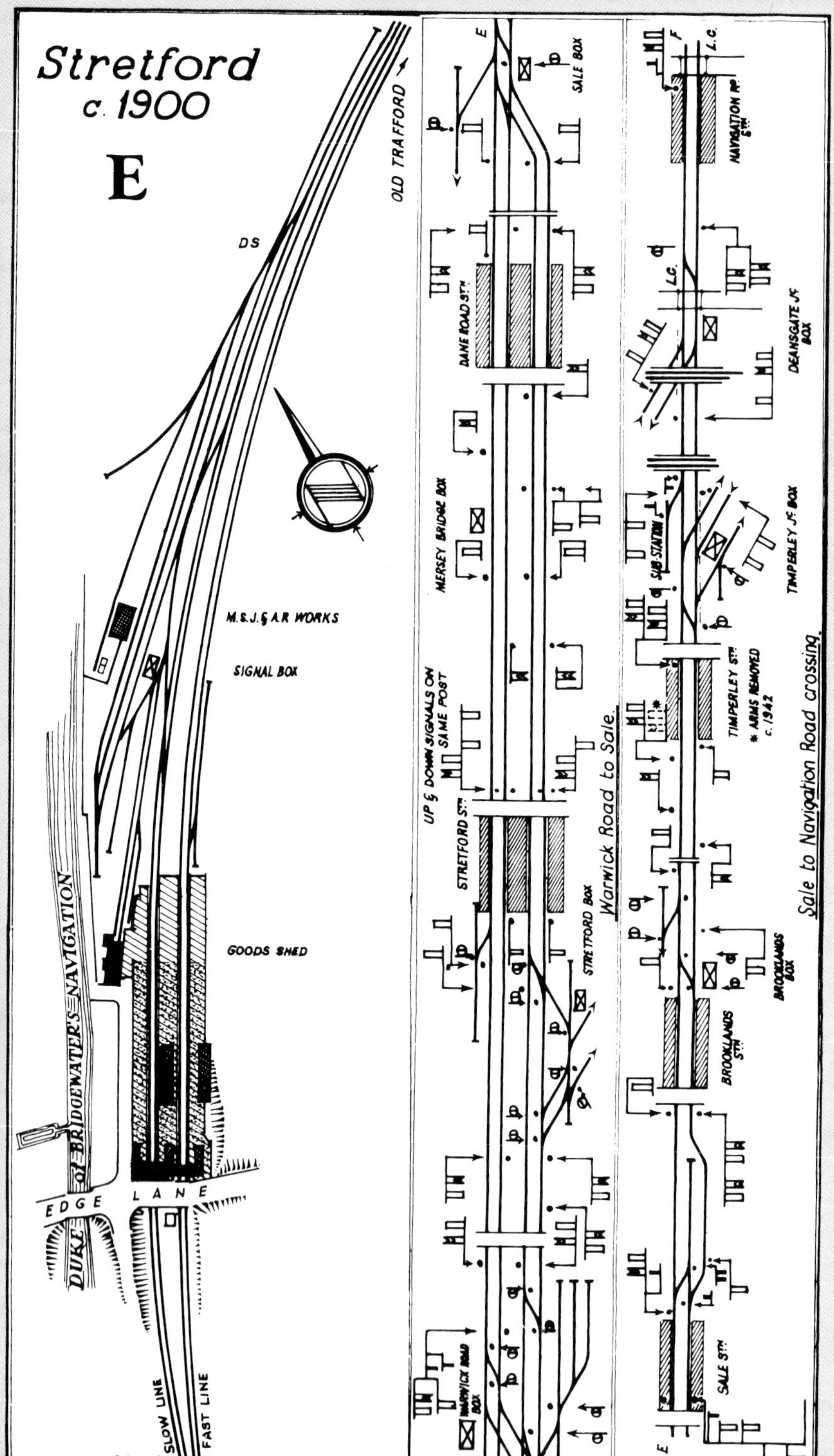

Stretford
c. 1900
E
OLD TRAFFORD
DS
M.S.J. & A.R. WORKS
SIGNAL BOX
GOODS SHED
DUKE OF BRIDGEWATER'S NAVIGATION
EDGE LANE
SLOW LINE
FAST LINE
SALE
SALE BOX
DANE ROAD STN
MERSEY BRIDGE BOX
UP & DOWN SIGNALS ON SAME POST
STRETFORD STN
STRETFORD BOX
WARWICK ROAD BOX
D
Warwick Road to Sale.
L.C.
NAVIGATION RD STN
DEANSGATE JC BOX
SUB STATION
TIMPERLEY JC BOX
TIMPERLEY STN
* ARMS REMOVED c. 1942
BROOKLANDS BOX
BROOKLANDS STN
SALE STN
F
Sale to Navigation Road crossing.

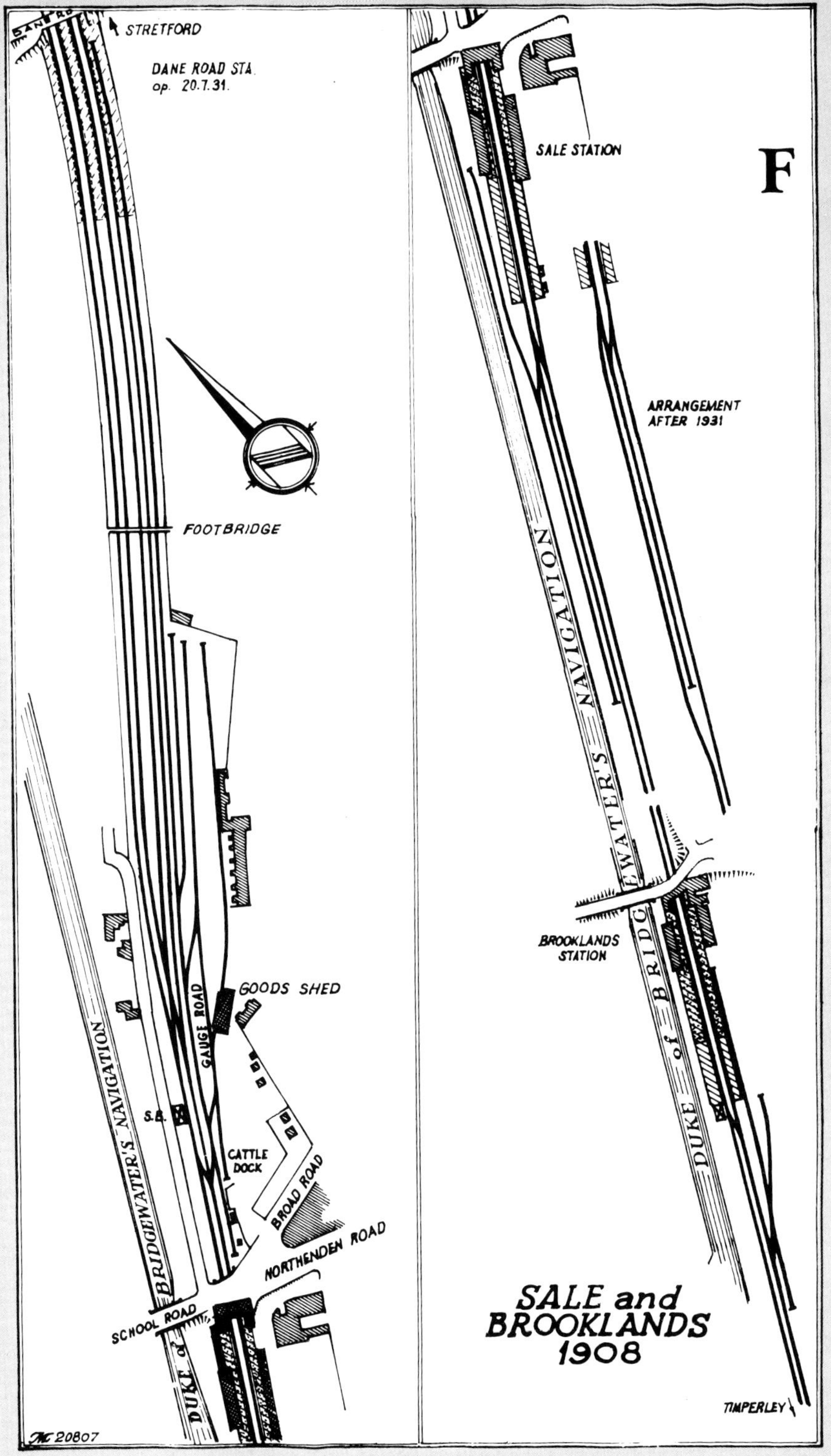
F
SALE and
BROOKLANDS
1908
STRETFORD
DANE ROAD STA.
op. 20.7.31.
FOOTBRIDGE
GOODS SHED
GAUGE ROAD
S.B.
CATTLE
DOCK
BROAD ROAD
NORTHENDEN ROAD
SCHOOL ROAD
BRIDGEWATER'S NAVIGATION
DUKE of
SALE STATION
ARRANGEMENT
AFTER 1931
DUKE of BRIDGEWATER'S NAVIGATION
BROOKLANDS
STATION
TIMPERLEY
20807

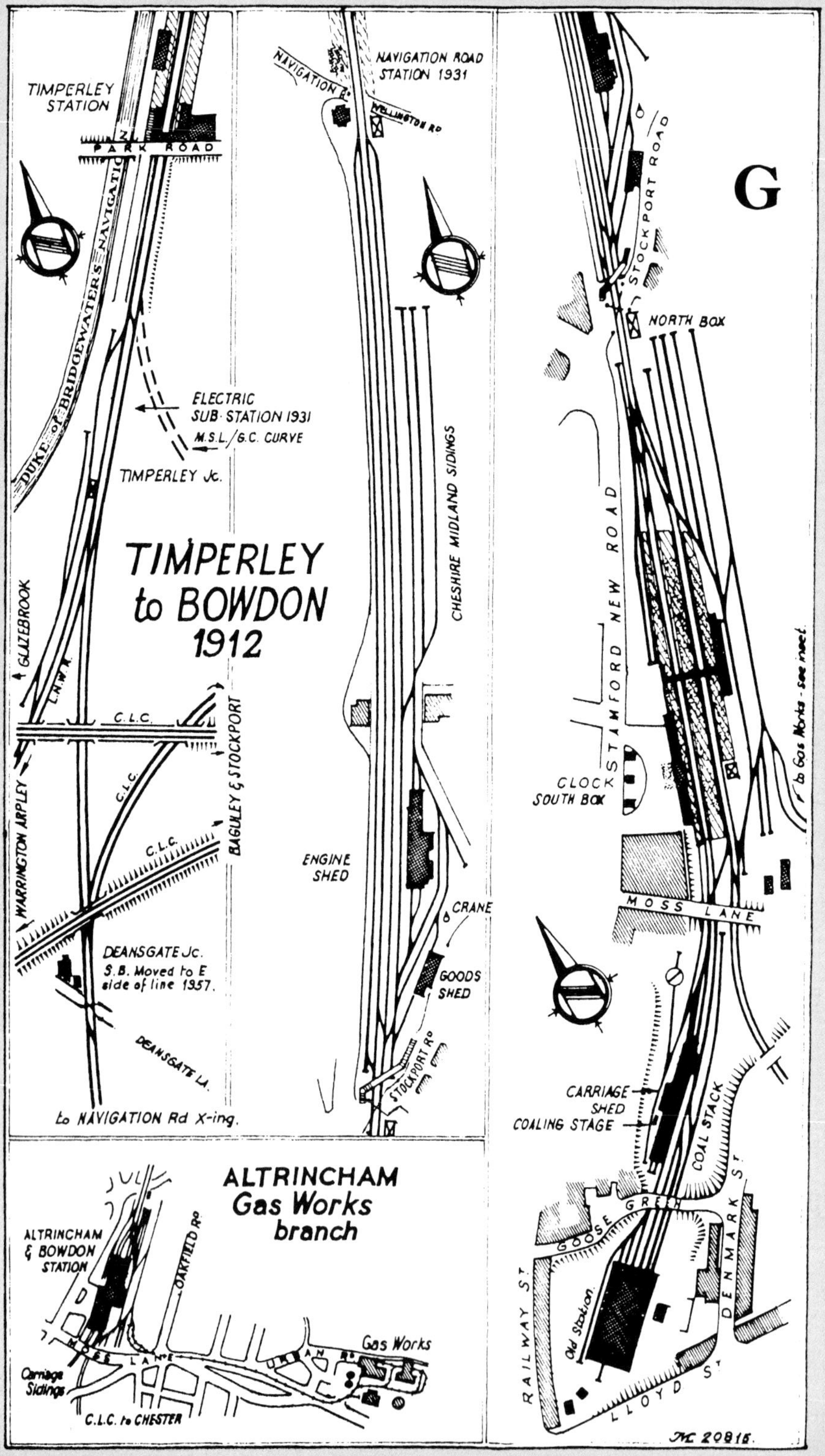
TIMPERLEY to BOWDON 1912
TIMPERLEY STATION
PARK ROAD
DUKE of BRIDGEWATERS NAVIGATION
ELECTRIC SUB-STATION 1931
M.S.L./G.C. CURVE
TIMPERLEY Jc.
GLAZEBROOK
L.N.W.R.
C.L.C.
C.L.C.
C.L.C.
BAGULEY & STOCKPORT
WARRINGTON ARPLEY
DEANSGATE Jc.
S.B. Moved to E side of line 1957.
DEANSGATE LA.
to NAVIGATION Rd X-ing
NAVIGATION Rd
NAVIGATION ROAD STATION 1931
WELLINGTON Rd
CHESHIRE MIDLAND SIDINGS
ENGINE SHED
CRANE
GOODS SHED
STOCKPORT Rd
G
STOCKPORT ROAD
NORTH BOX
STAMFORD NEW ROAD
CLOCK
SOUTH BOX
to Gas Works - see inset
MOSS LANE
CARRIAGE SHED
COALING STAGE
COAL STACK
GOOSE GREEN
DENMARK ST
RAILWAY ST
Old Station
LLOYD ST
MC 20815.
ALTRINCHAM Gas Works branch
ALTRINCHAM & BOWDON STATION
OAKFIELD Rd
MOSS LANE
Gas Works
Carriage Sidings
C.L.C. to CHESTER

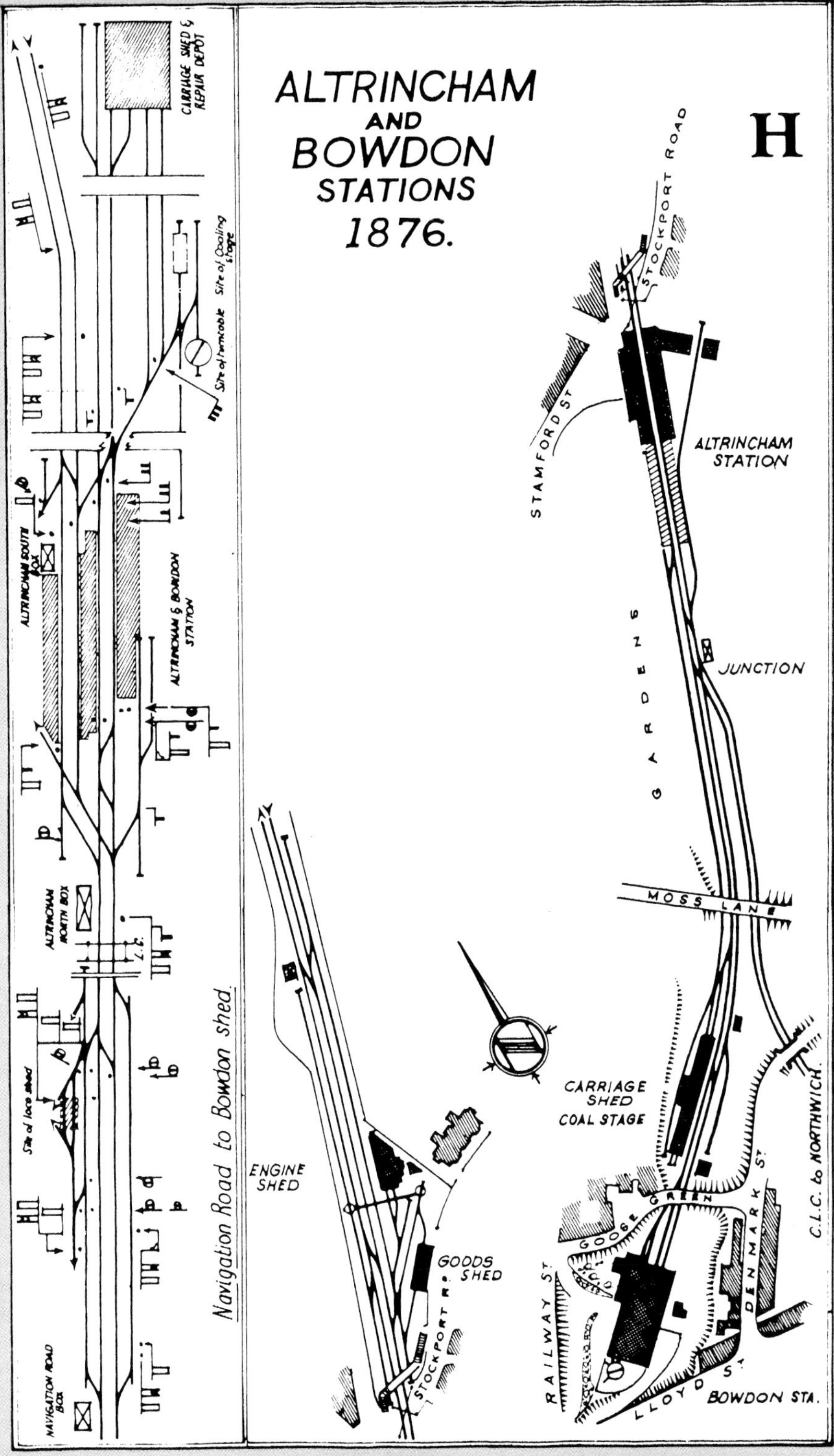
ALTRINCHAM AND BOWDON STATIONS 1876.
H
STOCKPORT ROAD
STAMFORD ST
ALTRINCHAM STATION
GARDENS
JUNCTION
MOSS LANE
CARRIAGE SHED
COAL STAGE
C.L.C. to NORTHWICH.
GOOSE GREEN
DENMARK ST
RAILWAY ST
LLOYD ST
BOWDON STA.
ENGINE SHED
GOODS SHED
STOCKPORT RD.
Navigation Road to Bowdon shed.
CARRIAGE SHED & REPAIR DEPOT
Site of Coaling stage
Site of turntable
ALTRINCHAM SOUTH BOX
ALTRINCHAM & BOWDON STATION
ALTRINCHAM NORTH BOX
Site of loco shed
NAVIGATION ROAD BOX

Bibliography

The basic bones of the MSJA's history can be found in several easily-accessible sources, and all I had to do was tie all the loose ends together to make a respectable-looking skeleton and add a bit of meat, which was obtained from the sources mentioned in the 'Acknowledgements' section.

The following works were of great use: H.C. Casserley – *Britain's Joint Lines* (1968); George Dow – *Great Central* (1960s); R.P. Griffiths – *The Cheshire Lines* (1949); W. Harrison – *History of the Manchester Railways* (1882); J.R. Kellet – *The Impact of Railways on Victorian Cities* (1969); H. Linecar – *British Electric Trains* (1948); E.T. MacDermot – *The Great Western Railway*, as were various local history books such as Alfred Ingham's *History of Altrincham & Bowdon* (1879) and R.W. Procter's *Memorials of Manchester Streets* (1874). Also of use were the official MSJA souvenir booklets issued in 1899, 1931, and 1971 and the *Railway Magazines* for 1899, 1914, 1931 and 1971.

* * * * *

A number of other publications were often referred to during the preparation of the Second Edition of this book, in particular: E. Ogden and J. Senior – *Metrolink Official Handbook* (1991) and D. Holt – *Manchester Metrolink* (1992). *Light Rail and Modern Tramway, Modern Railways, Rail, Railway Magazine, Railway World* and newspapers were consulted for various articles and news items. Other references were J.C. Gillham's *The Age of The Electric Train* (1988) and the first two 'Railfilms' videos about the line: *Electric Trains to Manchester* (1990) and *Many Short Journeys and Absolute Reliability* (1992). (At the time of writing, a third video is expected shortly.)

A particularly important source of information was *Live Wires*, the journal of the Altrincham Electric Railway Preservation Society, which has recorded many of the changes that have taken place along the line over the past 20-or-so years.

Warwick Road station on 22nd April, 1951 with a 3-coach electric train to Altrincham. *H.C. Casserley*